Social Control of

D. Richard Laws

Social Control of Sex Offenders

A Cultural History

D. Richard Laws
Pacific Behavioural Assessment
Victoria, British Columbia, Canada

ISBN 978-1-137-39125-4   ISBN 978-1-137-39126-1   (eBook)
DOI 10.1057/978-1-137-39126-1

Library of Congress Control Number: 2016940978

Cover illustration: © Cultura RM / Alamy Stock Photo

Printed on acid-free paper

This Palgrave Macmillan imprint is published by Springer Nature
The registered company is Macmillan Publishers Ltd. London

*To my colleagues, associates, and friends who have supported, guided,
disagreed, and collaborated with me for nearly half a century.
Also to those ex-offenders who have pulled up their socks and are trying to
live responsible offense-free lives in the face of daunting challenges.*

Acknowledgments

I am indebted to many people. Thanks are due to the following: Julia Willan, my editor at Palgrave Macmillan, who encouraged me to stick with the project when I considered giving it up; to Dominic Walker at Palgrave Macmillan for excellent editorial assistance; to Shadd Maruna, who shared some of the initial ideas with me; to Tony Ward, who provided strong encouragement for the project throughout; special thanks to Karl Hanson, who provided much information that helped me better understand actuarial assessment; to Brian Abbott and Karen Franklin, for providing Appendix 1; for a little help from my friends, thanks to Maia Christopher, Andrew J.R. Harris, Randal Kropp, Christopher Lobamov Rostovsky, and Caroline Logan; thanks very much to the international perspectives contributors: Lawrence Ellerby, Mark Blandford, Anne-Marie McAlinden, Caoilte Ò Ciardha, Martin Rettenberger, Jules Mulder, Andreas Mokros, Leni Helle Rivedal, Niklas Långström, Aini Laine, Petr Weiss, David Cohen, Andrew Day, Gwenda M. Willis, Chi Meng Chu, and Judy Hui; finally, and not the least, to my wife Cynthia Mills, who kept me going when the going got tough.

Contents

1

Introduction: What This Book Is About

Overall Purpose of the Work

The evidence available today indicates that the serious social problem called sex offending does not appear to be resolvable by any of the means currently employed. A large array of procedures are used in the attempt to control this difficult population. These include, to name only the major ones, imprisonment, institutional and community treatment, community monitoring by probation and parole, electronic monitoring, registration as a sex offender, community notification of an offender's status, strict limits on behavioral movement in the community, and residence restrictions. These constraints on behavior are almost completely a result of public outrage regarding sensational and heinous sex crimes, overreaction of media coverage that produces wildly inaccurate statements of potential community risk, and the efforts of the legal professionals and politicians to quell this anger and foreboding by enacting legislation that supposedly confronts the risk. Thus we in the United States have erected a massive edifice of community control that is socially and politically rather than empirically driven, which has largely failed to contain sexual crime.

© The Editor(s) (if applicable) and The Author(s) 2016   **1**
D.R. Laws, *Social Control of Sex Offenders*,
DOI 10.1057/978-1-137-39126-1_1

There is an openly declared war against sex offenders which has been underway for nearly 100 years. In the early years of the republic, sex offending was a minor problem that communities could deal with by reintegrating the offender in a gentle fashion or sometimes more severe consequences such as whipping or branding were used. As population increased and the commercial and industrial economy grew, the prevalence of sex crimes increased and more elaborate measures of containment such as asylums and prisons were required. The war against sex offenders as we understand it today began around 1915. To those implementing the various provisions of the legislations helping the struggle, they are simply doing what needs to be done. Throughout the twentieth century up to the present time there has existed a moral panic regarding sexual crime. It has ebbed and flowed throughout this period but it has never gone away and shows no sign of abating. Although it has increased in intensity and complexity for 100 years, the result of these control efforts has been the production of a seemingly endless proliferation of federal and state laws, local ordinances, and community regulations that has thrown an ever-widening net over the civil behavior of sex offenders. This book argues that the regulatory net makes it virtually impossible for sex offenders under supervision in the community to live peaceful and productive lives, maintain stable marriages and relationships, and care for their children.

There is a huge literature on sexual deviance and sex offending. Much of that literature is descriptive, examining various aspects of the phenomena. Little of it is precisely prescriptive and almost none of it is conclusive. Sexual deviance and sex offending, while not particularly difficult for mental health and forensic professionals to understand, remain mysterious and incomprehensible to most people. Much of the information regarding sex offenders comes to both the professional and lay public through sensational television, online, and print media. Much of it is inaccurate and a lot of it is actually false. There is no question that there are dangerous people among us who must be identified, processed legally, and contained. However, there are far fewer of them than the public supposes. This book attempts to provide a clear picture of the risk posed by sex offenders.

The purpose of this book is not to argue for complete overthrow of the existing regulatory system. It is rather to show the strengths and weaknesses of that system, to inform the relevant publics of the futility of many of these efforts, and to prepare them to request the repeal of the regulatory system where possible. In the author's view, it makes no sense to try to understand the punitive and failed policies in force today without understanding how they got that way. This is the major goal of the book.

What This Book Is Not About

The reader will find nothing in this work about:

- *Internet offenses.* Many sex offenders have access to child pornography; some collect it and some trade it with other offenders. There is much currently being written about Internet offenses. This attracts a lot of attention because no one seems to know what to do about it, if anything can be done, or even if anything *should* be done about it. It is considered a serious offense in some jurisdictions; in others it is not. A good general source in this area is M. Seto (2013). *Internet sex offenders.* Washington, DC: American Psychological Association.
- *Pornography.* Pornography has historically been suspected of promoting sexual offending. While this is certainly an undesirable social product, there is mixed and insufficient evidence that it is causally related to deviant sexual behavior. This ambiguity, particularly in the pre-Internet days, may be seen in the review by M.C. Seto, A. Maric, and H.E. Barbaree (2001). The role of pornography in the etiology of sexual aggression. *Aggression and Violent Behavior, 6,* 35–53. Based on evidence available at that time, the authors concluded that "individuals who are already predisposed to sexually offend are the most likely to show an effect of pornography exposure and are most likely to show the strongest effects" (p. 35).
- *Victims.* There is also a huge literature on the victims of sexual offending. The author's professional experience has been exclusively with adult male sex offenders and he is therefore not qualified to write about victims. A good resource in this area is J.A. Cohen, A.P. Mannarino, and E. Deblinger (2006). *Treating trauma and traumatic grief in children and adolescents.* New York: Guilford.

- *Diagnosis of sexual deviance.* This is a very murky area for most forensic professionals. While there is an extensive literature on assessment for purposes of diagnosis, the risk of false positives remains high. Some deviant behavior is clearly defined and obviously criminal, but much of it is not. For a general view, interested readers should consult Laws and O'Donohue's *Sexual deviance* (2nd ed) published in 2008. A more specific treatment of problems in diagnosis may be found in W. O'Donohue (2016). Problems in the DSM-5 classification and diagnosis of the paraphilias: What is the evidence? In D.R. Laws and W. O'Donohue (Eds.). *Treatment of sex offenders: Strengths and weaknesses in assessment and intervention.* New York: Springer.
- *Evaluation and treatment and its effects.* Laws and Ward (2011) argued that criminological statistics suggest that very few persons actually receive treatment. While short-term follow-up indicates that completed treatment is effective in reducing recidivism, it is not reasonable to assume that this effect will persist for decades into the future, as a sort of inoculation. What the reader will find here is an outline of what should be included in sex offender treatment and how those goals are expressed in two major schools of thought today. Some evidence is provided regarding the efficacy of these approaches. A wide-ranging review of sex offender treatment and its effects is beyond the scope of this book. There are many texts available in this area. A good, general, contemporary work is W.L. Marshall, L.E. Marshall, S.E. Serran, and Y.M. Fernandez (2006). *Treating sexual offenders: An integrated approach.* New York: Routledge.

What This Book Is About

In this work the reader will find information about:

- *Moral panic.* This is a phenomenon that has been evident in Western society for centuries. A moral panic occurs when an event that is seen as an outrage against social order occurs in a community. At first usually minimal information is taken up by the media which exaggerate the threat. Senior community members, politicians, law enforcement, and other concerned persons demand that something be done to contain the threat. The most egregious moral panic was probably the witchcraft crazes of the sixteenth century. In more recent times we have seen moral panic in allegations of satanic ritual abuse, inflated crime rates, or a war on drugs. The current laws regarding registration, community notification, and residency restrictions are the product of moral panic.

- *Early historical treatment.* Information is presented on treatment interventions from colonial times through the nineteenth century and into the early twentieth century. Although sex offenses could result in execution, more often less serious consequences such as a fine, whipping, or public shaming were used. In some cases offenders were welcomed back into the community following punishment. As time wore on, society became more complex, requiring ever more elaborate means of managing social deviance. Thus, we see a progression from family care in colonial times to almshouses, to workhouses, to penitentiaries, and ultimately, to maximum security prisons or "treatment" centers.

- *Sexual psychopath laws.* These statutes are extremely important in that they prefigure much of what is happening today in dealing with sex offenders. Here we encounter the belief that sexual crime is so incomprehensible that it must be the result of a mental illness. Sexual psychopath laws, first introduced in 1937, were seen as a scientific approach to the control of sexual crime. Prior to 1937, sex offenders were seen as simply criminals. Subsequently they were judged to be not only criminals but also *mentally ill* criminals. It followed that they could possibly be "treated." In 1977 the Group for the Advancement of Psychiatry recommended repeal of these laws, stating that they represented an experiment that had failed. Professionals, they argued, lacked the skills to predict future behavior or to treat sexual violence. The laws were slow to die but most were repealed by the 1980s. They have been resurrected in recent times in the enactment of civil commitment statutes aimed at "sexual predators." These statutes also require a diagnosis of mental illness.

- *The medicalization of sexual deviance.* Seeing sex offenders as mental patients stretches from the 1930s to the present time. Despite the noted objection of the professional psychiatric community, efforts to treat sex offenders have relentlessly persisted. An important review published in 1989 stated, not that treatment could *not* be effective, but that it was not possible to determine up to that time whether early efforts had been successful (Furby, Weinrott, & Blackshaw, 1989). Since that time a number of models have emerged which purport to be effective although the long-term outcome of those remains to be determined. The belief persists that sexual deviation is a mental illness, that there is something special about it, and that it remains incomprehensible to most people. Perhaps the strongest support for that belief has been the emergence of civil commitment of "sexual predators" and indeterminate confinement in "special" commitment, from which few are ever released.

- *Assessment of risk to reoffend: Historical background.* The historical background can be found both in the USA and Europe. Early efforts focused upon dangerous criminals as classes rather than as individuals. Methods became more sophisticated in the mid-nineteenth century to the early twentieth century, when fingerprinting was introduced as the major identification method. Many of the early efforts were crude and lacked reliability, but the rudiments of those systems are clearly evident in contemporary assessment instruments.

- *Assessment of risk to reoffend: Actuarial assessment versus risk formulation.* Since the introduction of the *Violence Risk Assessment Guide* (VRAG) (Quinsey, Harris, Rice, & Cormier, 1998) an entire generation of psychologists, psychiatrists, social workers, and probation/parole officers has been heavily influenced by the use of actuarial risk assessment methods. Because of its prominence today, the background of this approach has largely been ignored. In fact, generations of criminologists have been similarly influenced since the introduction of risk assessment in their profession from 1923. The development of this mode of risk assessment is described as well as its formidable alternative, risk formulation. The latter approach is well illustrated in the *Risk for Sexual Violence Protocol* (Hart et al. 2003).

- *Sex offender registration and community notification.* Registration as a sex offender in the community is governed by a number of major laws that have been enacted and modified over the past 25 years. As might be expected, these statutes have become more restrictive and oppressive as time passes. At least one of them has become so restrictive and expensive to implement that some jurisdictions have declined to proceed. The registration and reporting laws provide an excellent example of how politics and media can drive legislation of highly questionable value. While there are many persons, lay and professional, who believe that "I know these laws protect kids," there is actually little evidence for that assertion.

- *Community restrictions on sex offender behavior.* These restrictions form a package with the registration and reporting laws. The restrictions on sex offender behavior in the community are typically state laws or local ordinances. Most are of a go/no-go variety. Some appear to make some sense while others are simply absurd or irrelevant. In order to provide a flavor of these restrictions, Chap. 9 provides a potpourri of them from across the USA. There are restrictions that are very important. These refer to where an offender may live with regard to proximity to schools, churches, playgrounds, swimming pools, bus stops, and other places where children may be expected to congregate. As might be expected, as the restrictions grow tighter, it becomes apparent that there are few places where an offender may lawfully be and virtually no place where an offender may live. These routines can drive offenders underground and thus compound risk.

- *The international picture of registration, notification, and community restrictions.* Colleagues in other countries were contacted to attempt a determination of the international extent of these social control policies. The correspondents were asked to provide information on offender registration, community notification, and community restrictions on social behavior. Responses were obtained from Canada, England, Northern Ireland, Republic of Ireland, Norway, Sweden, Finland, Switzerland, the Netherlands, Germany, Czech Republic, Israel, Australia, New Zealand, Hong Kong, and Singapore. With some similarities, it is apparent that none of these countries support policies of the severity seen today in the USA.

- *Psychological treatment: Risk reducer or life enhancer?* The evidence base for general correctional treatment is quite strong. That base largely resides in the work of Andrews and Bonta (2010a) and their colleagues over the past 30 years. These researchers are the originators of what has come to be called the "Risk–Need–Responsivity (RNR) model" of treatment. This approach focuses attention on risk, need, and responsivity. Scarce resources should be devoted to *high-* and *moderate-risk* clients; treatment should be targeted to *criminogenic need* (dynamic risk factors), and it should be *responsive* to the intellectual capability and learning style of the offender. Andrews and Bonta (2010a) identified eight major risk/need factors that should guide interventions. Meta-analyses have supported the RNR model for treatment of general criminal offenders. Hanson, Bourgon, Helmus, and Hodgson (2009) examined the extent to which the RNR model was applied to sex offenders and found equally strong support.

Critics have argued that the RNR model, while impressive, is primarily useful for managing risk and alleviating some prominent behavioral deficits in offenders. In recent years the Good Lives Model (GLM; Laws & Ward, 2011; Ward & Maruna, 2007) has been advanced as an alternative approach whose central focus is on building client strengths. Willis, Yates, Gannon, and Ward (2013) stated that the GLM is not necessarily a competitor but it is complementary to the RNR model. Preliminary research has suggested that the GLM can actually enhance an RNR-based treatment, particularly by improving client engagement in treatment.

Chapter 11 provides a full description of both of these contemporary treatment models. It is important to remember that neither of these approaches considers sexual deviation to be a treatable mental illness. Rather it is viewed as criminal behavior of varying severity that may be brought under control by a variety of means.

Conclusions and Future Outlook

The future outlook is not particularly bright, but there is some hope for moderation of the oppressive regulatory net that exists today. Some regulations appear to be so useless that they may be struck from the books. Others may be modified and the more restrictive elements lifted. One hopes that more humanistic and person-oriented methods of offender management may be developed. Most importantly, the general public and the legal and law enforcement professionals need to be better educated regarding the facts of the issues of concern. Certainly, sex offenders present a social problem, but it is not of the magnitude or seriousness that politicians and the media would have us believe. If the book can find an audience receptive to these ideas, it will have done its work.

References

Andrews, D. A., & Bonta, J. (2010a). *The psychology of criminal conduct* (5th ed.). New Providence, NJ: LexisNexis.

Cohen, J. A., Mannarino, A. P., & Deblinger, E. (2006). *Treating trauma and traumatic grief in children and adolescents.* New York: Guilford.

Furby, L., Weinrott, M. R., & Blackshaw, L. (1989). Sex offender recidivism: A review. *Psychological Bulletin, 105*, 3–30.

Hanson, R. K., Bourgon, G., Helmus, L., & Hodgson, S. (2009). The principles of effective treatment also apply to sexual offenders: A meta-analysis. *Criminal Justice and Behavior, 36*, 865–891.

Hart, S. D., Kropp, P. R., Laws, D. R., Klaver, J., Logan, C., & Watt, K. A. (2003). *The Risk for Sexual Violence Protocol (RSVP): Structured professional guidelines for assessing risk of sexual violence.* Burnaby, BC: Simon Fraser University, Department of Psychology, Mental Health Law and Policy Institute.

Laws, D. R., & O'Donohue, W. T. (Eds.). (2008). *Sexual deviance: Theory, assessment and treatment* (2nd ed.). New York: Guilford.

Laws, D. R., & Ward, T. (2011). *Desistance from sex offending.* New York: Guilford.

Marshall, W. L., Marshall, L. E., Serran, G. A., & Fernandez, Y. M. (2006). *Treating sexual offenders: An integrated approach.* New York: Routlege.

W. O'Donohe (2016). Problems in the DSM-5 classification and diagnosis of the paraphilias: What is the evidence? In D.R. Laws and W. O'Donohue (Eds.). *Treatment of sex offenders: Strengths and weaknesses in assessment and intervention* (pp. 1–18). New York: Springer.

Quinsey, V. L., Rice, M. E., Harris, G. T., & Cormier, C. A. (1998). *Violent offenders: Appraising and managing risk* (1st ed.). Washington, DC: American Psychological Association.

Seto, M. C. (2013). *Internet sex offenders.* Washington, DC: American Psychological Association.

Seto, M. D., Maric, A., & Barbaree, H. E. (2001). The role of pornography in the etiology of sexual aggression. *Aggression and Violent Behavior, 6*, 35–53.

Ward, T., & Maruna, S. (2007). *Rehabilitation: Beyond the risk paradigm.* London: Routledge.

Willis, G. M., Yates, P. M., Gannon, T. A., & Ward, T. (2013). How to integrate the Good Lives Model into treatment programs for sexual offending: An introduction and overview. *Sexual Abuse: A Journal of Research and Treatment, 25*, 123–142.

2

Moral Panic: Threat to the Social Order

Becker (1963) has provided definitions of social deviance that are widely accepted. Relevant to the aim of this chapter is Becker's contention that deviance is a social construct, that a community or a society condemns a specific act or practice as deviant and unacceptable. His definitions are straightforward:

> The simplest view of deviance is essentially statistical, defining as deviant anything that varies too widely from the average .... [The] statistical view seems simple-minded, even trivial. Yet it simplifies the problem by doing away with questions of value that ordinarily arise in discussions of the nature of deviance. (pp. 4–5)
>
> A less simple but much more common view of deviance identifies it as something essentially pathological, revealing the presence of a "disease" .... Sometimes people mean the analogy more strictly, because they think of deviance as the product of mental disease. (p. 5)
>
> Some sociologists ... discriminate between those features of society which promote stability (and thus are "functional") and those which disrupt stability (and thus are "dysfunctional"). (p. 7)

© The Editor(s) (if applicable) and The Author(s) 2016
D.R. Laws, *Social Control of Sex Offenders*,
DOI 10.1057/978-1-137-39126-1_2

These definitions are highly germane to the positions taken in this chapter.

In conversations with sex offenders, I have often been asked, "What's *deviant* behavior anyway?" My reply has always been, "Deviant behavior is what most people *don't* do. Most people don't rape other adults, they don't sexually molest children, they don't expose their genitals in public, and they don't grope other people on public transit." Many sex offenders do not accept this as an adequate definition. The general public, on the other hand, has no difficulty in identifying the above behaviors as deviant. Some of these behaviors are heinous crimes, such as the kidnapping, rape, or murder of a child. When such incidents become public knowledge, the community is angry, disgusted, fearful, and worry that what they now know about may be only one instance of a much wider phenomenon. In that perception of a possibly wider menace lie the roots of a moral panic about sexual deviation.

Background of the Concept

Goode and Ben-Yehuda (2009) have defined the moral panic as:

> From time to time in every society, charges of terrible and dastardly deeds committed by evildoers erupt; sides are chosen, speeches are delivered, enemies are named, and atrocities are alleged. In some such episodes, the harm is alleged but imaginary, in others, the threat or harm is real but exaggerated. However, when the moral concern felt by segments of the society or the community is disproportionate to the threat or harm, sociologists refer to them as "moral panics," and the threatening agents, "folk devils." (pp. 16–17)

The term "folk devil" is typically attributed to the sociologist Stanley Cohen in his 1972 study of youth gangs in England in 1964. The gangs were representative of two extremes of British youth culture. The Mods (sharply dressed on expensive motor scooters) were opposed to the Rockers (leather-clad bikers). They fought in the spring of 1964 across seaside resort towns in southern England. Cohen stated that the violence in these encounters was probably no more extreme than youth brawls at seaside resorts and after football games in later decades. However, the media turned these events into symbols of delinquency and social deviance, referring to the clashes as being of "disastrous proportions." Cohen states that the media even used faked interviews to keep the story alive. Some of the youths went to trial where prosecutors argued that these were young people who lacked respect for law and order. A Member of Parliament called for increasingly severe measures to control hooliganism. Given what we have witnessed in the succeeding 50 years, these events seem mild. However, the soubriquet "folk devil" lingers in the sociological literature.

However, Cohen's description (cited by Goode & Ben-Yehuda, 2009, p. 23) provides an early template for the phenomenon of moral panic:

> A condition, episode, a person or group of persons emerges to become defined as a threat to societal values and interests; its nature is presented in a stylized and stereotypical fashion by the mass media; the moral barricades are manned by editors, bishops, politicians and other right-thinking people; socially accredited experts pronounce their diagnoses and solutions; ways of coping are evolved or (more often) resorted to; the condition then disappears, submerges or deteriorates and becomes more visible. Sometimes the object of the panic is quite novel and at other times it is something which has been in existence long enough, but suddenly appears in the limelight. Sometimes the panic passes over and is forgotten, except in folklore and collective memory; at other times it has more serious and long-lasting repercussions and might produce such changes as those in legal and social policy or even in the way the society conceives itself.

Cohen's summary expresses the essential features of the moral panic and suggests its limits. Krinsky (2013) described Cohen's analysis as a *processual* model because it focused on the social and cultural development of moral panics. Goode and Ben-Yehuda (2009), on the other hand, advanced what Krinsky called an *attributional* model, that is, specific features of events (missing children) or individuals (sexual deviants) cause concern, fear, or possibly threat to the social order. Probably due to its explicit expression, the Goode and Ben-Yehuda model has provided a framework for studying moral panic.

Elements of the Moral Panic

Goode and Ben-Yehuda (2009) describe five key attributes of moral panics (pp. 37–41):

- *Concern.* This attribute can be measured. The level of anxiety regarding a perceived threat can be determined through the amount of media attention to an event, opinion polls, public commentary, proposed legal remedies, or arrests for engaging in a particular activity.
- *Hostility.* An identifiable group (e.g., sexual deviants, drug dealers) must be seen as responsible for the supposed threat to social order. Members of this category are identified as the enemy who must be pursued, apprehended, and punished.
- *Consensus.* For a moral panic to take hold there must be a widespread belief that the threat actually exists, that it is of a serious nature, and that the identified culprits are responsible.
- *Disproportion.* The level of public concern is typically wildly out of proportion to the actual threat posed. Numbers are an essential element of disproportion [for example, claims of 50,000 missing children].
- *Volatility.* Moral panics may erupt quickly and fade away quickly. However, they sometimes leave behind enduring changes in the society [for example, the enmity toward sex offenders never goes away].

Goode and Ben-Yehuda additionally advance three theories to explain why moral panics occur (pp. 55–69). Krinsky (2013, p. 7) refers to these as a "concise taxonomy of commonly held scholarly models of, or theoretical perspectives on, the evolution of such episodes":

- *The grassroots model.* This theory asserts that the general public generates and maintains moral panics. There is a widespread belief that something of value to society is believed to be under threat. Goode and Ben-Yehuda cite examples (pp. 56–58). A broadly based example is the Salem witchcraft trials of the 1600s. Urban legends that arise and quickly dissipate would include allegations that the Central Intelligence Agency (CIA) or Federal Bureau of Investigation (FBI) is distributing drugs in the ghettos to poison African Americans; M&M's have an aphrodisiac in them; or the Jockey shorts manufacturer puts a chemical in its underpants to make men sterile. The fear and loathing of sex offenders may have grassroots origins which are then amplified by exaggerated media and political attention. The role of "moral entrepreneurs" (Becker, 1963) can be critical here.

- *The elite-engineered model.* This model "... argues that the ruling elite causes, creates, engineers, or 'orchestrates' moral panics, that the richest and most powerful members of the society undertake campaigns to generate and sustain concern, fear, and panic on the part of the public over an issue that is not generally regarded as terribly harmful to the society as a whole" (p. 62). Said another way, "(T)he ruling elite create a 'red herring,' a diversionary and false enemy to divert attention away from society's real problems" (p. 64). This is a rather paranoid vision that would require an extremely gullible public (or devoted Marxists) to be accepted.

- *The interest-group model.* Goode and Ben-Yehuda claim that this is the most common generator of moral panics. "In the interest group perspective, professional associations, police departments, portions of the media, religious groups, educational organizations ... may have an independent stake in bringing an issue to the fore ...." (p. 67). Again, description of the moral entrepreneur by Becker (1963) is prominent here. In the area of sex crimes, there are numerous examples of parents of kidnapped, sexually assaulted, or murdered children who have become central to keeping alive the moral panic about sex offenders.

Another point of view is the argument of McRobbie and Thornton (1995) that folk devils can fight back. These groups are "able to respond instantly to the media demonization of the group they represent, and ... provide information and analysis designed to counter this representation" (p. 566). Possibly the least successful in this approach are the pro-pedophile groups who advocate for "inter-generational" consensual sex (e.g., the North American Man/Boy Love Association). On the other hand, advocates for legalization of marijuana and gay marriage have seen considerable success. In light of these successes, we sometimes forget that homosexuals have been demonized throughout history and that "reefer madness" was demonized not that long ago.

Moral Panic About Sex Offenders

Jenkins (1998) produced a major work in this area of study. From the perspective of the late 1990s he noted that there were a number of allegations regarding the threat posed by sex offenders that were accepted as facts in the American population. These allegations persist to this day (pp. 1–2):

• Children face a terrible danger of being sexually abused.
• Sexual abuse is a problem of wide dimensions.
• Sex offenders are compulsive and offend frequently.
• Sex offenders cannot be cured or rehabilitated.
• Sexually deviant behavior can escalate to murder.
• Sex with adults causes lasting harm to victims.
• Sexual abuse can produce the so-called cycle of abuse such that abused children will later perpetrate the same act against new victims.

Jenkins (1998) stated that the preceding list of allegations contain only fragments of truth. "(A)ll concepts of sex offenders and sex offenses are socially constructed realities: all are equally subject to social, political, and ideological influences, and no particular framing of offenders represents a pristine objective reality" (p. 4). These social constructions regarding sex offenders and sex offenses have waxed and waned throughout the twentieth and the early years of the twenty-first centuries:

> Originating in the Progressive Era, the imagery of the malignant sex fiend reached new heights in the decade after World War II, only to be succeeded by a liberal model over the next quarter century. More recently, the pendulum has swung back to the predator model; sex offenders are now viewed as being little removed from the worst multiple killers and torturers. (p. 2)

The historical construction of sex crime from colonial times to the present will be treated at length in the following chapter. Following are a few examples intended to demonstrate that the so-called self-evident facts listed above have persisted throughout the twentieth-century America:

- There were sex crime panics in the 1940s and 1950s. "*Colliers* reported that sex crime by 'the rapist, the psychopath, the defiler of children' had 'virtually gone out of control.'" (p. 52).
- FBI director "Hoover ... warned that parole boards were all too often guilty of 'in effect, releasing a predatory animal,' and in 1937 he claimed that the 'sex fiend' was 'most loathsome of the all the vast army of crime.'" (p. 55)
- Hoover further stated: "The most rapidly increasing type of crime is that perpetrated by degenerate sex offenders .... (I)t is taking its toll at the rate of a criminal assault every forty-three minutes, day and night." (pp. 55–56)
- The persisting myth of menacing stranger also comes from this period. "The agency [ed: FBI] distributed posters urging children to beware of 'stranger danger': 'Boys and girls, ... for your protection, remember to turn down gifts from strangers, and refuse rides offered by strangers.'" (p. 56)
- The sense of threat was also marketed by commercial cinema. "Although censorship made it impossible to deal overtly with ... rapists, or child molesters, the subject of warped killers did not fall under the same restrictions .... Fictional explorations of sex crime thus concentrated on the most serious aspect of the problem, namely the 'maniac killer,' whose sexual motivation could be subtly implied." (p. 56)

During this same period there were more balanced appraisals of the social threat. Jenkins (1998, pp. 65–66) cites the New York City Mayor's Committee for the Study of Sex Offenses (1940). "The committee devoted a great deal of space to challenging myths about sex fiends .... Given the city's vast population [ed: nearly 7.5 million in 1940], the two or three thousand people who were arrested each year for sex offenses should be considered a 'phenomenally low' figure .... (F)irst time offenders committed the majority of sex crimes, and when sex offenders had previous records, they were usually for nonsexual misdeeds ... .' The habitual sex offender, who specializes in the commission of sex crime, is the least conspicuous figure among the offenders with criminal records." Three quarters of a century later, findings such as these are common.

The sociologist Paul Tappan, a technical consultant to the New Jersey Commission on the Habitual Sex Offender (1950), produced findings that largely replicated those of the New York Mayor's Committee. Commenting on the myths about sex offenders, Tappan concluded "'That tens of thousands of homicidal sex fiends stalk the land, … that the victims of sex attack are 'ruined for life,' … that sex offenders are usually recidivists,… that sex psychopathy or sex deviation is a clinical entity …. the vast majority of sex deviates are minor offenders …. Most of the persons adjudicated are minor deviates, rarely if ever sex fiends'" (p. 70). Tappan's findings showed that about 5% of convicted sex offenders actually used force or inflicted injury. That 5% reoffense rate attributed to the most dangerous offenders, later confirmed empirically by Wolfgang, Figlio, and Sellin (1972), has persisted in the criminological and forensic psychological literature ever since.

Actors in the Moral Panic About Sex Offenders

Goode and Ben-Yehuda (2009) described this framework originally outlined by Cohen (1972). The following illustrates the roles that each of these actors plays in the drama where sex offenders are seen as the object of threat to the social order.

The Media

In the author's view, the print and visual media play the central role in generating and maintaining a moral panic. With sex offenders this is particularly easy to do. Goode and Ben-Yehuda (2009) have noted: "(I)t is important to point out that *many* moral panics are about sex …. Sex is a special and *unique* sphere in which rules are abundant, and strict, and within which the human drama plays out and the status of wrongdoing and abnormality is applied" (p. 18). There is a nostrum in journalism that says "If it bleeds, it leads." Thus, when instances of sexual deviation that produce horrible consequences such as rape or murder occur, the media seizes upon the details, often blows them out of proportion, subtly (or not so subtly) suggests that the instant event may be "just the tip of the iceberg," and implies that the phenomena currently observed are things to be very concerned about. This approach feeds public fear and can generate a moral panic. "The Boys of Boise" is a good example of media distortion (Goode & Ben-Yehuda, 2009, pp. 11–13). Several adult males in Boise, Idaho, were arrested following allegations that they had had sexual relations with teenaged boys. Rumors began to circulate that these were probably not the only adults involved in these practices. "*Time* magazine ran a story claiming that 'a widespread homosexual underworld that involved some of Boise's most prominent men ... had preyed on hundreds of teen-age boys for the past decade." As time went on, the amount of misinformation grew to huge proportions. This moral panic lasted for the better part of two years. Since 1990, moral panics about sex offenders have resulted in the enaction of legislation intended to indefinitely confine and "treat" dangerous sex offenders who have committed serious crimes. Many scholars have argued that these laws are punitive rather than rehabilitative.

The Public

Sex and deviant sexuality are threatening issues to much of the general public. It is not surprising that intense media coverage of sex crimes can readily arouse anger, disgust, and fear in a community. Serani (2011, p. 2) has stated that "fear-based media has become the staple of popular culture. The distressing fall-out from this trend is that children and adults who are exposed to media are more likely than others to

- Feel that their neighborhoods and communities are unsafe.
- Believe that crimes rates are rising [ed: when they are in fact falling].
- Overestimate their odds of becoming a victim, and
- Consider the world to be a dangerous place."

Persons who feel so threatened are apt to demand action to stop the spread of whatever sexually criminal events that they perceive to be taking place.

Law Enforcement

The Boise example illustrates the role of the police and courts. As the rumors spread more widely, the City Council demanded the arrest and conviction of all arrested homosexuals. Five homosexuals were sentenced to prison. If there was a ring of homosexuals preying on large numbers of boys, the leaders of this organization were never named. In the end, over 1500 people were interviewed during the investigation. Long after the panic had subsided, the prosecuting attorney had this to say: "We had to get 'those guys,' he said, 'because they strike at the core of the society, I mean the family and the family unit. And when you get those guys crawling around the streets, you've got to prosecute to save the family'" (Goode & Ben-Yehuda, 2009, p. 13).

Politicians and Legislators

Like the general public these individuals can be swept up in a moral panic. They are asked by the press and the public: "You can see that we're in an awful situation here. Everybody is scared to death. What are you going to do about it?" As an illustration of "doing something," Jenkins (1998) described the acceleration of the growth of sex psychopath legislation from the late 1930s through the 1940s. In the 1940s the statutes had come under severe criticism from the psychiatric and legal professionals alleging that the approach was a failed experiment and should be abandoned.

> But the faster the criticisms accumulated in the late 1940s, the more enthusiastically legislatures passed new sex offender legislation. By 1960, a majority of American states had acquired sex psychopath statutes founded on exactly the principles that the medico-legal experts derided [ed: that sex crime was a treatable mental illness] …. Lawmakers and police faced overwhelming pressure to do something about sex crime, and special legislation directed against sex psychopaths was the natural quick fix. In the desperate public mood of 1938 or 1949, it would have taken suicidal courage to oppose or even question a bill ostensibly intended to protect the innocent from sex fiends, even if a legislator knew perfectly well that the measure would be less than useless. (pp. 71–72)

Regrettably today, in the twenty-first century, legislators face the same paradox and continue to make the same mistakes.

Action Groups

"At some point, moral panics generate appeals, campaigns ... which arise to cope with the newly-existing threat. The leaders who launch these groups are 'moral entrepreneurs' (Becker, 1963) ... who believe that existing remedies are insufficient" (Goode & Ben-Yehuda, 2009, p. 26). An overheated press, an aroused public, a determined combination of police and courts, and legislators fearful of reprisal may be more than adequate to be characterized as action groups. However, in the sex offender moral panic there are some notable moral entrepreneurs. Outstanding examples are parents of missing or slain children who take it upon themselves to lead a crusade demanding that something be done. These individuals stand out as spokespersons for community outrage. They often appear in print and visual media making statements such as: "If you (police, courts, probation, parole) had done your job, my child would still be alive!" It is impossible not to sympathize with such people and they must be accorded a prominent role in the drama of the sex offender moral panic.

A Final Word

Historically and presently, moral panics appear to be a constant in the world of the sex offender. Most panics erupt suddenly, find a peak, and subside quickly or gradually, sometimes leaving something behind and sometimes simply disappearing. Moral panic about sex offenders is one that does not subside and may never go away. That is a fearsome prospect for some members of the public, for law enforcement, for sex offense victims, and for tense legislators. There are not only losers in this drama. For other professions, who make sex crime their professional business—lawyers, psychiatrists, forensic psychologists, working for the defense or the prosecution—it is a gift that keeps on giving.

References

Becker, H. S. (1963). *Outsiders: Studies in the sociology of deviance*. New York: Free Press.

Cohen, S. (1972). *Folk devils and moral panics*. London: MacGibbon & Key.

Goode, E., & Ben-Yehuda, N. (2009). *Moral panics: The social construction of deviance* (2nd ed.). Chichester: Wiley-Blackwell.

Jenkins, P. (1998). *Moral panic: Changing concepts of the child molester in modern America*. New Haven, CT: Yale University Press.

Krinsky, C. (2013). Introduction: The moral panic concept. In C. Krinsky (Ed.), *The Ashgate research companion to moral panics* (pp. 1–14). Burlington, VT: Ashgate.

Mayor's Committee for the Study of Sex Offenses. (1940). New York City: Mayor's Committee for the Study of Sex Offenses.

McRobbie, A., & Thornton, S. L. (1995). Rethinking "moral panic" for multi-mediated social worlds. *British Journal of Sociology, 46*, 559–574.

Serani, D. (2011). If it bleeds, it leads: Understanding fear-based media. *Psychology Today*, June 7. New York: Sussex.

Tappan, P. W. (1950). *The habitual sex offender: Report and recommendations of the Commission on the Habitual Sex Offender*. Trenton, NJ: The Commission.

Wolfgang, M. E., Figlio, R. M., & Sellin, T. (1972). *Delinquency in a birth cohort*. Chicago: University of Chicago Press.

3

Early Historical Treatment of Social Deviance

Colonial America

We can trace the legal and social treatment of sex offenders from the eighteenth century. The major problem in attempting to study sex offenses in the early republic is that the behaviors provoked such disgust that they often were not clearly identified and usually not described in detail. Instead, we find cryptic statements such as "A crime not to be named among Christians" (which could be anything) as well as (and still prevailing in some statutes) "The infamous crime against Nature." Sodomy, for example, was on the books but not clearly described. Today it is defined as anal sex or oral copulation with no specification of who is doing what to whom. In colonial times sodomy referred to sexual penetration that would not end in procreation. This would include sex between men, sex with an underage child of either sex, or sex with animals.

Regarding sex with underage children, Jenkins (1998) noted that "(t)he American colonies followed the common law principle that, before a certain age, a girl was too young to give valid consent to sexual activity. Most jurisdictions defined sexual intercourse with a girl younger than ten as rape or carnal abuse, while sexual interference short of intercourse would

© The Editor(s) (if applicable) and The Author(s) 2016
D.R. Laws, *Social Control of Sex Offenders*,
DOI 10.1057/978-1-137-39126-1_3

generally be classified as indecent liberties, 'lewd and lascivious acts.' Offenses were felonies if committed against children below the age of ten, but acts with slightly older girls were commonly misdemeanors" (p. 24).

Other actionable sex crimes included adultery, the vaguely defined "fornication," exhibitionism, public masturbation, sex with young males, and transvestism.

Following are some common examples of sex crime and punishment in the eighteenth century. There is no intention here to provide a comprehensive history but rather to provide a flavor of the times and how colonial Americans dealt with unconventional sexual behavior.

Olson-Raymer (undated) has stated that, in the colonial period, jury trials and imposition of punishment were a deliberate social drama. These were public spectacles of retribution intended to show the unpleasant consequences of crime. These included:

- Admonition. A lecture on good and evil, probably by parents, judges, or the local pastor.
- Fines. Rich people could buy their way out of consequences, the poor suffered punishment.
- Public penance. Time in the stocks.
- Confinement. Time served in a stockade or local jail.
- Branding. Various images to denote the crime, for example, "A" for adultery, "R" for rape.
- Disenfranchisement. Denial of the right to vote.
- Banishment. This refers to exclusion from the community, not the country (retrieved July 6, 2015, from: users.humboldt.edu/ogayle/hist110/unit1/criminal justice.html).

Rothman (2008, p. 48) added to this list the pillory and the public cage, noting that one or a combination of all these techniques was used. One ingenious method was to have the convicted person stand on the gallows for an hour with a rope around his neck, after which he was freed. Jails were used but typically the person was held in custody only while the legal proceedings were carried out.

Ramsey (2013) has described how colonial Americans enforced laws against adultery and other offenses.

Adultery, even with a consensual *ménage à trois*, was still adultery, a punishable crime. "(T)obacco planters…Edward Hudson and Richard Holt shared a roof, a business, and…the sexual favors of Holt's wife…..After Holt complained that his wife and her lover intended to kill him, the court sentenced Hudson to be whipped with thirty lashes and banished from the county. Dorothy was ordered to endure fifty lashes, but the court later commuted both whippings to fines. The court also prohibited Dorothy from living as man and wife with Hudson, although he later fathered two of her children." (p. 197)

A group of women in Virginia attempted to "define the sexual identity of a neighbor who had male genitalia but dressed as a woman and displayed skill in sewing. The female 'searchers' of Thomasine (or Thomas) Hall's body objected to designating a person with a penis as female. The General Court's compromise—ordering Hall to wear masculine clothes adorned with an apron—demonstrated the informal influence of women upon the outcome of sexual cases" (p. 199).

There were mild punishments, such as shaming rituals directed at cuckolds or henpecked husbands. "[Moral] policing embraced bawdiness and riot and placed the blame on different actors (the cuckold, rather than the adulterer)….Nailing horns to a man's door, literally or figuratively, amounted to a communal judgment that he was unable to control his wife's sexual habits" (p. 206).

"(Y)oung Samuel Terry of Springfield, Massachusetts distressed his neighbors when, during the Sabbath sermon, he stood outside the meeting house 'chafing his yard to provoak lust'" (D'Emilio & Freedman, 2012, p. 15). For public masturbation Mr. Terry suffered a lashing. He was later charged with premarital intercourse, considered a crime at that time. He was fined. Twenty-three years later he was fined again with a group of men for "immodest and beastly play," probably fondling and mutual masturbation. Again he was fined. The notable feature of Mr. Terry's punishment was that he accepted it and was, therefore, considered a citizen of good standing. He eventually became a town constable.

Punishments Varied In the Chesapeake Colony, fines and whipping were common punishments for adultery, sodomy, rape, or the bearing of illegitimate children. In the Massachusetts Bay Colony, on the other hand, the death penalty was imposed for adultery, sodomy, or rape. These behaviors were equated with capital offense such as treason, murder, or witchcraft (D'Emilio & Freedman, 2012, p. 11).

> In Plymouth Colony, two women were convicted of unspecified 'leude behavior each (with) the other upon a bed,' but the penalty was far different from the death sentence that a man could expect. One was required to make public acknowledgement of her 'unchast (sic) behavior.' The other received *no* penalty. In Massachusetts Bay Colony a female servant was flogged, partly because of 'unseemly practices betwixt her and another maid'. (Painter, 2005, p. 6)

Early America was a mainly agricultural society, so there was ample opportunity for sex with animals (called "buggery"). Citizen William Hacketts, "'found in buggery with a cow, upon the Lord's day,' had to witness the execution of the cow before his own hanging took place. Sixteen year old Thomas Granger...confessed to 'buggery with a mare, a cow, two goats, five sheep, two calves, and a turkey.' The court ordered a lineup of sheep at which Grazer identified his sexual partners, who were 'killed before his face' and then 'he himself was executed'" (Ben-Atar & Brown, 2014, p. 22).

In "the autumn of 1796, eighty-five-year-old John Farrell...(was)... convicted by the Massachusetts Supreme Judicial Court of engaging in 'a venereal affair with a certain Brute Animal called a Bitch'....Almost exactly three years later...eighty-three-year-old Gideon Washburn was also convicted of buggery" when the jury determined that he "hath lain with beasts or brute Creatures by carnal copulation" (Ben-Atar & Brown, 2014, p. 4). The appeal of these convictions dragged on for a considerable period. Eventually one was executed and the other died in custody. Not all crimes of buggery resulted in so grim a fate. "(I)n 1794 eleven-year-old Jeffry Skuse was caught with his penis 'fasten'd' to a dog, but 'on account of his Youth the court tho't fit to shown him Compassion, and order'd him discharge'd'" (Ben-Atar & Brown, 2014, p. 19).

A Rhode Island court convicted a man of "an Attempt of Buggery with a doge." He was fined, had a thumb branded with the letter R (for rape), was publicly humiliated and whipped, and had to stand in stocks for

3 days wearing a sign that stated "heare I stand ffor Commiting the Most Horrid and Beastly Sin of Bugery or Sodomy with A dog" [ed: errors in original] (Ben-Atar & Brown, 2014, p. 27).

In colonial America, marriage and the bearing of children were considered paramount to maintain social cohesion. Sex was best practiced within these confines. An illustrative example is that of Stephen Temple's wife. Mrs. Temple accused her husband of sexual intercourse with their 14-year-old daughter. She wanted her husband to change his behavior and did not seek a divorce. They were reconciled when he apologized and promised to reform. This was common practice at the time. If an offender seemed to repent, he or she was welcomed back into the church or official positions in the society (D'Emilio & Freedman, 2012, p. 25).

Punishment was also meted out by gender. "Sodomy and rape were men's crimes. Although adultery, fornication, and bastardy involved couples, women…were more likely than men to be prosecuted and convicted for these sexual offenses.…Men more often had to pay fines and court costs, while women who had less access to property, had to accept whipping.…Most…colonies adopted the death penalty for adultery, although it was rarely enforced" (D'Emilio & Freedman, 2012, p. 28).

Sodomy, as it was conceived at that time, was not the same thing as the modern conception. Rather, as stated earlier, it referred to nonprocreative sexual acts of various kinds. However, "(M)en convicted of 'sodomitical acts,' such as 'spending their seed upon one another,' received severe and repeated whipping, burning with a hot iron, or banishment." There was no category specifically recognizable as homosexuality. "Like other sinners, women or men who were punished for unnatural acts did not acquire a lifetime identity as 'homosexuals,' and they could be reintegrated into the fold" (D'Emilio & Freedman, 2012, pp. 30–31).

Nineteenth-Century America

At the dawn of the nineteenth century, America remained a primarily agricultural society. The eighteenth-century public theater of show trials and punishments persisted for a time as the major methods of sexual control.

Punishable acts still included adultery, fornication, incest, bestiality, and sodomy. The printing and selling of obscene pictures or books were now included on the list but these victimless crimes attracted less attention as time wore on (Carlisle, 2009, p. 148).

> Public punishments were a visible part of daily life….(H)owever, this began to change as lawmakers began to view criminals as people who could be rehabilitated, rather than as hardened criminals who had to be physically punished – or executed….People's interest in privacy, seclusion, and control of emotions…meant that public hangings were too inflammatory for the public to view. Society and lawmakers came to see self-discipline, moderation, and sobriety as the hallmarks of a republican society. (Carlisle, 2009, p. 152)

"Rehabilitation" had a different meaning in the early nineteenth century. As American society became increasingly industrialized the population swiftly increased. In 1749 the population was roughly 1,000,000. By 1775 it had more than doubled to 2,400,000. At the time of the second census in 1800, it had doubled again to 5,308,483. What this meant for the criminal justice system was that the small colonial jails and stockades would be insufficient to house the growing numbers of convicted criminals, the socially deviant, the poor and dependent, and the mentally ill. Rothman (2008, pp. xxviii–xxx) described this development:

- Incarceration became the outstanding method for punishment and treatment.
- Whether the purpose of the institution was correcting criminal behavior to treatment of the mentally ill, all institutions had the same pattern of organization.
- Institutions were deliberately set physically apart from society in general, clearly defining the boundaries between "Us" and "Them."
- Daily activities were rigorously routinized.
- The heart of these routines was work, solitude, steady labor, and isolation.
- Almost all of the institutions housed the lower orders of society.

In such a controlled setting, "rehabilitation" meant that the convict, social deviant, or mentally ill person could seriously contemplate the error of his or her ways and consider how their life could be conducted in an orderly, law-abiding, nonviolent fashion. Rothman's (2008) description strongly resembles the description of the "total institution" by Goffman (1961)

The asylum or prison as a solution to uncomfortable social problems would, according to Rothman (2008):

> at once rehabilitate the inmates, thereby reducing crime, insanity, and poverty, and would then, through the very success of its design, as an example for the larger society…It was a grand and utopian vision, one that sought to ensure the safety of the republic and promote its glory. (p. xxxiv)

Such hopes, of course, proved in the end to be nonsense. Incarceration may have been preferable to the lash, branding, or other forms of public humiliation and degradation. Private degradation and humiliation through numbing routines or meaningless work in total silence was a heavy burden on the inmates. Rehabilitation in such a setting seems a highly unlikely outcome.

Laws (2009) has described some of the details of life in the prison community:

- Solitary cells for eating, sleeping, and working.
- Private yards for exercise.
- Inmates spoke only to selected visitors.
- Reading confined to morally uplifting literature.
- Inmates hooded when moving about so they could not see or be seen by other prisoners.

These methods were heralded as halting corruption by separation from evil influences. As time wore on, the notion of rehabilitation was abandoned. The ruling philosophy became:

- Separation
- Obedience
- Labor

The regime was very military in nature and persisted into the early twentieth century. At Sing Sing Prison in New York, the guiding rule was: "To labor diligently, to obey all orders, and preserve an unbroken silence." As the nineteenth century progressed, as might be expected of such grim situations, the hopefulness vanished from the enterprise. Prisons and asylums became warehouses that were overcrowded and understaffed, a not unfamiliar sight a century later. If society wanted to keep the deviant out of sight, this was a compelling solution.

Laws (2009) noted further that there was more to this effort than just locking up inconvenient people. In the early nineteenth century the roots of deviant behavior were sought. These included:

- Family disorganization
- Community corruption
  - Taverns
  - Brothels
  - Theaters
  - Gambling houses
  - Street life

The assumption was that the delinquent moved inexorably from minor to major crime. The belief emerged that society was disintegrating and something had to be done. Measures had to be taken to preserve public order and isolate troublesome people.

Finer Definitions of Deviance

Who were these troublesome people? Many were the same as those identified in colonial times. As the century progressed efforts were made to completely understand deviant sexual behavior. Classification schemes and more complete descriptions of deviant behaviors of various types would not fully emerge until the twentieth century. What follows is not intended to be comprehensive but rather to provide a flavor of the times.

Incest, Child Molestation, Statutory Rape

The Social Science Research Council (Mintz, 2012, p. 1) noted:

> That the young were sexually abused was well known to nineteenth-century Americans. In New York City, between 1790 and 1876 between a third and a half of rape victims were under the age of 19; during the 1820s the figure was 76%...[A historian]...found more than 500 published newspaper reports of father-daughter incest between 1817 and 1899 ....
>
> At first, public concern focused on the very young, those ten or younger. But beginning in the late nineteenth century, philanthropists and reformers brought attention to a somewhat older group of those aged eleven to seventeen. Reformers fought to raise the age of consent to sixteen and to enact laws to prevent those younger than sixteen from entering any place that sold intoxicants, pool halls, and dance halls ....
>
> In courthouses, the treatment of sexual abuse was colored by a young person's age, gender, and willingness to conform to cultural stereotypes. For a long time, jurors treated young girls very differently from boys and older girls. Sexual activity with young girls was clearly regarded as pathological by the late nineteenth century, but proving cases of abuse proved very difficult. Jurors expected a young girl to reveal her innocence by using vague, simple, euphemistic language, while expecting older girls to put up resistance or demonstrate immaturity and a lack of sexual understanding. Interestingly, men charged with sodomizing pubescent boys were convicted in the same proportions of those whose victims were young boys, but this was not the case with girls.
>
> At first, the focus was on physical harm to the young person or the ruin of their reputation; nothing was said about the psychological scars caused by abuse until the 1930s. 30 (sic) percent of statutory rape cases from 1896 to 1926 sought to resolve the case by marriage or financial payment.

The resolutions noted for incest, child molestation, and statutory rape were available only to those who could buy off the complainant or persuade her to marry. The poor went to jail. The issues described in the preceding section are treated in considerable detail by Robertson (2005) and a review of that work by Fass (2006). It was not until the early twentieth century that the perpetrators of these offenses against children would come to be called monsters, sex fiends, and perverts, the real folk devils.

Rape

Block (2009) has provided descriptive accounts of rape law for the period 1830–1900. Jurisprudence was initially guided by English common law. This was modified as time passed.

> Judges began to stray from or alter English common law doctrines.... For example, a majority of American courts rejected the common law requirement of proof of seminal emission to show that penetration had occurred....On the other hand, American judges in many jurisdictions made it easier for defendants to attack the reputation of their accusers.... (p. 1391)

That has a familiar sound to it. Block noted further that Americans in the nineteenth century used language to describe rape that would be barely recognizable today because the clinical terms did not exist. "There were no 'rapists' or 'sexual offenders' in the 19th century. Men 'outraged' women, they did not 'sexually assault' them. The medicalization of rape language did not occur before the 20th century..." (p. 1392).

In the antebellum era if a white man raped a slave woman that would not be recognized in a court of law. Slaves were, by definition, chattel property and owners could use their own property as they saw fit. White slave owners sometimes forced male slaves to impregnate female slaves. The law did not recognize this as rape although it bore all of the descriptors of that crime (p. 1393).

The rape of a black woman by a white man was treated much the same in the antebellum era. In the Reconstruction period following the Civil War, black women fared somewhat better in that, on occasion, they could bring official charges against their assaulters. "What mattered in these cases was not so much the race of the defendant but the class of the complainant. A lower-class woman who brought the charge was more suspect and her accusation more scrutinized" (Block, 2009, p. 1395).

Then, as now, few women were willing to report sexual assault. What is striking is the fact that, 150 years later, defendants and complainants seem to be treated much the same in American courts.

Sodomy

As we have seen, the word "sodomy" was a catchall for several varieties of deviant sexual behavior in the eighteenth century. This continued into the nineteenth century. Today it exclusively refers to anal intercourse or oral copulation.

Painter (2005) stated that, under English common law, sodomy referred only to anal intercourse between two men or a man and a woman, or sexual intercourse with an animal of the opposite sex. The prescribed punishment was death. "Cunnilingus, fellatio, tribadism, interfemoral intercourse, and mutual masturbation were not to be included in the act. An early English case ruled that fellatio with a minor, including the emission of semen, 'did not constitute the offense of sodomy.' Fellatio, interfemoral intercourse, and mutual masturbation, were not punished…with death, whereas anal intercourse was" (p. 6).

Hamowy (1977) stated that the common law description of sodomy, anal intercourse between men or between a man and a woman, remained the major prohibition against sexual deviance through most of the nineteenth century. Toward the end of the century, doctors, psychiatrists, and legislators began to consider other unconventional sexual acts as worthy of legal notice.

> The original statues – all of which prohibited "sodomy," "buggery," "the crime against nature," or any combination of these terms – did not explicitly specify which acts were included within the meaning of the law. Traditionally the common-law interpretation prevailed, thus limiting the prohibition to anal intercourse. However, because of the vagueness of the language, when a particular "unnatural" act was charged as being in violation of the statute, the courts had the option of extending the sense of the statute by construing it as covering the particular act before it.
>
> (B)eginning in 1879…legislatures were encouraged to expand their statutory prohibitions to cover fellatio, cunnilingus, and other "unnatural"

acts, which medical science had shown to be the product of diseased and perverted minds. (p. 250)

While the mechanisms of the law were closing in on acts deemed to be sexually deviant, it is worth noting that some of these behaviors which would be deemed highly deviant today—intercourse with females over the age of 10 or 12, solicitation of sexual intercourse—were not considered illegal in 1880.

Because the arm of the law was not long toward the end of the century, there is every reason to suppose that deviant subcultures were established by the mid-nineteenth century. For example, Walt Whitman (1900) celebrated his "body electric" as he openly described cruising the sidewalks of his beloved New York, his "city of orgies":

> To-day, I go consort with nature's darlings – to-night too;
> I am for those who believe in loose delights – I share the
> midnight orgies of young men;
> I dance with the dancers, and drink with the drinkers;
> The echoes ring with our indecent calls;
> I take for my love some prostitute – I pick some low person
> for my dearest friend,
> He shall be lawless, rude, illiterate – he shall be one condemn'd
> by others for deeds done;
> I will play a part no longer – why should I exile myself from my
> companions? (p. 127)

Jenkins (1998, p. 27) described some aspects of deviant subculture in the late nineteenth and early twentieth centuries:

> Among the varieties of perversion that came under scrutiny in America were pedophilia and homosexuality....Confirming the magnitude of the pervert danger was the evidence produced by Progressives and muckrakers about the vice districts of American cities, where gay and pederastic subcultures were apparent to any investigator....At the end of the century, social reformers venturing into the vice underworlds...found evidence of child prostitution involving both girls and boys....A vice investigation in

Philadelphia in 1912 reported "the corruption of hundreds of young boys for the use of perverts. 'Numbers of boys in knee pants are commercializing themselves openly on our streets for the practice of perversion.' This use of boys from eight to fourteen has developed in the last five years to an appalling extent."

Medicalization of Sexual Deviance

In the late nineteenth century, psychiatry was a new branch of medicine. This new discipline was distressed that the arm of the law was not long enough to capture those offenders deemed to have "diseased and perverted minds."

> The shift in American criminal law at the end of the 19th century which subjected so much conduct to legal restraint was occasioned by…the intrusion of medicine and psychiatry into the legislative process….By the 1880s…the profession was prepared to forcibly remold the entire society in the interests of mental health. In this respect physicians, and particularly psychiatrists, exhibited the same presumptuousness in meddling in the private affairs of people as was shown by others active in the reform movements of the period [ed: the early Progressive Era]. (Hamowy, 1977, p. 253)

As we shall see, this "presumptuousness" was a strong force well into the twentieth century. Szasz (cited in Hamowy, 1977, p. 232) traces the onset of meddling in private affairs to Benjamin Rush, the eighteenth-century physician considered to be the father of American psychiatry. He described Rush as:

> (T)he first American physician to urge the medicalization of social problems and their coercive control by means of "therapeutic" rather than "punitive" sanctions.

It is to the medicalization of sexual deviance that we now turn.

References

Ben-Atar, D. S., & Brown, R. D. (2014). *Taming lust: Crimes against nature in the early Republic.* Philadelphia: University of Pennsylvania Press.

Block, M. R. (2009). Rape law in 19th century America: Some thoughts and reflections on the state of the field. *History Compass, 7*(5), 1391–1399.

Carlisle, R. P. (2009). *Handbook to life in America* (Vol. 2). New York: Facts on File.

D'Emilio, J., & Freedman, E. B. (2012). *Intimate matters: A history of sexuality in America* (3rd ed.). Chicago: University of Chicago Press.

Fass, P. S. (2006). Crimes against children: Sexual violence and legal culture in New York City, 1880–1960 (review). *Journal of Social History, 40*, 231–233.

Goffman, E. (1961). *Asylums: Essays on the social situation of mental patients and other inmates.* Garden City, NY: Anchor Books.

Hamowy, R. (1977). Medicine and the crimination of sin: "Self-abuse" in 19th century America. *Journal of Libertarian Studies, 1*, 229–270.

Jenkins, P. (1998). *Moral panic: Changing concepts of the child molester in modern America.* New Haven, CT: Yale University Press.

Laws, D. R. (2009, April). *The recovery of the asylum: Observations on the mismanagement of sex offenders.* Keynote presentation at the Tools to Take Home conference, Lucy Faithfull Foundation, Birmingham, UK.

Mintz, S. (2012). *Placing childhood sexual abuse in historical perspective.* Retrieved December 15, 2014, from blogs.ssrc.org/tif/2012/07/13

Olson-Raymer, G. (n.d.). Syllabus from: *The Evolving Colonial Criminal Justice System,* History 110, Department of History, Humboldt State University, Arcata, CA.

Painter, G. (2005). *The sensibilities of our forefathers: The history of sodomy laws in the United States.* Portland, OR: Gay and Lesbian Archives of the Pacific Northwest.

Ramsey, C.B. (2013). Sex and social order: The selective enforcement of colonial American adultery laws in the English context. *Yale Journal of Law and the Humanities, 10*, 191–228.

Robertson, S. (2005). *Crimes against children: Sexual violence and legal culture in New York City: 1880–1960.* Chapel Hill, NC: University of North Carolina Press.

Rothman, D. J. (2008). *The discovery of the asylum: Social order and disorder in the new republic.* Piscataway, NJ: Aldine Transaction.

Whitman, W. (1900). *Leaves of grass* (Electronic classics series). Hazelton, PA: Pennsylvania State University.

4

The Medicalization of Deviance: Sex Offender as Mental Patient

What Is Medicalization?

The fifth version of *The Diagnostic and Statistical Manual of Mental Disorders* (*DSM-V*; American Psychiatric Association, 2013) states that most people with atypical sexual interests do not have a mental disorder. According to *DSM-V*, a diagnosis of paraphilic disorder requires that the affected individual:

- Experience personal distress about their behavior, not distress about society's reaction to their behavior, or
- Have a sexual desire or behavior that involves psychological distress, injury, or death of another person, or a desire for sexual conduct with unwilling persons or persons unable to give consent.

The majority of sex offenders do not experience personal distress about their behavior but a substantial number may cause psychological distress or injury, or force themselves on unwilling persons. It is important to remember that sex offending is a disorder of sexual interest, not a mental illness in the sense of the individual experiencing delusions and

© The Editor(s) (if applicable) and The Author(s) 2016
D.R. Laws, *Social Control of Sex Offenders*,
DOI 10.1057/978-1-137-39126-1_4

hallucinations. It is equally important to remember that if that disordered behavior appears in the *DSM-V* nomenclature—exhibitionism, fetishism, frotteurism, pedophilia, sexual masochism, sexual sadism, transvestism, or voyeurism—it is considered a psychiatric disorder worthy of intervention.

Medicalization of social deviance, in this case atypical sexual behaviors, then "refers to the tendency to define deviance as a manifestation of an underlying sickness, to find the causes of deviance within the individual rather than the social structure, and to treat deviance through the intervention of medical personnel" (Horowitz, 1981, p. 750). Conrad (1992, p. 211) states that "medicalization occurs when a medical frame or definition has been applied to understand or manage a problem .... The interest in medicalization has predominantly focused on previously nonmedical problems that have been medicalized (and, often, thought to be inappropriately medicalized)." For example, an atypical sexual orientation, transsexualism, the belief that one is actually a member of the opposite sex, can be unhelpfully medicalized as "gender dysphoria." The following imaginary colloquy between a psychiatrist and his client, suspected as being a transsexual, illustrates this problem.

> Psychiatrist: (confident) When did you first realize that you were a woman trapped in a man's body?
> Client: (amused) I never thought that. I just like to dress up in women's clothes. Can't you tell that I'm just an old drag queen?

Related to the preceding hypothetical example, Newburger and Bourne (1978) note that socially marginal individuals are more likely to be defined as deviant and in need of "treatment." The more the client resembles the examining psychiatrist (or other medical professional), the less likely he/she be assigned a deviant label. "Professionals ... engage in an intricate process of selection, finding facts that fit the label which has been applied, responding to a few details set within a panoply of entirely acceptable conduct" (p. 601). In such a model, persons are examined in terms of what is "wrong" with them, a search for the defining characteristics of deviance.

"(M)edicalization is a broad definitional process, which may or may not directly include physicians and their treatments (although it often does)" (Conrad, 1992, p. 211). At the institutional level, psychiatric control has always been prominent. However, at the institutional and community levels, other professionals such as psychologists, social workers, counselors, probation and parole officers, and psychiatric nurses are all woven into the medicalization web. And all are bound to some extent by the scripture of the *DSM*.

To put sex offenders into this context, consider that deviant behaviors once viewed as sinful or criminal are now characterized as a medical problem. A problem previously dealt with by a civil court or a church has, through medicalization, become the responsibility of psychiatry (Link, 2009, p. 3).

Medicalization of Sexual Deviance

The preceding section cites literature from the late twentieth to the early twenty-first centuries. Medicalization may be a phenomenon recognized as a subject for study in the twentieth century, but its practice began in the mid-nineteenth century.

The narrative thus far has shown that, in the eighteenth through much of the nineteenth centuries, sexual deviants were not classified as such. Instead they were treated as common criminals who committed crimes such as sodomy (loosely defined and incorporating homosexuality), incest, rape, child abuse, or bestiality, the offenses most commonly named. The previous chapter noted that it was the father of American psychiatry, Benjamin Rush, who urged that social deviants be treated therapeutically, albeit in a manner unspecified, rather than punished. This resolution proved to be a long time coming. By the late nineteenth century, psychiatrists began to categorize various paraphilias because they wanted a more descriptive system than legal or religious concepts such as "sodomy" or "perversion."

Defining Deviant Sexuality

Much of the theorizing about deviant sexuality as a group of specific psychiatric disorders began to appear in the late nineteenth and early twentieth centuries. In 1896, Sigmund Freud scandalized the Vienna

Society for Psychiatry and Neurology with his seduction theory of childhood sexuality. The conference chair, Richard von Krafft-Ebing, replied to Freud, "It sounds like a scientific fairy tale" (Hunt, 1993, p. 181). The cold reception did not deter Freud. In 1905, he published *Three Essays on the Theory of Sexuality*, the book that made his early reputation. It was publicly denounced but well received in professional circles (Hunt, 1993, p. 191).

In the twenty-first century, many professionals continue to believe that Freud was the father of the study of deviant sexuality. This is inaccurate. His voice was one of many. Gay (1998, pp. 143–144) noted that in the mid- to late-nineteenth century many scientists were considering the varieties of human sexual behavior. In 1845, Adolf Patze, a German physician, observed sexual behavior in children 3–6 years of age. Infantile sexuality was similarly noted in 1867 by Henry Maudsley, a British psychiatrist. In 1869 the word "homosexuality" was introduced by Karoly Maria Benkert. In the same year, Carl Friedrich Otto Westphal advanced "contrary sexual feeling" as a similar description. Published in 1886, Richard von Krafft-Ebing's *Psychopathia Sexualis* remains one of the most detailed descriptions of deviant sexuality ever published. In 1896 Albert Moll followed Krafft-Ebing with *Perversions of the Genital Instinct*. This tradition carried into the twentieth century, notably in the writings of Havelock Ellis and Magnus Hirschfeld. What is apparent from the preceding examples is that what today we refer to as sexology was well established academically by the time Freud published his *Three Essays* (Laws, 2003, p. 22; Laws & Marshall, 2003, pp. 76–77).

In this same time period, unlike the writings of Freud and other psychodynamic thinkers, a strictly behavioral theoretical account was developing to account for the development of deviant sexual behavior. In the early 1900s Alfred Binet (of intelligence testing fame) advanced the theory that sexual deviation was a learned behavior that developed through accidental experience with deviant behavior. A decade earlier Norman noted that deviant sexual interest could be developed by repeated masturbation to sexual fantasies of specific deviant behaviors. By the mid-twentieth century it was generally acknowledged that specific expressions of sexual behavior were learned (see, e.g., Ford & Beach, 1952; Kinsey, Pomeroy, & Martin, 1949; Laws & Marshall, 2003, p. 77).

Prior to the mid-century writings noted, it is clear that the major pronouncements regarding deviant sexual behavior were made by medical doctors. In the early twentieth century, MacMillan (2013, p. 263) cited a view of deviant sexual behavior typical of the time by the German psychiatrist Emil Kraepelin: "There is not the slightest doubt that contrary sexual tendencies develop from the foundation of a sickly, degenerate personality." He was speaking of homosexuality but the condemnation could easily be applied to any deviant sexual behavior.

Hamowy (1977) has summarized the takeover of the treatment and management of deviant social behavior by psychiatry in this period.

(W)hile, during the 19th century, the prohibition of sexual immorality played a comparatively unimportant role in American criminal law, the medical profession arrogated to itself the task of dealing with moral questions .... (B)y substituting "treatment" of disease for legal punishment of moral transgression, placed itself in the position of enforcer of virtuous conduct. Medicine was so successful in assuming this function that, by the end of the century, it had enlisted the great mass of the literate public in support of its findings respecting the connection between sexual behavior and mental disease. At that point it became possible to encompass the conclusions reached by the psychiatric and medical professions and to criminalize sexual immorality under the guise of legislating in the area of preventive medicine. (p. 229)

The Progressive Era

Running consecutively with the preceding developments was the onset of the progressive era (1890s–1920s). Progressive programs stood in bold contrast to the treatment of social deviants that was prominent in the nineteenth century. The programs were not necessarily led by medical doctors and included social reformers from universities and workers from settlement houses. Rather than viewing social deviants as a class of criminal offenders, they focused on the individual case. Their approach was on a case-by-case basis, the goal being to understand the life history of the offender and devise a treatment specific to the individual (Rothman, 2002, p. 5). This intensive study of the individual case is highly similar to later criminological research by Glueck and Glueck (1950) and Sampson and Laub (1993).

> (A)ll Progressive programs assumed one outstanding feature: *they required discretionary responses to each case* [ed: italics in original]. Rules could not be made in advance. Each person had to be treated differently. Fixed codes of set procedures were both unfair and ineffective. (Rothman, 2002, p. 6)

The preceding statement represents the positive side of Progressive thinking. In reality things did not go quite that well. There was understandably considerable opposition to such radical and sweeping reforms. The Progressives intended their reforms to be *substitutes* to confinement; in fact, they became *supplements* to confinement.

> [Re]formers were never deeply disturbed by the fact that administrative convenience had become so well served in their programs for they were convinced that their innovations could satisfy both goals, that the same person and the same institution could at once guard and help, protect and rehabilitate, maintain custody and deliver treatment …. In the end, when conscience and convenience met, convenience won. When treatment and coercion met, coercion won. (Rothman, 2002, pp. 9–10)

Despite the failure to fundamentally alter the practice of institutionalization, the Progressives remained staunchly anti-institutional, and some of the reforms enacted in the period 1900–1920 persist to the present day. These included probation, parole, indeterminate sentences for adults, juvenile courts for delinquents, and the foundation of outpatient clinics for the mentally ill. These changes altered the entire picture of incarceration (Rothman, 2002, p. 43).

Early Treatment of Sex Offenders

Efforts to control sex offenders followed several streams from the late nineteenth to the mid-twentieth centuries. Legal remedies competed with therapeutic ones, the latter being defined in a variety of ways. Although not so intended, Krafft-Ebing's term *psychopathia sexualis* implied that all sexual deviance was a mental disease, and the term *psychopathy* gained a prominence which would persist for half a century.

There was also the belief that sexual deviance was associated with mental deficiency, hence the appearance of the term "defective delinquent." Jenkins (1998, p. 39) has described this development:

> Criminological writing of the era also focused on the mentally defective, or individuals of very low intelligence…. In a daring intellectual leap, mental deficiency was linked to the moral deficiency of the psychopath, on the grounds that morality and intelligence were associated characteristics. For both the morally and mentally defective, a lack of conventional inhibitions increased the tendency to lawbreaking … By the end of the nineteenth century, controlling "defective delinquents" became the most important issue for those wishing to reduce the incidence of violence and sex crime.

There were brutal options. If the sex criminal was morally and intellectually unfit, it was believed that these tendencies could be transmitted to the offspring.

> Perversion, like alcoholism, crime, epilepsy, and insanity, was a byproduct of the "genetic rubbish" polluting the social gene pool and would stubbornly resist conventional legal solutions. In 1893 Dr. F.E. Daniel argued that castration was the appropriate treatment for perverts: "rape, sodomy, bestiality, pederasty and habitual masturbation" should involve the loss of all rights, including the right of procreation. (Jenkins, 1998, p. 42)

As noted previously, institutionalization alone, the separation of the offender from society, coupled with the provision of strict routine and stable work, was thought to provide a therapeutic environment that could potentially rehabilitate him or her.

> Criminologist Enrico Ferri wrote in 1884, "As the sick person is kept in the hospital just as long a time as is necessary for his cure, and as the insane patient remains in the asylum all of his life until cured and leaves it when he is cured, so it should be with the delinquent." (Jenkins, 1998, p. 40)

Some practices change very slowly. Eighty-five years later the author was employed in a large maximum security hospital that was famous for its "treatment" of over 500 confined sex offenders. The patients were transferred from penitentiaries where they had been serving time for a sex offense. They had been termed "mentally disordered sex offenders" and were sent to a secure hospital for treatment until they were "no longer a danger to themselves or others." In fact, the patients had very little to occupy themselves. Such jobs as were available were mostly make-work with no recompense. Educational opportunities were minimal and were typically monopolized by stronger, aggressive offenders. Psychiatric staff controlled the institution but actually did not engage in treatment other than the conventionally medical. Treatment took two forms. Patients attended therapy groups several times a week. These were conducted by psychologists, social workers, interns, and psychiatric nurses. They tended to be unfocused and vaguely psychodynamic in nature. The other treatment stream was simply termed "milieu therapy." This resembled the situation described by Ferri above. Just being in the institution was deemed therapeutic; if the patient "got with the program" he might "get better" and eventually "go home." If he did not get with the program he was likely to be sent back to prison. The notion of milieu therapy is nonsense. According to Rothman (2002, p. 144) a system of incarceration, whether it be called a prison or a secure hospital, can never both incapacitate and rehabilitate.

The situation that the author experienced in 1970 had been established in the late 1920s to the early 1930s when psychologists and psychiatrists went to work in prisons. Ostensibly they were bringing new therapeutic skills that would benefit the inmates. This did not work any better then than it did in the early 1970s.

> (T)he skills that the new professional brought to the institutions... (did not) ...prove very helpful .... (T)heir classification schemes were static and descriptive, not dynamic or analytic .... In essence there were only three categories: the better sort, the hardened, and the defective. (Rothman, 2002, pp. 132–134)

Life in mental institutions as described by Rothman persisted in the author's experience through the 1960s in a different, more common mental hospital. As in the subsequent decade there were vaguely focused psychodynamic therapy groups, music therapy, bibliotherapy, experimentation with newly developing psychoactive drugs, as well as occupational therapy. While appearing to be an active therapeutic institution, it was a warehouse for the troublesome and inconvenient and included some sex offenders. The institution was sited on a hill overlooking the adjacent rural community. The hospital dated from 1869 and was at one time totally self-sufficient in that it grew its own crops, slaughtered livestock, maintained a dairy, and operated shops to maintain the institution. But, in the 1960s, was it very different from what it had been, say, in the 1920s? Probably not. Rothman (2002, p. 340), speaking of that earlier era, put it this way:

> If improvement and discharge did not take place within a few months, as was all too true for the great majority of cases, the hospital routine moved into a second and very different phase. Now the patient received a ward assignment, determined almost entirely by his behavior in the institution. The quiet and orderly patient went to one ward, the noisy to another, the violent to still another. The classification was not by illness or by prescribed treatment, but how easy or difficult it was to control the patient.

For sex offenders, change from this sort of routine did not begin to occur until the 1950s.

Nonbehavioral Treatment of Sex Offenders

If sex offenders, as previously believed, were in fact intellectually and morally deficient it would not be expected that they could profit from treatment. The discovery that they could be engaged in conventional treatment laid the basis for later, more direct behavioral interventions. In addition, research on the classification of subtypes of sex offenders (e.g., Gebhard, Gagnon, Pomeroy, & Christenson, 1965) provided details on the characteristics of sex offenders that could become targets of treatment. The details provided enabled sex offenders to be differentiated from non-sexual offenders as well as nonoffenders (Laws & Marshall, 2003, p. 85). That was the good news. The bad news was that psychotherapeutic programs in this era suffered from the lineage that they bore from previous efforts. While therapists were optimistic that their treatments were successful, this did not prove to be the case. An influential early review of sex offender treatment (Furby, Weinrott, & Blackshaw, 1989) found that most of these efforts were faulted in a variety of ways and it could not be demonstrated at that time that the early varieties of treatment had an effect on the recidivism of sex offenders. However, the fact that the programs were faulted led to the search for alternatives.

The Movement Against Medicalization

Behavioral Treatment of Sex Offenders

Some of those alternatives first appeared in the late nineteenth and early twentieth centuries. Laws and Marshall (2003, p. 77) have noted some of these early attempts. The earliest published account of an attempt to treat homosexuality by what we today would call masturbatory reconditioning (Laws & O'Neil, 1981) was reported by Charcot and Magnan in 1882 and Schrenk-Notzing in 1895. In 1911 Moll, using a series of successive approximations, was able to shift sexual interest from boys to young women. In the 1960s this technique would be refined as a shaping procedure called fading (Barlow & Agras, 1973). In 1892 Norman argued that deviant sexual interest was a result of repeated masturbation to deviant fantasies. That hypothesis would be elaborated in 1965 by McGuire, Carlisle, and Young. Thus, there were precursors to behavioral intervention but not yet a movement in that direction.

The movement that eventually emerged was a reaction to the imprecision and vagueness of treatment efforts directed at sex offenders in the early twentieth century. We have noted that the main theme of the Progressive Era was that progress toward behavior change could only be achieved by intensive examination of the individual case, by prediction and control of behavior. Thus the historical moment was right when, in 1913, John B. Watson published *Psychology as the Behaviorist Views It*, the behaviorist manifesto. Hunt (1993, p. 258) stated that, in 56 words, the manifesto proclaimed three essential principles that would subsequently guide treatment: (1) the content of psychology should be behavior, not consciousness; (2) its method should be objective, not introspective;

and (3) its goal should be the prediction and control of behavior, not a fundamental understanding of mental events. These principles were later expanded in Watson's *Psychology from the Standpoint of a Behaviorist* (1919) and *Behaviorism* (1924).

Laws and Marshall (2003, p. 79) described why, at this moment, behaviorism was what needed to happen:

> It was precisely this appeal to science, the assertion that behaviorism was the first scientific psychology, that sold the idea in America. Although many psychologists would not wish to acknowledge it, in academia at least, behaviorism of one sort or another was the reigning psychology from 1920 to the late 1960s. It was scientific. It was experimental. It was practical. It was commonsensical, and it was useful. In its more modern form, it is still all of these things.

Probably the key moment in the development of what would come to be called "behavior therapy" was the publication of paper "Effects of Psychotherapy" by Eysenck (1952). Although this paper is today often dismissed by clinicians, it began the process of unraveling established beliefs about the value of the then-reigning dynamic psychotherapy. Eysenck argued that traditional methods of psychotherapy had failed to demonstrate efficacy. At the time this was a revolutionary statement and paved the way for the birth of behavior therapy, first in South Africa, then in England, and ultimately in the USA.

In 1958 the South African psychiatrist Joseph Wolpe published *Psychotherapy by Reciprocal Inhibition*. A treatment called systematic desensitization emerged which was successfully applied to anxiety disorders. It was subsequently applied to deviant sexual behavior (Laws & Marshall, 2003, p. 82).

Wolpe's work was influential in the development of behavior therapy in both England and North America. An array of procedures appeared that were scientifically respectable, based on laboratory procedures with animals, and were practical and easy to apply. Early descriptions of behavior therapy with sexual deviants were primarily individual case studies using some variation of aversive therapy. The usual procedure was to pair a noxious stimulus with either images of the target behavior (Pavlovian conditioning) or the enactment of the deviant behavior (operant conditioning). For example, injection of a nausea-inducing agent (apomorphine) was associated with sexual activities or images. Electrical aversion, where a shock to the arm or leg was associated with deviant images or acts, replaced apomorphine. Electric shock was easier to administer and could be precisely paired with the deviant image or act. This became the treatment of choice with homosexuals as well as transvestites and fetishists. Other aversive stimuli included noxious odors, covert aversive images, and the use of shame and embarrassment. Unfortunately most of these studies were performed with homosexuals who were coerced into treatment. However, their publication led directly to the application of behavior therapy to sex offenders rather than merely sexual variants (Laws & Marshall, 2003, p. 83).

It should be mentioned here that the examples given served more as demonstrations of various behavior therapy interventions. There is a notable lack of long-term investigations of the efficacy of behavior therapy. It is often forgotten by practitioners that, while behavior therapy can produce dramatic effects in the short term, those effects will diminish and fade away if the procedure is not repeatedly administered. In this sense, behavior therapy may be seen as a form of social control for sex offenders. Some of the techniques such as olfactory aversion (e.g., Laws, 2003) are easily self-administered and may be used to control fantasies as well as avoiding risk in vivo.

Medicalization had not gone away during this period. Almost all of the procedures reported above were administered by or under the control of psychiatrists and were performed in a hospital setting. Thus, even a new development with its roots firmly placed in psychology was co-opted and controlled by psychiatric medicine.

Behavior therapy was instrumental in changing the focus of treatment of sex offenders. The institutional programs that were devoted to altering sex offenders' personalities to reduce or eliminate sexual crime were mostly failures. As noted previously, such recidivism data as were available could not distinguish between treated and untreated sex offenders (Furby et al., 1989). The prime contribution of behavior therapy was the focus on the problem behavior itself. The notion of mental illness was dismissed and sexual deviation was viewed as a conscious choice in the present.

Most historical influences were not considered. The focus sharpened and was directed toward the elimination of deviant sexual preferences and behavior. Gradually the elements of treatment that could accomplish this end began to be packaged. Sets of treatments began to be directed to a set of clearly related problems (e.g., pro-offending attitudes). Toward the mid-1970s many treatment programs began to adopt this approach. This type of behaviorally oriented intervention was the precursor of what today we refer to as cognitive–behavioral therapy (Laws, 2003). Although some elements of dynamic psychotherapy are present in some programs, the interventions have largely moved away from medical control and the diagnosis of mental illness. Although there is typically a psychiatric presence, administrative control of these programs is largely in the hands of psychologists, social workers, and criminal justice personnel.

At this writing (2015) there are two major therapeutic schools of thought governing the treatment of sex offenders. These are *The Psychology of Criminal Conduct* (the RNR model) (Andrews & Bonta, 2010a) and the *Good Lives Model* (GLM) (Laws & Ward, 2011; Ward & Maruna, 2007). A detailed consideration of these approaches appears in Chap. 11.

References

American Psychiatric Association (APA). (2013). *Diagnostic and statistical manual of mental disorders* (5th ed.: DSM-5). Arlington, VA: American Psychiatric Association.

Barlow, D. H., & Agras, W. S. (1973). Fading to increase heterosexual responses in homosexuals. *Journal of Applied Behavioral Analysis, 6*, 355–366.

Conrad, P. (1992). Medicalization and social control. *Annual Review of Sociology, 18*, 209–232.

Eysenck, H. J. (1952). The effects of psychotherapy: An evaluation. *Journal of Consulting Psychology, 16*, 319–324.

Ford, C. S., & Beech, F. A. (1952). *Patterns of sexual behavior*. London: Methuen.

Furby, L., Weinrott, M. R., & Blackshaw, L. (1989). Sex offender recidivism: A review. *Psychological Bulletin, 105*, 3–30.

Gay, P. (1998). *Freud: A life for our time*. New York: Norton.

Gebhard, P. H., Gagnon, J., Pomeroy, W., & Christenson, C. (1965). *Sex offenders: An analysis of types*. New York: Harper and Row.

Glueck, S., & Glueck, E. (1950). *Unraveling juvenile delinquency*. New York: Commonwealth Fund.

Hamowy, R. (1977). Medicine and the crimination of sin: "Self-abuse" in 19th century America. *Journal of Libertarian Studies, 1*, 229–270.

Horowitz, A. V. (1981). The medicalization of deviance. *Contemporary Sociology, 10*, 750–752.

Hunt, M. (1993). *The story of psychology*. New York: Doubleday.

Jenkins, P. (1998). *Moral panic: Changing concepts of the child molester in modern America*. New Haven, CT: Yale University Press.

Kinsey, A. C., Pomeroy, W. B., & Martin, C. E., (1949). *Sexual behavior in the human male*. Philadelphia: Saunders.

Laws, D. R. (2003). Penile plethysmography: Will we ever get it right? In T. Ward, D. R. Laws, & S. M. Hudson (Eds.), *Theories and controversial issues in sexal deviance* (pp. 82–102). Thousand Oaks, CA: Sage.

Laws, D. R., & Marshall, W. L. (2003). A brief history of behavioral and cognitive behavioral approaches to sexual offenders: Part 1. Early developments. *Sexual Abuse: A Journal of Research and Treatment, 15*, 75–92.

Laws, D. R., & O'Neil, J. A. (1981). Variations on masturbatory conditioning. *Behavioural Psychotherapy, 9*, 111–136.

Laws, D. R., & Ward, T. (2011). *Desistance from sex offending*. New York: Guilford.

Link, S. (2009). *The medicalization of deviance*. Retrieved January 3, 2015, from: www.dswleads.com/Ebsco/The%20Medicalization%20of%20deviance.pdf

MacMillan, M. (2013). *The war that ended peace*. Toronto: Penguin.

Newburger, E. H., & Bourne, R. (1978). The medicalization and legalization of child abuse. *American Journal of Orthopsychiatry, 48*, 593–607.

Rothman, D. J. (2002). *Conscience and convenience: The asylum and its alternatives in Progressive America*. New York: Aldine de Gruyter.

Sampson, R. J., & Laub, J. H. (1993). *Crime in the making: Pathways and turning points through life*. Cambridge, MA: Harvard University Press.

Ward, T., & Maruna, S. (2007). *Rehabilitation: Beyond the risk paradigm*. London: Routledge.

Watson, J. B. (1919). *Psychology from the standpoint of a behaviorist*. Philadelphia: Lippincott.

Watson, J. B. (1924). *Behaviorism*. Chicago: University of Chicago Press.

5

The Sexual Psychopath/Predator Laws: Legal Construction of Deviance

To this point I have argued that, in the late nineteenth and early twentieth centuries, the discipline of psychiatry had successfully medicalized and demonized the "sexual psychopath" as surely a mentally ill and possibly dangerous person. Attempts to treat this condition had been piecemeal and yielded variable outcomes. There was, as yet, no systematic attempt to confine and ultimately treat sexual psychopaths on a large scale. A series of initiating events occurred in the late 1930s which spawned a movement that lasted for over the next 40 years. This was the era of the sexual psychopath laws.

There were actually three eras (Leon, 2011, p. 4):

- *The sexual psychopath era (1930–1950)*. This was a result of a moral panic that engendered belief that sex crime was increasing, that these crimes were committed by mentally ill "fiends," and that strict legislation was required to bring the problem under control.
- *The rehabilitative era (1950–1980)*. The focus here shifted from harsh, punitive measures to a concern with the mental health of sex offenders. The belief was that, with proper treatment that focused on the individual case, many sex offenders could be restored to useful life in society.

© The Editor(s) (if applicable) and The Author(s) 2016
D.R. Laws, *Social Control of Sex Offenders*,
DOI 10.1057/978-1-137-39126-1_5

- *The containment era (1980–present)*. As in the 1930s, public outcry over a number of heinous sex crimes and murders shifted attention back to the solution of incapacitation, the focus again being the worst of the worst. What made this era different was the emergence of the containment model, of which institutionalization was only one component. The other component was a model of social control that included criminal justice and treatment personnel who constructed a model for community monitoring.

Background to the Sexual Psychopath Laws

The background to these events shows that the situation of detected sex crime and punishment in the early twentieth century did not differ greatly from what we observe today. In 1940, for example, the New York City Mayor's Committee for the Study of Sex Offenses reviewed the situation that prevailed in the period 1930–1939. Vague terms like "impairing morals" covered a broad range of activities which included varieties of child molestation and sexual activities as well as nonsexual behaviors such as "gambling" or "sleeping in room with female child" (Mayor's Committee, 1940, pp. 54–55). The only sex offense with a reasonable degree of specificity was rape (forcible, statutory, and attempted) while others had vague titles such as "carnal abuse," "sodomy," or "seduction" (Lave, 2009, p. 550). Then as now, overworked courts and prosecutors made plea bargains that reduced serious sex offenses to crimes of a lesser degree or converted a felony to a misdemeanor. Offenders often accepted the plea rather than admit to an offense such as rape or sodomy which would lead to more serious consequences. Offenses against children were likely to be dropped due to the difficulty of obtaining credible evidence and relying upon the testimony of children (Jenkins, 1998, pp. 76–78). Ultimately the Mayor's Committee recommended a sexual psychopath law

> which would make it possible to retain convicted sex offenders who are not reasonably safe to be at large, in institutional confinement even after expiration of sentence. This would make it possible to retain custody over abnormal sex offenders who are neither mentally defective nor insane, but who because of constitutional penchants for abnormal

methods of satisfying sexual passions are dangerous to be at large. (Mayor's Committee, 1940, p. 9)

Was there really a wave of sex crime that required this level of legal response? Three child assaults and murders in the New York City area in the spring and summer of 1937 were given broad coverage in the local and national press. "In 1937 alone, there were 143 articles published about sex crimes in the *New York Times*... sex offenders were described as a national menace" (Lave, 2009, p. 550). The public was outraged and demanded that something be done.

That outrage was repeated in many communities across the country.

Lave (2009) has noted that such data as was available nationally was not a reliable index of the actual incidence of sex crimes. In 1930 the Federal Bureau of Investigation (FBI) began collecting arrest data from police departments and compiling it into the Uniform Crime Reports (UCR). The UCR reports data for the following seven index offenses: (1) murder, (2) nonnegligent manslaughter, (3) forcible rape, (4) burglary, (5) aggravated assault, (6) larceny, and (7) motor vehicle theft. Arson was later added to the list. Child molestation was not considered an index offense then, nor is it today. On the face of it, the UCR is clearly not a good measure of sex crime.

Today, a better index overall, the National Crime Victimization Survey (Bureau of Justice Statistics, 2013) lumps all sex crimes into a single category, "rape and sexual assault."

A major problem with the UCR was that, initially, the FBI could not compel police departments to report any arrests. In the first year, only 300 police departments participated. Forty years later 7800 departments (covering 96% of the USA) were reporting. Thus, if you compare the arrests for rape in 1950 with 1930 it might appear that there was an enormous increase in sexual offenses when in fact more police agencies were reporting.

During this period the population was also increasing. So, reported sex crimes kept pace with this increase which appeared to some that crime rates were increasing.

There was imprecision in specification of the nature of a sex crime. An accusation of rape by a woman had to have corroborating evidence. Police could ignore such a complaint if they believed that rape had not occurred. A woman's mode of dress or her sexual history could also be used against her. Thus, actual rapes may have been underreported.

Because it was not an index offense there was no data on child moles-tation. If a politician stated that child sex crimes were rising this could not be confirmed or denied. Such ambiguity only served to stoke public anxiety (Lave, 2009, pp. 553–554).

> Some of the sexual assault statistics are compelling nonetheless. In 1935, there were 4,106 rapes known to police as compared with 10,634 in 1955. Not only was this an absolute increase of 159%, but it was an increase in the rate per 100,000 population. In 1935, there 7.2 rapes per 100,000 population. By 1955, the rate had increased to 13.2 per 100,000. Thus, the number of rapes per 100,000 population increased by 83% during this twenty year time period. (Lave, 2009, p. 555)

Had the general public been able to appreciate this statistical description, they would have been very alarmed indeed.

The Sexual Psychopath Era (1930–1950)

Public alarm began to be translated into official reaction in the late 1930s as a result of pressure by medical, legal, and civic groups. These groups believed that sex crimes were a result of mental disorder that should be treated rather than punished:

> As evidenced in popular literature of the times, the sexual psychopath stat-utes reflected the public's anxieties about sex crimes. The propositions were: (W)omen and children were in danger because of the prevalence of serious sexual crimes. The serious sex crimes were committed by sexual psychopaths, who were referred to as "creatures" in one magazine. Sexual psychopaths had no control over their impulses. Therefore, they had a mental defect that did not make them responsible for their behavior. Because of their inability to control their behavior, the sexual psychopath would continue to commit serious sex crimes throughout his life. (Blacher, 1994–1995, p. 899)

As a result of pressure from professional and civic groups as well as the broad publication of information about sensational sex crimes, demands began to be made to do something definitive about the "sexual psycho-path." The psychiatric profession was armed and ready.

The invention of the "sexual psychopath" as a category of person consti-
tuted, to a large extent, an attempt on the part of psychiatrists to occupy an
entire field of legal regulation (one they deemed too complex for lawyers):
that of "deviant" sexual behavior. It also accomplished, for some time at
least, the identification of a whole class of people who required psychiatric
intervention and who were poorly served by a legal system that understood
only their bad acts and not their ill minds. (Schmeiser, 2008, p. 187)

The preceding could be seen as a rather measured approach to the problem, albeit a biased one. At the same time, prominent public figures such
as J. Edgar Hoover published an article in the *New York Herald Tribune*
entitled "War on the Sex Criminal" in which he breathlessly stated: "The
sex fiend, most loathsome of all the vast army of crime, has become a
sinister threat to the safety of American childhood and womanhood"
(Hoover, September 26, 1937). The professional and public worlds were
now adequately prepared and anxious for the introduction of the sexual
psychopath laws to control this perceived menace because ordinary legislation did not provide sufficient protection.

To a greater or lesser extent, all subsequent sexual psychopath/predator
laws have been based on seven central fallacies regarding sex crimes (Leon,
2011, pp. 23–24):

- *The stranger fallacy.* The biggest threat is posed not by people known to
  us but by random sex attacks by monsters.
- *The bogeyman fallacy.* People who commit sex crimes have a unique
  essential identity. They are of a different kind—distinct from the
  general population in terms of their deviant and compulsive sexual
  interests, criminal offense patterns, and likelihood of reoffending.
- *The singular sex offender fallacy.* All sex offenders are equally deviant,
  dangerous, harmful, and incurable. There is no reason to differentiate
  among them—all require the harshest response.
- *The continuum fallacy.* There is a continuum of deviance on which
  every sex crime exists, and offenders will inevitably escalate from non-
  contact offenses to murder.
- *The victim-or-offender fallacy.* To promote therapeutic rehabilitation for
  offenders is to deny the harm caused by the offense or to favor offenders
  over victims. Sex offenders neither deserve nor respond to treatment.

- *The knowledge-is-power fallacy.* By keeping convicted sex offenders under public scrutiny, the community can participate in policing offenders and can prevent recidivism.
- *The new law fallacy.* New laws will prevent victimization. If previous penal strategies proved ineffective, those problems can be remedied by new laws.

The problem in dealing with these fallacies lies in their immutable persistence. It does not seem to matter how many times any of the preceding fallacies can be demonstrated to be false. They have taken on a life of their own and, regrettably, strongly influence public policy.

The pioneering statute was enacted in Michigan in 1937. The law stated that:

> a person convicted of a sex crime could be identified as a "sex degenerate or pervert or (as suffering) from (a) mental disorder with marked sex deviation and tendencies dangerous to public safety." The court examined the individual with the assistance of two physicians, and the diagnosed psychopath would be indefinitely committed to a mental hospital. (Jenkins, 1998, p. 81)

If it was determined that the defendant was indeed a threat to public safety, the court could order him committed to a hospital or institution until such time as he had "ceased to be a menace to the public safety because of said mental condition." If a determination was ultimately made that he no longer posed a threat, he could be released or remanded to prison to serve his sentence (Lave, 2009, p. 571).

The statute was challenged and declared unconstitutional. The court ruling stated that it took the form of a criminal proceeding without the protection of a jury trial and violated the principle of double jeopardy.

In 1938 Illinois passed a similar law but avoided the constitutional issues. Committal as a sexual psychopath could occur without a criminal trial. The proceeding was conducted as an insanity hearing rather than a criminal trial. The person, if found to be a sexual psychopath, would be committed to a mental institution but could face criminal charges once released. This statute passed the constitutional tests and was widely imitated in other states.

Blacher (1994–1995, p. 901) stated that the sexual psychopath statutes rested on a two-tiered legislative objective: (1) protect society by incapacitating the sexual psychopath so long as he remains a threat to others, and (2) subject him to treatment in order that he may recover from his mental illness and be rehabilitated. As we shall see, and as we see in the contemporary sexual predator laws, incapacitation became the actual but unstated goal. Blacher also noted that the authority for enacting sexual psychopath statutes "rested on both the police power of the state and the doctrine of *parens patriae* [ed: the government, or any other authority, regarded as the legal protector of citizens unable to protect themselves]. The statutes were presented as "the appropriate measures… to protect society more adequately from aggressive sexual offenders… (and) that society as well as the individual (sex offender would) benefit" (p. 901).

From 1938 onward, the sexual psychopath statutes appeared in three different varieties (Swanson, 1960, p. 216):

- Sixteen statutes provided that the offender *must* have been *convicted* of *some* crime, or of a specific sex crime before the court could proceed to determine if he could be committed for treatment.
- Seven statutes merely required that the offender be *charged* with *some* crime, or a sex crime.
- The remaining five statutes did not even require that a charge be brought against the person, but simply demand that cause be shown that he probably was a sexual psychopath.

What type of proof was required to warrant confinement? Again, states differed in their requirements. The following are some samples (Lave, 2009, p. 573):

- "A mental disorder existing for one year coupled with criminal propensities to commit sex offenses; not mentally ill or feeble-minded so as to be criminally irresponsible."

- "A predisposition to commit sex offenses dangerous to others plus any of the following: mental disorder, psychopathic personality, or marked departure from normal mentality."
- "A habitual course of misconduct in sexual matters evidencing an utter lack of power to control sexual impulses and likely to attack or otherwise inflict injury, loss, pain or other evil."

The ambiguity of definition and the potential for misuse and abuse are obvious in these prescriptions.

How many people were actually committed under these statutes? Lave (2009, pp. 576–578) noted that:

> Although the state statutes were expansive in defining who could fall under the law, few people were actually committed as sexual psychopaths.... (Prosecutors) only resorted to the sexual psychopath laws when they did not think that they would be able to get a criminal conviction due to a lack of evidence.

Further, statements from administrators revealed a lack of enthusiasm for the procedures.

California	435 committed during the first 10 years of statute operated through the 1970s	Leaves much to be desired. An ineffectual law
Illinois	16 cases in 10 years	Requires change; little, interest in administering present statute
Indiana	Between 1949 and 1956, about 23 individuals committed per year	
Minnesota	Over 200 cases in 10 years	No triumph for justice of the protection of society
New Hampshire	0 cases	These cases should not be sent to a state hospital. No treatment facilities
New Jersey	35 cases in 6 months	
Washington, DC	14 cases in 1950	A star chamber procedure with inadequate diagnostic and treatment facilities

By 1950 the programs in Massachusetts, Michigan, Vermont, Washington, and Wisconsin were inoperative. Considering the enthusiasm with which the sexual psychopath laws were greeted, that initial response had waned considerably within the first 15 years, although California held on until the bitter end in the early 1980s.

Swanson (1960) has provided an extensive comparison of all sexual psychopath statutes in force in 1960. As indicated above, "in force" does not necessarily mean "in use." At this date 27 states had sexual psychopath laws on the books. Swanson's tabulation showed comparisons of the following conditions (pp. 228–235):

- Citation—the archival reference to the statute
- Designation of condition—what the diagnosis was called
- Elements of definition—how exactly the condition was defined
- Who initiated proceedings—prosecuting attorney, judge, or other
- Basis of jurisdiction—conviction of sex crime or other crime
- Medical examination—psychiatrist or "qualified" physician
- Tribunal and proceedings—court, jury trial, or neither
- Procedure for release—typically administered by the institution
- Nature of release—absolute, probation, or return to court
- Effect of commitment on criminal proceedings—various

What is clear from examining this long table is that, while the overall scheme of the laws was similar, the details varied remarkably from state to state.

There were many problems with the laws. The early sexual psychopath laws, like the sexual predator laws in force today, provided for indeterminate and possibly life commitment. As stated previously, the person could be released only when the confining institution determined that he was either cured or able to be released as no longer posing a risk of dangerousness to others. Tappan (1950) described this problem:

It will be noted that, except for New Jersey, the several statutes provide for an indeterminate commitment without a terminal maximum. This fact together with the tendency to commit a large proportion of minor offenders has resulted in a situation in which individuals whose conduct is no more than a nuisance in the community may be incarcerated for long periods of time … with the disinclination of hospital authorities to assert that the patient is cured. (p. 34)

After the statutes had been in effect for nearly 25 years, Swanson (1960, pp. 220) described the major problems with the laws which persisted to their eventual overturn. These criticisms continue to the present day with respect to the sexual predator laws:

> [T]he various provisions of the sexual psychopath statutes have been the objects of considerable legal controversy. The usual attacks have been that the statutes deny due process and equal protection of the laws, impair the right to trial by jury and the privilege against self-incrimination, place the offender in double jeopardy, and contradict the constitutional guarantees against cruel and unusual punishments. Although the courts generally have not found these contentions sufficiently persuasive to defeat any of the sexual psychopath statutes … it cannot be assumed that these contentions are invalid.

The most typical attacks were (Swanson, 1960, pp. 220–224):

- Denial of due process and equal protection of the laws due to improper classification. The concepts used for classification were meaningless and incomprehensible because abnormality could not be assessed by objective medical and legal standards. Determinations were left to judges, juries, and physicians who might make their judgments based on subjective notions of what is "normal."
- The statutes did not distinguish between types and degrees of mentally abnormal sexual behavior. No distinction was often made between truly dangerous offenders such as sadistic rapists and relatively harmless sexual deviants such as voyeurs, exhibitionists, or fetishists.
- Were the proceedings under the laws *criminal* or *civil?* If they were criminal the accused might be put in double jeopardy, be forced to testify against himself, not guaranteed the right of public hearing, notice, personal attendance, counsel, habeas corpus, jury trial,

presentation of evidence, subpoenaing of witnesses, cross-examination, and appeal.

- Sexual psychopath proceedings have all the consequences of a criminal trial. If the proceedings are construed to be civil, then the end result must provide for treatment, not punishment. In states where conviction of criminal charges preceded hearings for commitment as a mentally disordered sex offender, the defendant was tried a second time for the same crime with the likely result being a longer sentence under the sexual psychopath statute.
- The privilege against self-incrimination should be respected in sexual psychopath proceedings. The defendant risked too much by possibly disclosing information that could lead to discovery of past crimes.
- The right to a jury trial was not always guaranteed.
- If an offender was detained in an institution where adequate treatment facilities did not exist, and held for a time not in proportion to the actual criminal offense, such detention could be construed as punishment, even cruel and unusual punishment.

By the 1970s questions such as the preceding were again raised. Once again the issues were lack of due process and protections, doubts about whether a person could be detained indefinitely without treatment, lack of access to counsel, inability to confront hostile witnesses, and notably, whether an examining psychiatrist was an independent, objective professional, or merely a tool of the court.

Jenkins (1998, pp. 115–117) chronicled the demise of the sexual psychopath laws:

- In 1973, in *Davy v. Sullivan*, a US District Court struck down Alabama's statute based on its requirement that release from an institution should meet the impossible criterion of "full and permanent recovery" from psychopathy. The decision also criticized the statute's broad and unscientific definitions and the mixing of civil and criminal elements.
- The laws required that offenders be treated by experts but treatment regimes in the institutions came under increasing scrutiny for use of

intrusive procedures such as electroconvulsive therapy (ECT) or noxious chemical and electrical stimuli. Anthony Burgess' *A Clockwork Orange* (1962) provides a good fictional example of such procedures.

• In such an environment, conditioning procedures, however beneficial their intent, were often viewed as cruel and unusual punishment, if not torture.

• In 1975 convicted pedophiles in Connecticut successfully sued to end the rule that they could only gain parole if they underwent painful aversion therapy involving electric shocks to their genitals. Since the procedure was linked to release, it was obligatory.

• By the early 1970s it was the statutes themselves rather than the offenders that became the outstanding social problem. Assaulted from all sides, the existing laws and treatment programs were overwhelmed. Repeal of some laws began while others were simply considered dead and inoperative.

Janus and Prentky (2009, p. 91) noted how rapidly the statutes faded away.

> In its first incarnation, from the late 1930s through the 1970s, sexual psychopath laws were adopted by over half the states. In a brief period of time, between 1975 and 1981, half of those statutes were repealed. By 1985, these statutes existed in only thirteen states, and were regularly enforced in only six states.

Did these laws serve any useful societal purpose? Freedman (1987, p. 106) argued that, in a rather roundabout way, they served to clarify a number of unresolved historical issues:

> The response to the sexual psychopath ... confirms that ... the fear of sexual violence can provide an extremely powerful tool for mobilizing public support against nonconforming individuals. The ultimate historical legacy of the response to the sexual psychopath, however, was to expand the public discourse on sexuality, to focus attention on male violence, and so heighten the importance of sexuality as a component of modern identity. In so doing, the sexual psychopath helped to redefine the boundaries of acceptable sexual behavior in modern America.

The Rehabilitative Era (1950–1980)

The central characteristic of this era is the image of the treatable offender. Leon (2011, p. 61) put it this way:

> This image of the reformable sex offender reveals a crucial aspect of rehabilitative logic – rather than trying to remake subjects who are further from the ideal, sex offenders "most amenable to treatment" were those not incapacitated by sexual disorders or those acting out of violence, but only those who were slightly mixed up. These offenders, though temporarily inpatients in the civil commitment facility, were really thought of as "outpatients" who could quickly return to society. The patient image signals a pathology that is amenable to treatment, not an identity.

According to Leon (2011, p. 66) in 1963 the California Department of Mental Hygiene provided a highly exaggerated portrait of the typical sex offender, one that reinforced the rehabilitative nature of the era. The offender was

> white, married, a father, about 35 years of age, born of American parents, a blue collar worker, Protestant, and a veteran. He has some high school education, but is not a graduate.

A regular guy. Not a hopeless deviant, not a violent criminal, not mentally defective, has ties to the society in general, and has a problem that we can work with. This picture is sharply at variance with popular belief.

From the late 1930s until the early 1980s California was a major player in both the sexual psychopath and rehabilitative eras. Throughout both periods the state confined the largest number of sex offenders in the country. In the rehabilitative era California scaled back its efforts in experimenting with the treatment of "nearly all offenders, no matter how bad." Instead the focus of commitment turned to those offenders who could possibly be "useful citizens." These offenders were diverted from prison while those who were most unlike the treating staff and considered more dangerous were sent to prison (Leon, 2011, p. 78).

Despite these efforts, it all came to an end in much the same way as it occurred in the 1930s and 1940s. A series of heinous sex crimes and murders once again led to demands that harsh measures be taken against the responsible offenders, now called a "sexual predator" rather than a "sexual psychopath" or "sex fiend."

The Containment Era (1980–present)

A New Approach

Unlike the sexual psychopath and rehabilitative eras, the containment era is composed of two major elements. First, the sexual predator statutes were intended to capture and indeterminately confine the worst of the worst. Second, and more far reaching, was the emergence of what has come to be known as "the containment model" of community control. To be sure, in the past police agencies, probation, parole, and various mental health agencies had exerted efforts to control sex offenders in the community. However, these efforts typically operated independently and did not work together. The containment model was originally advanced by English, Pullen, and Jones (1997) under the auspices of the American Parole and Probation Association. Leon (2011, p. 114) listed its ideal major components:

- A philosophy that values public safety, victim protection, and reparation for victims as the paramount objectives of sex offender management.
- Implementation strategies that rely on agency coordination, multidisciplinary partnerships, and job specialization.
- A containment approach that seeks to hold sex offenders accountable through the combined use of both the offenders' internal controls and external criminal justice measures, and the use of the polygraph to monitor internal controls and compliance with external controls.
- Development and implementation of informed public policies to create and support consistent practices.
- Quality control mechanisms, including program monitoring and evaluation, that ensure that prescribed policies and procedures are delivered as planned.

The preceding series sounds like a wish list. Reduced to its essentials, the containment model is intended to target the offender from a variety of perspectives. Specifically, this means implementation of the federal *Jacob Wetterling Act* (1994) and the federal *Megan's Law* (1996) governing registration as a sex offender and community notification. These statutes were repealed by the *Adam Walsh Act* and the *Sex Offender Registration and Notification Act* (2006). These statutes are treated in more detail in Chap. 8.

Background of the Current Sexual Predator Laws

Probably because the original sexual psychopath laws faded away so slowly through the 1970s and 1980s, whatever lessons the experience had taught were largely forgotten or set aside. However, at the end of that decade several horrific sex crimes redirected attention to a perceived need to identify and confine presumably highly dangerous sex offenders. As in the previous incarnation legislators were pressured by civic groups and police agencies to take action against an obvious social menace. Janus (2006, p. 9) commented on this process:

> In the struggle to reach and hold the moral – and political – high ground, politicians and others use toughness, the idea of "zero tolerance," as a club to beat down those concerned with civil liberties or alternative approaches. But zero tolerance is a chimera, a hoax. The bluster about toughness often hides a failure to address the huge part of sexual violence that is not in the news, that is not flashy, and that is appallingly common.

The first major sexual predator law enacted was the *State of Washington Community Protection Act* in 1990. In 1989 a mentally defective male with a long history of sadistic sexual assault was convicted of the rape and murder of a 7-year-old child. The ensuing public outrage resulted in the Washington legislature convening a task force to determine what should be done. Lieb (1996, p 2) stated that "Every proposal for reform was tested against the key question: Would it offer the state the necessary power to contain someone … who had reached the end of his maximum criminal sentence, and yet clearly posed extreme risks to the public?" The solution reached was to enact legislation that focused upon persons designated as sexually violent predators (SVPs) who:

- Had been convicted of, or charged with, a sexually violent crime, and
- Suffered from a mental abnormality or personality disorder which made them likely engage in predatory acts of sexual violence.

The law authorized prosecutors or the Attorney General to initiate civil proceedings against that person. Following a probable cause hearing the individual would be confined for evaluation. A trial would then determine whether the individual met the legal definition of an SVP. If the state's case could be proven beyond a reasonable doubt, the person would be confined for treatment until it was determined that he was safe for release. Although this law was subjected to legal challenges that would beset subsequent sexual predator laws, it provided the template for what was to come. Although it used different words to describe the sex offender, it is clear that the Washington statute had much in common with the original sexual psychopath laws. In 2010, the Association for the Treatment of Sexual Abusers (ATSA) noted that 20 states and the District of Columbia had adopted such legislation.

These new laws have suffered the same challenges as the original sexual psychopath laws. The argument in these challenges was primarily that the laws were punitive and violated constitutional protections. Among these were double jeopardy, ex post facto lawmaking, denial of due process of law, conflating criminal and civil laws, and importantly, failure to prove "mental disorder"—a key element of all these statutes. The major cases that tested these issues were *Kansas v. Hendricks* (1997), *Selig v. Young* (2001), *Kansas v. Crane* (2002), and *US v. Comstock* (2010). State and federal courts and the Supreme Court have consistently upheld the constitutionality of the statutes.

All of the sexual predator laws contain a conundrum that has never, and possibly never will be, resolved. It concerns the problem of release from this type of confinement. Ewing (2011, p. 22) has concluded that

"In most states, the vast majority of offenders appear to be held more or less permanently." This appears to be due to three factors:

- The belief, reinforced by psychiatric diagnoses, that the offenders are mentally ill. Diagnoses that have been used to satisfy the mental illness requirement for SVP commitment (and described in the *Diagnostic and Statistical Manual of Mental Disorders* [DSM]) include pedophilia, exhibitionism, frotteurism, sadism, and voyeurism. Rape is not classified as a mental illness in the *DSM*. Sexual sadism is sometimes substituted. In an attempt to circumvent this difficulty, Doren (2002) created a fictional diagnosis, one that does not appear in the *DSM*. This was a "Paraphilia Not Otherwise Specified: Nonconsent." This was intended to provide a diagnosis for rape. Some courts have apparently accepted this. A major problem in meeting the criteria for SVP commitment is that many persons referred are not mentally ill or have a personality disorder.
- The view, reinforced by actuarial assessment, that these offenders are and always will be at risk for reoffending. The most common instrument considers static historical factors that cannot be changed. Two subsequent instruments consider dynamic factors that can be changed. The problem with the latter in the SVP environment is that factors such as homelessness, joblessness, and lack of a partner are irrelevant. Janus and Prentky (2009, p. 91) have observed that "The fundamental turn that the predator laws take is in asserting that the harm is manifested in *risky persons* (or the status of 'dangerousness') than *risky behavior*." These issues will be described more completely in Chap. 7.
- There is uncertainty about the effectiveness of treatment with individuals in these programs. How much is enough to make a determination of reduced risk and suitability for release? Treatment programs for sex offenders vary widely in scope and quality (see, e.g., the broad survey by McGrath et al., 2010). Some institutions have no treatment programs at all. This is a grave problem since SVP commitment is predicated on the need for treatment.

The efficacy of inpatient or outpatient treatment for sex offenders is typically measured by recidivism—rearrest or reconviction for a sex offense. Ewing (2011, pp. 33–34) provides some typical examples. Treated and untreated offenders are included here. Some of the individuals may have participated in SVP programs:

- US Department of Justice (2003). A 3-year follow-up of 272,111 prisoners released in 15 states in 1994 showed that 1.3% of nonsex offenders were arrested for a sex offense and 5.3% of sex offenders were rearrested for a sex offense.
- California Sex Offender Management Board (2008). A 5- to 10-year follow-up showed that 3.2% of 4204 were convicted at 5 years and 3.8% of 3577 were convicted at 10 years.
- Hanson and Bussière (1998). On average the recidivism rate was 13.4% at a 4- to 5-year follow-up: 18.9% for rapists and 12.7% for child molesters.
- Harris and Hanson (2004). A follow-up at 5, 10, and 15 years; for rapists, 14%, 21%, and 24%; for child molesters, 13%, 18%, and 23%.

Harris and Hanson (2004) (cited in Ewing, 2011, p. 35) concluded that:

> Most sexual offenders do not re-offend over time. This may be the most important finding of this study as this finding is contrary to some strongly held beliefs. After 15 years, 73% of sex offenders had not been charged with, or convicted of, another sex offenses. The sample was sufficiently large that very strong contradictory evidence is necessary to substantially change these recidivism estimates.

If sex offense recidivism is indeed a low base-rate phenomenon, what does that tell us about the rationale for the SVP laws? Rather than a necessary response to a poorly defined set of problems called "sexual violence" they seem more a product of the *Zeitgeist* of the 1990s. The product was a response to the outcries of a largely misinformed public, a response to media misrepresentation of the magnitude of the threat, and a hasty response to both of these by nervous politicians. Janus (2006) offers a highly critical appraisal:

> We have come to think of these men as archetypal sex offenders and we have shaped our public policy as if all sex offenders fit this mold. We are

blind to the true nature of sexual violence in our society, which is far different from what we think it is. Rape-murders are extremely rare, and sexual
predators represent but a small fraction – a thin sliver – of the sexual criminals in our country…. (T)hese new laws – although well intentioned – are
ill-conceived, bad policy. They were sold as innovative approaches to finding and incapacitating the worst of the worst, but there is little evidence
that they have succeeded in that important task … (O)ur way of thinking
about sexual violence is increasingly distorted. The distortion has led to the
predator laws, and the predator laws strengthen the distortion.

And later (p. 5):

We do not allow incarceration for the propensity to commit a crime. In our
system, the punishment should never precede the crime. Yet this is precisely what the predator laws seem to do – except that they do not call the
deprivation of liberty "punishment."

Conclusion

As the situation stands at this writing, the SVP laws are firmly in place, supposedly constitutionally grounded, and routinely implemented. Challenges
continue but they are largely ineffective. Constitutionally protected or not,
there remains gross unfairness in this system, a legal machine of social control that has had little or no effect upon the social problems it was designed
to address. What then might be the future of this effort of social control?
Janus and Prentky (2009, pp. 94–95) suggest some possibilities:

- States may simply run out of money to continue or implement these very
expensive programs. The cost per inmate is at least twice the cost of peni-
tentiary confinement. Registration with the police, community notification (see Chap. 8), and residence restrictions (see Chap. 9) appear to be
low cost to implement but the cost of enforcing them has proven to be
quite expensive. This, the authors say, is the most realistic outcome.
- Although problematic, and possibly not difficult to defeat on a local
level, would be a petition by aggrieved individuals challenging
improper implementation of a program, forcing a state to conform to

the law (and the Constitution). This approach, in my view, would require pressure (and a lot of supporting data) from a group such as the American Civil Liberties Union, a lot of television exposure, and strong endorsement by credible politicians.

- An alternative legal approach would be to claim that the SVP laws are "invalid as applied." This approach would have to demonstrate that the law has an improper (punitive) purpose based on persistent patterns of improper implementation. This would likely be linked to the approach described immediately above.

- The political and social framework supporting these laws needs to change. At this point the sex offender is characterized as very exceptional, a very high-risk "predator," a way to differentiate "Us" from "Them." A new framework would use a public health approach which sees sexual violence as a community problem, which sees this problem as everybody's business (Laws, 2003).

References

Blacher, R. (1994–1995). Historical perspective of the "Sex Psychopath" statute: From the revolutionary era to the present federal crime bill. *Mercer Law Review, 46,* 889–920.

Bureau of Justice Statistics. (2013). *Probation and parole in the United States, 2013.* Washington, DC: Office of Justice Programs, US Department of Justice.

Burgess, A. (1962). *A clockwork orange.* New York: Norton.

Doren, D. M. (2002). *Evaluating sex offenders: A manual for civil commitments and beyond.* Thousand Oaks, CA: Sage.

English, K., Pullen, S., & Jones, L. (1997). *Managing adult sex offenders in the community: A containment approach.* Washington, DC: National Institute of Justice, Office of Justice Programs, U.S. Department of Justice.

Ewing, C. P. (2011). *Justice perverted: Sex offender law, psychology, and public policy.* New York: Oxford University Press.

Freedman, E. B. (1987). "Uncontrolled desires": The response to the sexual psychopath, 1920–1960. *Journal of American History, 74,* 83–106.

Hanson, R. K., & Bussière, M. T. (1998). Predicting relapse: A meta-analysis of sexual offender recidivism studies. *Journal of Consulting and Clinical Psychology, 66,* 348–362.

Harris, A. J. R., & Hanson, R. K. (2004). *STABLE-2000/ACUTE-2000: Scoring manuals for the dynamic supervision project* (Unpublished scoring manuals). Ottawa, ON: Corrections Research, Public Safety Canada.

Hoover, J. E. (1937, September 26). War on the sex criminal. *New York Herald Tribune.*

Janus, E. S. (2006). *Failre to protect: America's sexual predator laws and the rise of the preventive state.* Ithaca, NY: Cornell University Press.

Janus, E. S., & Prentky, R. A. (2009). Sexual predator laws: A two-decade perspective. *Federal Sentencing Reporter, 21,* 90–97.

Jenkins, P. (1998). *Moral panic: Changing concepts of the child molester in modern America.* New Haven, CT: Yale University Press.

Kansas v. Crane, 534 U.S. 407 (2002)

Kansas v. Hendricks, 521 U.S. 346 (1997)

Lave, T. R. (2009). Only yesterday: The rise and fall of twentieth century sexual psychopath laws. *Louisiana Law Review, 69,* 549–591.

Laws, D. R. (2003). The rise and fall of relapse prevention. *Australian Psychologist, 38,* 22–30.

Leon, C. S. (2011). *Sex fiends, perverts, and pedophiles: Understanding sex crime policy in America.* New York: New York University Press.

Lieb, R. (1996). *Washington's sexually violent predator law.* Olympia, WA: Washington State Institute for Public Policy.

Mayor's Committee for the Study of Sex Offenses. (1940). New York City: Mayor's Committee for the Study of Sex Offenses.

McGrath, R. J., Cumming, G. F., Burchard, B. L., Zeoli, S., & Ellerby, L. (2010). *Current practices and emerging trends in sexual abuser management: The Safer Society 2009 North American Survey.* Brandon, VT: Safer Society Press.

Schmeiser, S. R. (2008). The ungovernable citizen: Psychopathy, sexuality, and the rise of medico-legal reasoning. *Yale Journal of Law & the Humanities, 20,* 163–240.

Selig v. Young. 531 U.S. 250 (2001)

Swanson, A. H. (1960). Sexual psychopath statutes: Summary and analysis. *The Journal of Criminal Law, Criminology, and Police Science, 51,* 215–235.

Tappan, P. W. (1950). *The habitual sex offender: Report and recommendations of the Commission on the Habitual Sex Offender.* Trenton, NJ: The Commission.

U.S. v. Comstock. 560 U.S. 126 (2010)

6

Assessment of Risk to Reoffend: Historical Background

The preceding chapters have traced the development of legal, medical, and social practices designed to protect society from the harmful behavior of sex offenders. Most of these approaches have not yielded the promised benefit, a safer society, and some clearly have marginal or questionable value. This chapter and the one following will consider the development of instruments intended to assess the risk to engage in sexually offensive behavior. This approach can take two forms. First, it might be possible to assess the *likelihood* that an individual *might* offend in the future, although he/she has never done so previously. This is legally untenable because it threatens punishment for something that has not happened. There are, undoubtedly, many who would favor such a proactive, anticipatory move to prevent possible future crimes. For example, Jones, Harkins, and Beech (2015) offer an assessment procedure focused on future risk and discuss the implications of this approach. Second, when an individual has been positively identified as a sex offender, the more likely course would be to develop a method that would permit *prediction* of *future* criminality. The instruments available today, with modest empirical support, are believed to do just that. A considerable faith has been invested in the accuracy of these instruments.

© The Editor(s) (if applicable) and The Author(s) 2016
D.R. Laws, *Social Control of Sex Offenders*,
DOI 10.1057/978-1-137-39126-1_6

In a recent book review Laws (2010) briefly described the basic beliefs underlying the idea of the preventive state, a risk-free society:

> The basic philosophy, of course, is that 'you can't be too careful.' If, as an ordinary citizen, you believe in 'the intransigence of evil' and fear the 'alien other,' you are likely to invoke 'the precautionary principle,' relying on the 'technology of categorical exclusion' (i.e. actuarial risk assessment) to 'criminalize uncertainty' resulting in 'actuarial justice,' nipping evil in the bud and leading to a peaceful 'pre-crime society'. (p. 506)

Many practitioners today appear to believe that actuarial risk assessment is virtually brand new, dating from the introduction of the *Violence Risk Appraisal Guide* (*VRAG*) and the *Sex Offender Risk Appraisal Guide* (*SORAG*) in the1990s (Quinsey, Rice, Harris, & Cormier, 1998). Applied to violent offenders and sex offenders, that is a more or less accurate conclusion. However, the tradition of offender risk assessment has a much richer history.

Prediction of Criminality by Descriptive Statistics

The observation of regularities in criminal behavior and the possibility of predicting future criminal acts had their origins in early nineteenth-century Europe. Laws and Ward (2011, pp. 27–29) have stated that the most consistently observed statistical regularity in all criminal behavior is the age–crime curve. In this statistic, the frequency of criminal acts is plotted against time, an age range. Criminal behavior is seen to increase in the teenage years, peak at various points in adulthood, and decrease slowly in later life. This phenomenon has been observed for over 180 years. It was first observed by Quételet, a Belgian astronomer and mathematician who introduced statistical procedures in sociology. In his search for regularities in criminal behavior, Quételet consulted the *Compte general de l'administration de justice criminelle en France*, the official census of criminal acts brought before the courts. Examining criminal statistics for the years 1826–1829, he found consistent regularities among persons accused and convicted of crimes against persons and property. While there was variation from year to year, there was considerable consistency. Beirne (1987, pp. 1153–1155) described these findings:

> The disproportionate and relentless presence of certain categories in the *Compte* between 1826 and 1829 also indicated to Quételet that young males, the poor, the less educated, and those without employment in lowly occupations had a greater propensity (*penchant*) than others to commit crimes and be convicted of them. These data seemed to enable Quételet to take issue with several conventional accounts of the factors that precipitated crime. In particular ... neither the presence of poverty nor the absence of formal education warranted the ... causal importance commonly claimed for them.

Beirne (1987, pp. 1155–1156) stated further that

> [H]e tabulated crimes according to the ages of their perpetrators and divided the number of crimes by the population in the respective age groups. The results show the propensity for committing crime at various ages. This propensity it at its weakest at both extremes of life.... The propensity for crime is at its strongest between the ages of 21 and 25.

After the passage of over 180 years, all of Quételet's research is consistent with what we continue to observe today. Similar data have been reported by Glueck and Glueck (1950), Gottfredson and Hirschi (1990), Laub and Sampson (2003), and Moffitt (1993). The age–crime curve for sex offenders has been illustrated by Hanson (2002) and Nicholaichuk, Olver, Gu, and Wong (2014).

Criminal Statistics and Risk Assessment, Nineteenth and Twentieth Centuries

Deflem (1997, pp. 155–157, 162–169) provided a brief history of the movement from simple collection of statistics on crime to classification of offenders by the type of crime, by the level of risk they posed as individuals, and by the early efforts at prediction of future offending.

This history shows, expanding on Quételet, that criminal statistics established the regularities of crime and, on that basis, it might be possible to calculate the probability of future crimes. Contemporary researchers working in this area believe that they have done just that.

- As they developed in the seventeenth and eighteenth centuries, statistics referred to the science of the state, a verbal, nonquantitative description of various aspects of the societies and government of the states of European empires.
- As Quételet empirically demonstrated in the 1830s, the investigations of governmental and social phenomena found that they showed a remarkable regularity over time.
- A tendency developed to have these descriptions presented in numbers. These tables emphasized the enumeration, computation, and quantification of social phenomena.
- By the mid-nineteenth century, mathematical theories of probability were introduced in descriptive statistics. The suitability of these methods applied to social and political problems was recognized.
- The conjunction of mathematical theory and descriptive criminal statistics offered the likelihood that future criminal behavior might be predicted. As noted previously, the Belgian astronomer Quételet was the first to measure the influences of various social factors on crime. By 1832 he concluded: "We might enumerate in advance how many individuals will stain their hands in the blood of their fellows, how many will be forgers, how many will be poisoners."
- Such findings suggested that human affairs follow a normal curve much like the curve of the probability of errors that mathematicians had discovered. The shape of the curve would show some irregularities as expressed in a single individual but, as group data, the curve would appear as a normal distribution.
- As the nineteenth century proceeded, it was argued that crime was committed by a specific type of person, the *homo criminalis* (the criminal person). In the earlier classical school, the criminal was defined as a person who simply broke the law. With the emergence of

the *homo criminalis*, society was seen as threatened, not by a mere law violator but by a dangerous criminal.

- In the early twentieth century there was movement toward the quantification of crime, specifically the types of crime, the number of crimes, and the fluctuations over time.

- In the 1920s and 1930s concern developed over the professionalization of crime. The perception that the crime rate was increasing stressed the need for accurate crime statistics, criminal statistics research, and the emergence of uniform crime reports to make data comparable across jurisdictions. More knowledge of the crime problem would then lead to a more efficient administration of criminal justice.

- Criminal statistics amounted to a precise description with a purpose: As risk assessment it collected information, and as risk management it predicted the crimes to be expected and prevented. Criminal statistics established the regularities of crime. On that basis, the probability of future crimes could be calculated.

- In the same time period the Uniform Crime Report appeared and interest was developed in the possible use of statistical data to predict success or failure of parole.

However, "[T]he rationality guiding contemporary forms of risk-based social control was already established in the previous (e.g., 19th) century." Deflem, 1997, p. 175)

Twentieth-Century Risk Assessment

Two major categories of risk assessment and prediction predominated in the twentieth century: clinical and actuarial. Clinical prediction involved observation of the offender by professionals who assessed risk based on their training and experience with offenders. Actuarial (statistical) prediction was made on the basis of how other offenders had acted in similar situations or the extent to which the individual being examined resembled members of other criminal groups (John Howard Society of Alberta [JHSA], 2000, p. 4).

Clinical Risk Assessment

The JHSA (2008, p. 4) has noted some of the basic elements of this approach:

- A professional, typically a forensic psychologist, psychiatrist, or social worker, interviews and observes the individual.
- The interviewer may use checklists or rating scales or ask the interviewee to complete a self-report.
- All available details regarding the nature of the crime, the individual's personality and behavior are considered.
- Risk factors differ for each individual and can change over time [for e.g., mental disabilities, attitudes, behavior, social skills].
- The individual characteristics examined give clinicians a picture of the person and a decision about the potential harm posed is made.
- Problem: The ability to distinguish between offenders who will recidivate from those who will not is questionable when using this method.
- Problem: Judgments made are subjective, often intuitive, based on the examiner's past experience with offenders.
- Problem: Laypersons, when given enough information, are able to make predictions that are as accurate as those made by clinicians.

Andrews and Bonta (2010a, p. 311) label this approach *First-Generation Risk Assessment*. Despite its limitations and the obvious problems surrounding clinical risk assessment by professionals, the method is frequently accepted as valid in courts of law. Clinical judgment in isolation will not be considered further in this chapter.

Actuarial Risk Assessment

This approach is generally believed to be superior to clinical risk assessment. In fact, some clinicians/researchers believe that it is so superior that it would be advisable to simply dispense with clinical judgment altogether (or as Dr. Strangelove would put it, "Dispense with human meddling!"). Janus (2006), pp. 56–58) has outlined the elements of this approach:

- The most important factors that are associated with risk of reoffense are isolated [e.g., past criminal history].
- These are combined through research into a formula that weights each factor optimally.
- The weighting produces a score for each individual based on the combination of risk factors.
- The formula is then applied to a large sample of offenders whose post-release history is then followed and reoffenses observed.
- The researchers then count, for offenders in the sample, the frequency of reoffense for each score level.
- This frequency is then taken to be the probability of recidivism associated with that particular score.
- There is substantial evidence that actuarial methods are more accurate than clinical risk assessment despite the fact that they cannot take into account many seemingly important individual features.
- Though they are less individualized they have the advantage of capturing important relationships in the data.

Actuarial risk assessment instruments look like ordinary psychological tests and there is, therefore, the tendency to regard the risk score as saying something unique about the offender. The usefulness of any actuarial test depends on the similarity of the offender being examined to offenders in the development sample. For critics of the approach, this is a long stretch. These assessments are statements of how *groups* of people will behave. The fundamental error in using this approach is to assert that a given offender will necessarily reoffend simply because his risk score is the same as that of a group of offenders in the development sample who did reoffend.

Despite the fact that there may be faults in the use of actuarial methods, proponents are adamant in their defense of the method: "What we are advising is not the addition of actuarial methods to existing practice, but rather the complete replacement of existing practice with actuarial methods.... Actuarial methods are too good and clinical judgment too poor to risk contaminating the former with the latter" (Quinsey et al., 1998, p. 171).

The Rise of the Actuarial Paradigm

The advent of actuarial prediction can be traced to the work of the sociologist Burgess in the 1920s (Burgess, 1928). I will treat the Burgess method at some length because his basic model has influenced all subsequent attempts to build a reoffense predictor. The first attempt to develop a formal risk assessment to predict success or failure on parole dates from this period. While parole board members had a wealth of information at their disposal (e.g., prior record, offense(s) committed, institutional adjustment, and program participation) there was no way to know what was significantly related to outcome. It was for this reason that the Illinois State Board of Parole approached Burgess to develop a predictive instrument that was based on data rather than clinical judgment alone. Harcourt (2007) considers Burgess to be the father of actuarial dangerousness prediction.

Burgess identified 22 variables believed to be associated with success on parole. These were (Hakeem, 1948, pp. 377–378):

- Nature of offense.
- Number of associates in the committing offense.
- Nationality of the inmate's father.
- Parental status, including broken home.
- Marital status.
- Type of criminal (first, occasional, habitual, professional).
- Type of criminal (farm boy, gangster, hobo, drunkard, ne'er-do-well)
- County from which committed.
- Size of community.
- Type of neighborhood.
- Resident or transient in community when arrested.
- Statement of trial judge and prosecuting attorney on recommendation for or against leniency.
- Whether or not commitment was upon acceptance of a lesser plea.
- Nature and length of sentence imposed.
- Months or sentence actually served before parole.
- Previous criminal record of the prisoner.
- Previous work record of the prisoner.

- Record of punishment in the institution.
- Age at time of parole.
- Mental age according to psychiatric examination.
- Personality type according to psychiatric examination.
- Psychiatric prognosis.

Burgess studied the cases of 3000 individuals paroled from three Illinois institutions, 1000 from each. The parolees had been released over a period ranging from two and a half to 6 years. All had been under parole supervision for at least 1 year (Hakeem, 1948, p. 377). The 22 predictor variables were scored as either "0=yes" or "1=no." So, if the question was *unstable work record* the item was scored as "1." The coded values were then added to create a predictor score, higher scores predicting a greater chance of success on parole.

The scale worked well. Burgess (1928) reported that, for men with the highest scores from 14 to 21, the rate of success was 98 %; for men with scores of 4 or less, the rate of parole success was only 24 %. The method of combining actuarial scores has come to be called the "Burgess method of unit-weighted regression." Hakeem (1948) reported that the Burgess method showed "remarkable accuracy in prediction" (p. 376). Although more advanced methods of statistical analysis have emerged since 1928, they do not show a clear advantage over unit-weighted methods (retrieved on February 23, 2015, at www.en.wikipedia.org/wiki/Ernest_Burgess).

Other researchers of the period had similar ideas. Warner (1923) also looked at factors determining success on parole from the Massachusetts Reformatory. The parole board considered four factors: (1) the nature of the offense, (2) the prisoner's conduct in the reformatory, (3) prior criminal history, and (4) time served. Of these, emphasis was placed almost exclusively on prior criminal history. Hart (1923) attempted a replication of Warner's work but increased the scale to 30 factors to produce a "prognostic score." Witmer (1927) and Borden (1928) produced similar scales (cited in Harcourt, 2007, pp. 48–51). The Burgess method received a lot of empirical attention in subsequent years. The main thrust of these studies was to reduce the number of predictor variables (e.g., Reiss, 1949; Glaser, 1954, 1955).

Not long after Burgess published his report a competing model appeared (Glueck & Glueck 1950):

> (T)he Gluecks conducted extensive investigation into the lives of 510 inmates whose sentences expired in 1921 and 1922. They focused on the parolee's experience during the first five years after their release. The Gluecks reviewed information about home life prior to the time spent in the institution, conducted interviews of the ex-convicts, and gathered information from parole agencies .... From that data, the Gluecks made four prediction tables that relied on a variety of pre-reformatory and reformatory statistics .... The parole-prediction instrument had seven factors, and, unlike Burgess, they weighted each factor using a simple method based on the subcategories of each factor. (Harcourt, 2007, p. 61)

The major difference between the Burgess and the Gluecks's approach involved the number and weighting of factors. Burgess weighted 22 factors equally while the Gluecks weighted their seven factors according to some approximation of importance. Subsequent research from the 1930s through the 1950s used a mix of these two approaches. The main focus was to reduce the number of predictive factors (Harcourt, 2007, p. 62).

Andrews and Bonta (2010a) classify the preceding study types as *Second-Generation Risk Assessment*, risk scales using static variables. Nearly 50 years after Burgess, Hoffman and Beck (1974), researchers for the United States Board of Parole, developed a Burgess-like second-generation risk scale called the *Salient Factor Score*. They started out with 66 factors which they subsequently reduced to nine. The factors were:

- Prior convictions
- Prior incarcerations
- Age at first commitment
- Auto theft
- Prior parole revocation
- Drug history
- Education grade achieved
- Employment
- Living arrangements on release

In 1974 Hoffman and Beck reported (p. 202):

> (T)his Salient Factor Score has been in use as an aid in Federal parole selection decisions throughout the United States since November 1, 1973, when it replaced an earlier version. Board members and hearing examiners have made over 3000 decisions using this instrument to date and appear well satisfied with its performance. Operationally, the Salient Factor Score requires no special skills to compute and can be completed in a short time; thus, it does not impose an undue administrative burden.

A very important development at this stage was the introduction of the *Level of Service Inventory* (*LSI*) (Andrews, 1982), subsequently revised (*LSI-R*) by Andrews and Bonta (1995). Harcourt (2007, pp. 78–81) states that the *LSI-R* is the most popular risk assessment instrument in the USA in that it targets both static and dynamic risk factors. Its main feature is the shift away from a minimum number of risk factors. *LSI-R* contains 54 questions grouped into 10 areas:

- Criminal history
- Education and employment
- Financial
- Family and marital
- Accommodations
- Leisure and recreation
- Companions
- Alcohol and drugs
- Emotional and personal
- Attitude and orientation

Interviewees are asked to reply "yes" or "no" to a series of questions ("Are you frequently unemployed?"). The interviewer scores the instrument and determines the offender's risk level. Scores are translated into odds of reoffending within a specified period. The *LSI-R* falls between two generations. It resembles a Burgess-type scale but now includes factors including family, marital status, socioeconomic conditions, and emotional outlook. This change would develop more fully.

Second-generation risk assessments form the richest period in the development of predictor scales. The period extends from the work of Burgess and his colleagues in the 1920s into the early twenty-first century. Other important instruments from this period include:

- The *Spousal Assault Risk Assessment* guide (*SARA*; Kropp, Hart, Webster, & Eaves, 1995).
- The *Historical-Clinical-Risk-20* (*HCR-20*; Webster, Douglas, Eaves, & Hart, 1997).
- The *Sexual-Violence-Risk-20* (*SVR-20*; Boer, Hart, Kropp, & Webster, 1997).
- The *Rapid Risk Assessment of Sex Offender Risk* (*RRASOR*; Hanson, 1997).
- The *VRAG* (Quinsey et al., 1998).
- The *SORAG* (Quinsey et al., 1998).
- The *Psychopathy Checklist—Revised* (*PCL-R*; Hare, 2003).

The preceding instruments are offered as representative examples of second-generation instruments. They hardly exhaust the list of available predictor scales. The handful of risk predictors most widely used today are those developed by Hanson and his colleagues in Canada. These are second- and third-generation instruments. Included here are:

- Static-99 (Hanson & Thornton, 1999, 2000).
- Static-2002 (Hanson & Thornton, 2003; Hanson, Helmus, & Thornton, 2010).
- SONAR (Hanson & Harris, 2000a, 2001).
- STABLE-2000/ACUTE-2000 (Hanson & Harris, 2004).
- STABLE-2007/ACUTE-2007 (Hanson, Harris, Scott, & Helmus, 2007).

These instruments are often used today in sexual predator evaluations and will be treated at greater length in Chap. 7.

The *LSI-R* falls into the grouping that Andrews and Bonta (2010a) call *Third-Generation Risk Assessment—Risk/Need Scales*. This category appears most relevant in relation to various theoretical propositions of Andrews and Bonta (2010a), which they call the *Psychology of Criminal Conduct*. This theoretical grounding sets this category apart from second-generation assessments. When they speak of "needs," they are referring to "criminogenic" needs, the dynamic risk factors in criminal behavior. The *LSI-R* is described above. Also included here would be the *Level of Service/Risk, Need, and Responsivity* (*LS/RNR*) (Andrews, Bonta, & Wormith, 2008). Andrews and Bonta (2010a, p. 317) state confidently that "the LSI-R has demonstrated considerable evidence as a predictor of criminal conduct."

Fourth-Generation Risk Assessment extends the reach of this approach. Here the concern is the integration of case management with risk/need assessment. At this writing, this is one of the major modes of risk assessment. According to Andrews and Bonta (2010a, p. 318), "This means more than adhering to the risk principle and targeting criminogenic needs. It also acknowledges the role of personal strengths in building a prosocial orientation, the assessment of special responsivity factors to maximize the benefits of treatment, and the structured monitoring of the case from the beginning of supervision to the end." They have an instrument that meets these criteria: *Level of Service/Case Management Inventory* (*LS/CMI*) (Andrews et al., 2004).

There is a final, nonactuarial category that is also fourth generation. It is not an actuarial, scorable category. Until recently, the *HCR-20* (Version 2; Webster et al., 1997) has been the most widely used violence risk-assessment measure in correctional, mental health, and forensic settings. The *HCR-20*, Version 3, has recently been released (Douglas, Hart, Webster, & Belfrage, 2013). This contains the basic features of Version 2 but sharpens the focus on individual risk factors to enable the preparation of a case formulation and the development of a risk management plan. The *Risk for Sexual Violence Protocol* (*RSVP*) (Hart et al., 2003) provides structured guidelines intended to go beyond the assessment of sexually violent risk and, like the *HCR-20*, Version 3, assists in the development of case formulation and risk management plans. (These items will be covered at greater length in Chap. 7).

Conclusion

The introduction of "truth in sentencing" laws in 1984 essentially stopped or curtailed the use of predictors of success on parole. These policies and laws are intended to curb or abolish parole, so that individuals serve the full or nearly full prison term. The argument for this development was that it made no sense to sentence a person for an indeterminate period, say 7–9 years, then release the inmate after on serving 5 or 6 years. It was necessary, advocates said, to be tough on crime, a sentiment that prevails today (retrieved from www.en.wikipedia.org/wiki/Truth_in_Sentencing, February 25, 2015).

As the twentieth century drew to a close, there was a recurrent wave of public belief, based on a handful of serious sex crimes, that, much like the moral panic of the 1930s and 1940s, something had to be done to capture and confine persons now termed "sexual predators." Despite the dismal failure of the earlier sexual psychopath laws, new legislation was proposed to find these individuals who posed a high risk for reoffense because they suffered from a mental disorder and confine them on an indeterminate basis. Because they supposedly had a mental illness that predisposed them to commit sexual offenses, treatment would be offered to help them get their behavior under control. In reality, this approach is intended to permanently incapacitate the worst of the worst; a large number of these offenders will never be released. This approach is often referred to as "selective incapacitation," originally attributed to Greenwood and Abrahamse (1982).

The data for selective incapacitation comes from the celebrated work of Wolfgang et al. (1972). This was a cohort study that collected data on every single male youth born in 1945 who lived in Philadelphia between the ages of 10 and 18. The total number for the study participants was 9945. Of these, 3475 had had at least one police contact by the age of 18. A smaller group, $n = 627$ (6.3 % of the total sample), were chronic offenders accounting for more than 50 % of crimes committed by the total cohort. A follow-up by Figlio, Tracy, and Wolfgang (1990) of a 1958 cohort found that 7.5 % individuals were high-rate offenders and accounted for 61 % of the crimes committed.

In this line of reasoning, the path to the future is clear. Harcourt (2007, pp. 88–89) put it this way:

> Selective incapacitation is based on the central insight that a small subset of repeat offenders is responsible for the majority of crime and that incapacitating this small group would have exponential benefits for the overall

crime rate…. The modern idea of selective incapacitation grew from this insight: locking up those 6 percent could cut crime in half. The problem became how to identify the 6 percent of chronic offenders. And the solution, naturally, was to turn to actuarial methods.

And later:

> The solution … was essentially to fall back on prior criminal history as a proxy for future dangerousness. All the studies—from parole prediction to selective incapacitation contexts—showed that prior correctional contacts (arrests, convictions, and incarcerations) were the single best predictor of recidivism. (p. 91)
>
> [T]he idea of relying so heavily on prior criminal history was precisely to capture the selective incapacitation effect without complicating the guidelines with the problem of false positives. (p. 97)

Chapter 7 will examine the most prominent of these actuarial methods that have held such promise for the past quarter century.

References

Andrews, D. A. (1982). *The Level of Supervision Inventory (LSI): The first follow-up*. Toronto: Ontario Ministry of Correctional Services.

Andrews, D. A., & Bonta, J. (1995). *The level of service inventory—Revised*. Toronto: Multi-Health Systems.

Andrews, D. A., & Bonta, J. (2010a). *The psychology of criminal conduct* (5th ed.). New Providence, NJ: LexisNexis.

Andrews, D. A., Bonta, J., & Wormith, S. J. (2004). *The Level of Service/Case Management Inventory (LS/CMI): User's manual*. Toronto: Multi-Health Systems.

Andrews, D. A., Bonta, J., & Wormith, S. J. (2008). *The Level of Service/Risk, Need, Responsivity (LS/RNR): User's manual*. Toronto: Multi-Health Systems.

Beirne, P. (1987). Adolphe Quételet and the origins of positivist criminology. *American Journal of Sociology, 92*, 1140–1169.

Boer, D. P., Hart, S. D., Kropp, P. R., & Webster, C. D. (1997). *Manual for the sexual-violence-risk-20: Professional guidelines for assessing risk of sexual violence*. Burnaby, BC: Simon Fraser University, Mental Health Law and Policy Institute.

Borden, H. G. (1928). Factors for predicting parole success. *Journal of Criminal Law and Criminology, 19*, 328–336.

Burgess, E. W. (1928). Factors determining success or failure on parole. In A. A. Bruce, A. J. Harno, E. W. Burgess, & J. Landesco (Eds.), *The workings of the indeterminate sentence law and parole in Illinois* (pp. 205–249). Springfield, IL: Illinois State Board of Parole.

Deflem, M. (1997). Surveillance and criminal statistics: Historical foundations of governmentality. *Law, Politics, and Society, 17*, 149–184.

Douglas, K. A., Hart, S. D., Webster, C. D., & Belfrage, H. (2013). *HCR-20: Assessing risk for violence (Version 3)*. Burnaby, BC: Simon Fraser University, Department of Psychology, Mental Health Law and Policy Institute.

Figlio, R. M., Tracy, P. E., & Wolfgang, M. E. (1990). *Delinquency in a birth cohort: II: Philadelphia, 1958–1986*. Ann Arbor, MI: Inter-University Consortium for Political and Social Research.

Glaser, D. (1954). *A reformulation and testing of parole prediction factors*. Ph.D. dissertation, Department of Sociology, University of Chicago.

Glaser, D. (1955). The efficacy of alternative approaches to parole prediction. *American Sociological Review, 20*, 283–287.

Glueck, S., & Glueck, E. (1950). *Unraveling juvenile delinquency*. New York: Commonwealth Fund.

Gottfredson, M. R., & Hirschi, T. (1990). *A general theory of crime*. Stanford, CA: Stanford University Press.

Greenwood, P. W., & Abrahamse, A. (1982). *Selective incapacitation*. Santa Monica, CA: RAND Corporation.

Hakeem, M. (1948). The validity of the Burgess method of parole prediction. *American Journal of Sociology, 53*, 376–386.

Hanson, R. K. (1997). *The development of a brief actuarial risk scale for sexual offence recidivism* (User Rep. 1997-04). Ottawa, ON: Department of the Solicitor General of Canada. www.ps-sp.gc.ca/res/cor/rep

Hanson, R. K. (2002). Recidivism and age: Follow-up data from 4,673 sex offenders. *Journal of Interpersonal Violence, 17*, 1046–1062.

Hanson, R. K., & Harris, A. J. R. (2001). A structured approach to evaluating change among sexual offenders. *Sexual Abuse: A Journal of Research and Treatment, 13*, 105–122.

Hanson, R. K., & Harris, A. J. R. (2004). *STABLE-2000/ACUTE-2000: Scoring manuals for the dynamic supervision project* (Unpublished scoring manuals). Ottawa, ON: Corrections Research, Public Safety Canada.

Hanson, R. K., Harris, A. J. R., Scott, T.-L., & Helmus, L. (2007). *Assessing the risk of sexual offenders on community supervision: The dynamic supervision proj-*

ect (User Rep.). Ottawa, ON: Corrections Research, Public Safety Canada. www.ps-sp.gc.ca/res/cor/rep

Hanson, R. K., Helmus, L., & Thornton, D. (2010). Predicting recidivism among sexual offenders: A multi-site study of STATIC-2002. *Law and Human Behavior, 34*, 198–211.

Hanson, R. K., & Thornton, D. (1999). *Static 99: Improving actuarial risk assessments for sex offenders* (User Rep. 1999-02). Ottawa, ON: Department of the Solicitor General of Canada. www.ps-sp.gc.ca/res/cor/rep

Hanson, R. K., & Thornton, D. (2000). Improving risk assessments for sex offenders: A comparison of three actuarial scales. *Law and Human Behavior, 24*, 119–136.

Hanson, R. K., & Thornton, D. (2003). *Notes on the development of the STATIC-2002* (User Rep. 2003-01). Ottawa, ON: Department of the Solicitor General of Canada. www.ps-sp.gc.ca/res/cor/rep

Harcourt, B. D. (2007). *Against prediction: Profiling, policing, and punishing in an actuarial age*. Chicago: University of Chicago Press.

Hare, R. D. (2003). *Manual for the Hare Psychopathy Checklist: Revised* (2nd ed.). Toronto: Multi-Health Systems.

Hart, H. (1923). Predicting parole success. *Journal of the American Institute of Criminal Law and Criminology, 41*, 405–413.

Hart, S. D., Kropp, P. R., Laws, D. R., Klaver, J., Logan, C., & Watt, K. A. (2003). *The Risk for Sexual Violence Protocol (RSVP): Structured professional guidelines for assessing risk of sexual violence*. Burnaby, BC: Simon Fraser University, Department of Psychology, Mental Health Law and Policy Institute.

Hoffman, P. B., & Beck, J. L. (1974). Parole decision-making: A salient factor score. *Journal of Criminal Justice, 2*, 195–206.

Janus, E. S. (2006). *Failre to protect: America's sexual predator laws and the rise of the preventive state*. Ithaca, NY: Cornell University Press.

John Howard Society of Alberta. (2000). *Offender risk assessment*. Edmonton, AB: John Howard Society of Alberta.

Jones, E., Harkins, L., & Beech, A. R. (2015). The development of a new risk model: The threat matrix. *Legal and Criminological Psychology, 20*, 165–175.

Kropp, P. R., Hart, S. D., Webster, C. D., & Eaves, D. (1995). *Manual for the spousal assault risk assessment guide* (2nd ed.). Vancouver, BC: British Columbia Institute on Family Violence.

Laub, J. H., & Sampson, R. J. (2003). *Shared beginnings, divergent lives: Delinquent boys to age 70*. Cambridge, MA: Harvard University Press.

Laws, D. R. (2010). Book review: B. McSherry and P. Keyzer (2009). *Sex offenders and preventive detention: Politics, policy, and practice.* Leichardt, NSW, Australia: The Federation Press. *Punishment and Society, 12,* 505–507.

Laws, D. R., & Ward, T. (2011). *Desistance from sex offending.* New York: Guilford.

Moffitt, T. E. (1993). Adolescence-limited and life-course persistent antisocial behavior: A developmental taxonomy. *Psychological Review, 100,* 674–701.

Nicholaichuk, T. P., Olver, M. E., Gu, D., & Wong, C. P. (2014). Age, actuarial risk, and long-term recidivism in a national sample of sex offenders. *Sexual Abuse: A Journal of Research and Treatment, 26,* 406–428.

Quinsey, V. L., Rice, M. E., Harris, G. T., & Cormier, C. A. (1998). *Violent offenders: Appraising and managing risk* (1st ed.). Washington, DC: American Psychological Association.

Reiss, A. J. (1949). *The accuracy, efficiency, and validity of a prediction instrument.* Ph.D. dissertation, Department of Sociology, University of Chicago.

Warner, S. B. (1923). Factors determining parole from the Massachusetts Reformatory. *Journal of Criminal Law and Criminology, 14,* 172–207.

Webster, C. D., Douglas, K. S., Eaves, D., & Hart, S. D. (1997). *HCR-20: Assessing risk for violence, version 2.* Burnaby, BC: Simon Fraser University.

Witmer, H. L. (1927). Some factors in success or failure on parole. *Journal of Criminal Law and Criminology, 17,* 384–403.

Wolfgang, M. E., Figlio, R. M., & Sellin, T. (1972). *Delinquency in a birth cohort.* Chicago: University of Chicago Press.

7

Assessment of Risk to Reoffend: Actuarial Versus Risk Formulation

This chapter will compare and contrast the two major approaches to assessment of risk to sexually offend in use today, the strictly actuarial and forensic case formulation.

As described in the preceding chapter, historically, actuarial risk assessment has depended heavily on static risk factors although there has been some movement in recent years to also consider dynamic factors in an actuarial format. Considerable research effort has been devoted to establishing the reliability and validity of these instruments. Evaluators using these methods are convinced that they represent the most accurate option for determining risk. Hart and Logan (2011, p. 86) state that:

> [B]ased on the information available to them, evaluators make an ultimate decision according to fixed and explicit rules, developed a priori.... It is also generally the case that the ... approach relies on empirical research to determine which information to consider, how to gather it, and how to weight and combine it. It is very specific in focus, designed to predict certain outcomes over certain timeframes in certain populations.

There are fewer instruments using the risk formulation format. I alluded to several in the preceding chapter. These instruments use *structured*

© The Editor(s) (if applicable) and The Author(s) 2016
D.R. Laws, *Social Control of Sex Offenders*,
DOI 10.1057/978-1-137-39126-1_7

professional judgment (SPJ) in making evaluations. Decisions about any given factor are guided by current scientific knowledge about that factor. The professional guidelines offered may thus be considered evidence based. The SPJ approach, according to Hart and Logan (2011, p. 88), "does not provide a formula or other algorithm for calculating risk based on the presence of various factors; instead, evaluators must use their discretion to consider, decide, and explain the relevance or meaningfulness of any factors that are present with respect to the risks posed and the management of those risks." "Scoring," such as it is, takes the form of making a judgment of whether any given risk is "low," "medium," or "high." The SPJ instruments typically provide a framework for combining these judgments into a case management plan.

There are enthusiastic, even fanatical, fans on either side of this divide. This is not a zero-sum game; both approaches will persist although, at this writing, actuarial approaches appear to have the edge.

Actuarial Assessment

Harcourt (2007, p. 24), a professor of law and criminology, provides a dismissive evaluation of this variety of assessment:

> Why should we assume that predictions of criminality and actuarial analysis will benefit society as a whole? There is no good reason. The fact that we do believe tells us something about *us* rather than anything about *them*. It tells us something about *our desire* to believe, *our desire* to predict, *our desire* to know the criminal. We are predisposed to *wanting* the actuarial model to be right—regardless of the empirical evidence.

In a more positive, explanatory fashion, Cooke (2011, p. 3) has offered the following description of the construction of an actuarial assessment instrument:

- *Groups* of offenders, usually *prisoners*, are evaluated in relation to a range of characteristics;

- The characteristics considered are those that are easily measured from file information [for example, age, marital status, history of offending, type of victim, relationship to victim];
- On occasion the cohort of offenders is followed-up to determine from their criminal records whether they have been reconvicted following release;
- More often the procedure adopted is a follow-back paradigm;
- The files of offenders who have been released, and whose conviction status is known, are reviewed;
- This information is then subjected to some form of statistical analysis [for example, Logistical regression];
- Then risk groups with different rates of reconviction—low, medium, high, very high—are created;
- This information is used to make prognostications about a new individual, the focus of a decision;
- This is an argument by analogue. The new individual is allocated to a group on the basis of the measured characteristics and then it is argued that his recidivism will mimic that of those in the group.

The Center for Sex Offender Management (CSOM, 2004, p. 5) has stated the limitations of the actuarial approach:

- *Commonly misunderstood is that the recidivism rate associated with an individual's score means that the rate applies to the specific individual.*
- Instead, scores reflect the recidivism rate of offenders in the development sample who had the same score as the current offender.
- These instruments are, therefore, very effective at predicting the reoffense rates of a *group* of similarly defined offenders, but cannot identify whether a *particular individual* offender with a specific risk group will or will not reoffend.

These limitations are too often overlooked and the risk score is considered to be a specific prediction of reoffense for an individual. Indeed, the test manual for the *Static-99*, the most frequently used actuarial instrument, provides a direct caution against making this mistake (Hart, 2009, p. 164).

Actuarial Instruments

Contemporary approaches to risk assessment have been influenced by the meta-analyses produced by Hanson and Bussière (1998) and later by Hanson and Morton-Bourgon (2005). These analyses pinpointed the risk factors most closely related to recidivism as well as others to be avoided in the development of assessment instruments. For purposes of illustration here, and to highlight the positive and negative features of this approach, I have chosen to focus on the suite of instruments developed by Hanson and his associates from 1997 to the present. Several of these have become so popular that they are *de rigueur* in sex offender evaluations. The package can be divided into two sections: Assessment of risk for recidivism and assessment of dynamic risk factors. To describe this suite, I have relied heavily on publications by Craig and Rettenberger (2016, pp. 19–44), Hanson (personal communication, December 18, 2014), and Harris and Hanson (2010, pp. 296–310) which provide detailed descriptions of this instrument package.

Risk of Recidivism

Included here are: (1) *Rapid Risk Assessment of Sexual Offender Risk* (*RRASOR*, Hanson, 1997); (2) *Static-99* (Hanson & Thornton, 1999, 2000); (3) *Static-99R* (Helmus, 2009); (4) *Static-2002* (Hanson, Helmus, & Thornton, 2010); and (5) *Static-2002R* (Hanson et al., 2010). The *Static-99* in its various iterations has become the most popular recidivism risk instrument in North America.

RRASOR (Hanson, 1997) This was a direct result of discovery of central static risk factors by Hanson and Bussière (1998). The initial instrument contained seven predictors (e.g., any male victims). Subsequent research reduced these to four. The scale proved moderately predictive.

Static-99 (Hanson & Thornton, 1999, 2000) This was a combination of two scales, the *RRASOR* and the *Structured Anchored Clinical Judgment—Minimum* (*SACJ-Min*; Grubin, 1998). The scale contained ten items and proved to be more accurate than either the *RRASOR* or the *SACJ-Min*, which were then abandoned.

Static-99R (Helmus, 2009) This is identical to the original *Static-99* except that it was recognized that risk ratings were less accurate with older offenders. The *Static-99R* changes the age factor into four bands ranging from age 19 to 60+ years.

Static-2002/Static-2002R (Hanson et al., 2010) This scale contains 14 items organized into three areas: age at release, sexual deviancy, and general criminality. It has proved to be slightly more accurate than the *Static-99*.

"The *Static-99* is the most used … and researched sex offender tool in the world and has repeatedly shown moderate levels of predictive accuracy in a large number of replication studies in multiple jurisdictions" (Harris & Hanson, 2010, p. 300). No other recidivism predictor can make that claim. Readers interested in the fine-grain intricacies involved in the development and implementation of the *Static-99* are referred to the developer's website www.static99.org.

Dynamic Risk Assessment

As the titles of the recidivism instruments indicate, they deal with permanent, unchangeable risk factors (e.g., number of previous convictions for sexual assault, age at release, and male victims). Hanson and his colleagues recognized the paucity of this approach and set about examination dynamic risk factors, those that might be amenable to change and thus form a better picture of the risk presented by the offender. They divided these into *stable risk factors*, well entrenched behaviors that could change, but probably slowly (e.g., attitudes and coping skills). In current parlance these are referred to as *criminogenic needs*, the targets of treatment. *Acute risk factors*, on the other hand, pose part of the threat picture but are malleable and open to change (alcoholism, drug addiction, joblessness).

To evaluate the presence of stable and acute risk factors, Hanson and Harris (1998, 2000b) examined whether supervising officers in the community could identify them reliably. In the study, called the *Dynamic Predictors Project*, officers were required to describe their supervisees' behavior in the month just preceding a reoffense and later, during a previous 6-month period. Analysis of these data enabled Harris and Hanson to separate them into stable characteristics of the offender as opposed to more transient states.

Sex Offender Need Assessment Rating (SONAR; Hanson & Harris, 2000a, 2001) The variables identified in the *Dynamic Predictors Project* led to the development of *SONAR*, according to Harris and Hanson, the first scale that attempted to track sex offender behavior change over time. It contained five stable and four acute factors. There was a problem. Other researchers identified important risk factors not included in *SONAR*. This led Harris and Hanson to refine their approach and develop two new measures.

STABLE-2000/ACUTE-2000 (Hanson & Harris, 2004) The effort here was to build more comprehensive instruments that would enable more precise tracking of behavior changes. The *STABLE-2000* contained 16 items in six categories: (1) significant social influences, (2) intimacy deficits, (3) sexual self-regulation, (4) general self-regulation, (5) cooperation with supervision, and (6) attitudes supportive of sexual offending. These risk factors, criminogenic needs, form the targets for treatment and long-term monitoring. The *ACUTE-2000* contained eight items dealing with current behavior: (1) victim access, (2) hostility, (3) sexual preoccupation, (4) rejection of supervision, (5) emotional collapse, (6) collapse of social supports, (7) substance abuse, and (8) a "unique" factor, something relevant to a particular individual. At this point the authors began a prospective study of dynamic risk predictors with a community sample, the *Dynamic Supervision Project* (DSP; Hanson, Harris, Scott, & Helmus, 2007). The project involved training community supervision officers on use of the *Static-99, STABLE-2000,* and *ACUTE-2000*, then tracking offenders for a median period of 41 months to determine who recidivated. Analysis showed that 10 of the 16 items of *STABLE-2000* were related to recidivism. This required another update.

STABLE-2007 (Hanson et al., 2007) Harris and Hanson (2010, p. 303) state that "*STABLE-2007* provides incremental validity to the prediction of all types of recidivism after controlling for the *Static-99*." As a result of the findings of the DSP the item categories were reduced by one. The first five categories of *STABLE-2000* were retained and category (6), attitudes supportive of sexual offending, was dropped. Hanson (personal communication, December 18, 2014) states that the items are rated on a three-point scale (no problem, unsure/small problem, and definite problem) by supervising officers, therapists, police, or other case managers. The total scores provide a global rating of the density of the offender's overall criminogenic needs (lower than average, average, and higher than average). Hanson further states:

> *STABLE-2007*, on its own, has a moderate relationship to recidivism (Eher, Matthes, Schilling, Haubner-MacLean, & Rettenberger, 2012; Eher, Rettenberger, et al. 2013; Hanson et al., 2007; Hanson, Helmus, & Harris, 2015). Its predictive accuracy increases when combined with a measure of static, historical risk factors, such as *Risk Matrix 2000* (Helmus, Hanson, Babschishin, & Thornton, 2015), *Static-99R*, or *Static 2002R* Hanson et al., 2007; Hanson et al., 2015). In the original development study, there was little change on *STABLE* scores during the 6- to 12-month reassessment period, and whatever change was observed was unrelated to recidivism.

ACUTE-2007 (Hanson et al., 2007) The DSP analysis showed that victim access, hostility, sexual preoccupation, and rejection of supervision were related to sexual, violent, and general criminal recidivism. Emotional collapse, collapse of social support, and substance abuse were not consistently related to recidivism. This led to a revision of the item categories separating sex and violence from general criminality. Victim access, hostility, sexual preoccupation, and rejection of supervision were now considered to be sex and violence factors. Emotional collapse, collapse of social supports, and substance abuse were now considered as general recidivism factors.

Hanson (personal communication, December 18, 2014) contrasts the *STABLE-2007* with the *ACUTE-2007*. The former deals with enduring, risk-relevant propensities, while the latter deals with rapid changes in the offender's current life. The seven items are rated on a four-point scale: 0 = no problem, 1 = slight problem, 2 = definite problem, and IN = intervene now. The full set of items are used to predict general (nonsexual) recidivism, while the first four items (victim access, hostility, sexual preoccupation, and rejection of supervision) are used to predict sexual and violent recidivism. Hanson (personal communication, December 18, 2014) further states:

> In the development sample, the most recent *ACUTE* rating predicted recidivism, as did the *ACUTE* ratings averaged over the past 6 months (Hanson et al., 2007); importantly, *ACUTE* scores changed over time and these changes were related to recidivism (Babchishin, 2013). I am aware of only one other study examining the predictive validity of *ACUTE-2007* (Smeth, 2013). Smeth (2013), however, only examined the initial (first) *ACUTE-2007*, which was coded approximately 9 months post-release. She found that the *ACUTE-2007* total score and the *ACUTE-2007* sex/violence score significantly predicted parole violations during the 3.5 year follow-up period.

Craig and Rettenberger (2016) take note of two additional studies:

> The *Stable-2007* had been cross-validated in only a few independent studies while the *Acute-2007* has yet to be cross-validated. Nunes and Babchishin (2012) conducted a construct validity study about the *Stable-2000* and the *Stable-2007* by examining correlations between selected items of the risk tools and validated independent measures of relevant constructs. The authors concluded that the results generally supported the construct validity of the stable risk measures but the degree of convergence was lower than expected (Nunes & Babchishin, 2012). In a currently published German study, Briken and Müller (2014) examined the utility of instruments like the *Stable-2007* for assessing criminal responsibility and the necessity for placement in a forensic psychiatric hospital ... The authors concluded that the specific items of the *Stable-2007* (e.g., deviant sexual interests, sexual preoccupations, or relationship deficits) and the *Acute-2007* (e.g., sexual preoccupation, emotional collapse, or collapse of social support) could be used as empirically well-established proxy variables beyond and additionally to formal diag-

nosis according to the international classification of diseases (ICD) and the diagnostic and statistical manual of mental diseases (DSM) criteria, in order to assess the severity of paraphilic disorders [ed: lower case in original].

The preceding studies may serve as examples of validation research on the DSP package. Dating from the early 2000s to the present, there have been a wide variety of studies on various combinations of the *Static-99, Static-99R, SONAR, STABLE-2000* and *STABLE-2007,* and *ACUTE-2000* and *ACUTE-2007.* There are far too many to attempt a summary here. The interested reader is referred to *www.offenderrisk.com* for a bibliography of these investigations.

How Do Dynamic Measures Fare in Practice?

Harris and Hanson (2010) state that the DSP demonstrated that community supervision officers could reliably rate both static and dynamic risk factors and predict sexual, violent, and general recidivism with high professional accuracy. Both the *STABLE-2007* and *ACUTE-2007* are the most widely used measures of dynamic risk in North America. The authors acknowledge that both instruments have strong face validity, but it remains necessary to continue to produce evidence for their validity.

Critical Appraisal of the Instruments

The *Static-99* in its various incarnations has sustained rather pointed criticism which appears to be largely directed at eliminating its use. *STABLE* and *ACUTE* have been less harshly treated.

Static-99 The argument for and against the *Static-99* and related actuarial risk assessment instruments (ARAIs) is conducted by two professional camps. Hart (2009) terms these groups "latitudinarian" and "orthodox" and makes the following distinctions (p. 148). The latitudinarians

[C]onsider evidence-based decision making to be a guiding philosophy, core value, or aspirational standard. They believe evidence-based describes the general process underlying a decision, not just the specific procedures used to make the decision. They emphasize that the evidence -base itself is always inadequate, flawed, or incomplete, and decision makers must always use their judgment or discretion to fill in the gaps. On the other hand are people who hold narrow views, who may be characterized as "orthodox." They consider decision making to be evidence-based only when the specific procedures used are directly derived from or supported (i.e., confirmed or validated) by empirical research. They emphasize the frailties and inadequacies of human cognition, and therefore attempt to find ways to minimize reliance on judgment or discretion.

Generally speaking, the latitudinarians are the persons supporting instruments using SPJs. Outstanding proponents of this approach would be Stephen Hart, David Cooke, Christine Michie, and Caroline Logan. The orthodox are the persons who strongly support strictly actuarial instruments. Major proponents of this approach would be Karl Hanson, Andrew J.R. Harris, Vernon Quinsey, the late Marnie Rice, and the late Grant Harris. Both sides are firmly convinced of the rightness of their vision. Here we are concerned with the orthodox viewpoint.

Hart and Cooke (2013) challenge the basic rationale of ARAIs, stating that their use is founded on analogical or inferential reasoning: "This man *resembles* offenders who were likely to recidivate, therefore he is likely to recidivate" (p. 82).

They offer the following syllogism to express this as a logical proposition (p. 82):

1. In the development sample for Test X, 52% of people with scores in Category Y committed violence during follow-up.
2. Mr. Jones has a score on Test X that falls in Category Y.
3. Therefore, the risk that Mr. Jones will commit future violence is similar to the risk of people in Category Y.

Cooke (2011, p. 5) labels this sort of reasoning a *fallacy of division*. This fallacy recognizes that it is not possible to make conclusions about an individual member of a group based on the collective properties of that group. Hart (2009, p. 163) expands on this:

> The recidivism estimates provided by the *STATIC-99* are group estimates based upon reconvictions and were derived from groups of individuals with these characteristics. As such, these estimates do not directly correspond to the recidivism risk of an individual offender. The offender's risk may be higher or lower than the probabilities estimated in the STATIC-99 depending on other risk factors not measured by this instrument.

As stated previously, instruments such as the *Static-99* provide percentage estimates of the probability of reoffense at 5, 10, and 15 years. This, say Hart and Cooke (2013, p. 99), is simply untenable:

> (I)t would be very surprising if ARAIs could make precise individual risk estimates of violence over periods of up to 15 years in the future using a small number of risk factors selected primarily on pragmatic grounds (i.e., they could be coded from files), without any idea about the … (experiences) … patients … (might have) … during the follow-up.

Even if one disagrees with the preceding challenges to the rationale underpinning *Static-99*, it is not possible to challenge the problems that have appeared in the course of its evolution from 1997 to 2014. It has been a very rough ride. Franklin and Abbott (2015) have provided a helpful timeline that traces these events over a 17-year period. This timeline appears as Appendix 1.

Sreenivasan, Weinberger, Frances, and Cusworth-Walker (2010) offer a critical appraisal from a psychiatric viewpoint. Despite contradictory findings about the degree of accuracy of prediction and wide divergence in replication samples (see Franklin & Abbott, 2015), these authors state that "the Static-99 scores have assumed an unassailable quality as almost the last word in risk assessment" (p. 401). They further note (p. 402):

- Normative data for *Static-99* and *Static-99R* are overwhelmingly based on unpublished findings (master's or doctoral theses, government reports).

- In 2010 these authors found only one article published in a peer-reviewed journal.
- Each dataset represents different custodial status: probation, release from a forensic hospital, prison release, or outpatient sex offender treatment.
- Variability in the samples undermines the rationale for new norms, i.e., those with better sample representativeness.
- It is difficult to understand how a person hospitalized in a forensic facility 20 years ago in Massachusetts could today be compared to a sex offender in outpatient treatment in Washington state.

Sreenivasan et al. (2010, p. 405) offer an apt conclusion to this section:

> Despite its limitations, this approach remains robust, largely because of the lure of quantification. Unlike other areas in mental health that seek to address potential risk of harm (for example, risk for suicide) where individual factors are weighted into the assessment, sexual recidivism risk seems to be stalled in "actuarial-land," with the veneer of "quantification" belied by shifting "norms." Although they purport be empirically based, the Static-99 and … Static-99R, violate the basic tenets of evidence-based medicine that require reasoned, not mechanical, application of group findings to the individual.

STABLE and ACUTE Hanson (personal communication, March 12, 2015) has offered a general summary:

> The major criticism of *STABLE/ACUTE* has concerned implementation. Although it was designed to be used by a wide range of professionals, it is unlikely to work without sufficient training and concientiousness [ed: close attention to completion of the rating sheets]. The other criticism is that the incremental effect of *STABLE* over *STATIC* is modest, so if all you want are risk categories, then certain jurisdictions have opted only to use *STATIC*.

Some Concluding Observations

The reader may reasonably ask, "Why is so much criticism leveled at the Static-99 in its various forms? Why aren't the same criticisms made of the ACUTE and STABLE? They are also actuarial instruments." The reason is straightforward. The proponents of the latitudinarian approach try to demonstrate that the various *Static* iterations are conceptually faulted and are the main bearers of weakness in this approach. It is true that the *Static-99* manual cautions that it should not be used in isolation. It is so used in that many forensic assessments stresses its purported ability to more or less precisely predict recidivism. It is tempting to believe that ten rather simple features could predict the occurrence of a highly complex behavior (e.g., prior sex offenses, never lived with a lover for at least 2 years, stranger victims, and male victims). This is what Sreenivasan et al. (2010) refer to as the "lure of quantification." The fault lines in the approach are amply demonstrated in the Franklin and Abbot (2015) timeline. However it is clear that its use will persist. The dynamic risk predictors such as *ACUTE* and *STABLE* do not suffer the same level of criticism probably because they closely resemble the various types of assessments that have been in use since the early years of the twentieth century. An instrument such as the Static-99 should always be buttressed by complementary dynamic risk assessments. My recommendation would be that, if a forensic evaluator insists upon using the Static-99, those data should be considered merely a foundational observation and not a precise predictor of reoffense.

While the *STABLE* and *ACUTE* are actuarial instruments, the item content of the risk categories bears close resemblance to other second-generation actuarial instruments such as the *Psychopathy Checklist—Revised* (Hare, 2003) as well as fourth-generation SPJ instruments such as the *Level of Service/Case Management Inventory* (*LS/CMI;* Andrews, Bonta, & Wormith, 2008) or the *Risk for Sexual Violence Protocol* (*RSVP;* Hart et al., 2003). This interpenetration and cross-fertilization of item content is rarely acknowledged. It is to these alternatives that we now turn.

Forensic Case Formulation

The latitudinarians have offered an alternative to actuarial risk assessment. These instruments employ SPJ. While their developmental course (1997 to the present) follows the same timeline as actuarial risk assessment, there are far fewer of them, they are less well known and, consequently, they are not widely used. Cooke (2011, p. 4) has provided a good summary of what the SPJ is and what it does:

- They are evidence-based, rely on evidence from empirical studies, as well as on evidence from best practice.
- They provide a comprehensive evaluation of a wide range of clinically and forensically relevant factors, not the restricted range of file information typical of actuarial approaches.
- They consider dynamic as well as static risk factors.
- Case-specific factors can be taken into account allowing a fuller understanding of unusual cases.
- SPJ focuses, not only on the presence, but also on the relevance of a particular risk factor to a particular case; relevance in regard to either the generation of violence or the disruption of risk management plans.
- While the output of an actuarial assessment is some type of estimate of likelihood that an individual will reoffend, the output from an SPJ approach focuses on managing putative risk.
- The explicit goal of an SPJ evaluation is violence prevention; the evaluation is designed to lead to a comprehensive risk management plan.

Hart and Cooke (2013, p. 98) note that SPJs do not make individual risk predictions or make any statements about the risk of future violence. The guidelines offered are intended to assist forensic evaluators to reach decisions on what kind of violence might be committed, against what sort of victim, and in what circumstances. Then the task is to make recommendations regarding how to prevent that violence. From the SPJ viewpoint, making individual predictions of violence risk is not necessary. As a codeveloper of one of these instruments, and a former user, I might also point out that SPJs, done properly, are a lot of work. Thus, the appeal of ARAIs as an alternative is understandable. The following are examples of two major SPJ instruments.

Sexual Violence Risk-20 (SVR-20; Boer, Hart, Kropp, & Webster, 1997)

In this procedure forensic evaluators rate the lifetime presence of 20 risk factors in four domains: psychological adjustment, social adjustment, history of sex offenses, and future plans. The factors are derived from an extensive review of the scientific and professional literature. Presence of a factor is coded on a three-point scale (absent, possible or partially present, and present). It might be tempting to numerically rate the items as 1–2–3 or 0–1–2, thereby converting the scale to an actuarial one. Instead, the manual requires raters to use symbols: N (No), ? (Maybe), Y (Yes), or O (Omit due to insufficient information). Evaluators consider the presence of case-specific risk factors, note any changes from previous evaluations, and make summary risk judgments (Low–Medium–High) (Hart & Cooke, 2013, p. 89). The final risk ratings are intended to indicate the degree of intervention that might be required in the case.

The following table shows the *SVR-20* risk factors (Boer et al., 1997):

Domain	Risk factor
Psychological adjustment	Sexual deviation
	Victim of child abuse
	Psychopathy
	Major mental illness
	Substance abuse problems
	Suicidal/homicidal ideation
Social adjustment	Relationship problems
	Employment problems
	Past nonsexual violent offenses
	Past nonviolent offenses
	Past supervision failure
History of sexual offenses	High density
	Multiple types
	Physical harm
	Weapons/threats
	Extreme minimization/denial
	Attitudes that support or condone
Future plans	Lacks realistic plans
	Negative attitude toward intervention

Hart and Boer (2010, pp. 282–283) reviewed a number of studies evaluating various forms of validity for the *SVR-20*.

Concurrent Validity: SVR-20 Versus RSVP Jackson and Healy (2008) compared presence ratings from the *SVR-20* with past and present ratings for the *RSVP*. Expectedly, the correlations ranged from high to very high.

Concurrent Validity: SVR-20 Langton (2003) compared the total lifetime presence scores on the *SVR-20* with several ARAIs: *RRASOR,* r = 0.20; *Static-99,* R = 0.36; and Minnesota Sex Offender Screening Tool – Revised (*MnSOST-R*), r = 0.46. Dietiker, Dittmann, and Graf (2007) compared *SVR-20* lifetime presence ratings with expert clinical ratings of sexual violence risk. The relationship was quite strong (AUC = 0.89). Rettenberger and Eher (2007) found a similarly strong correlation (0.78) between lifetime presence scores and total scores on the *SORAG*.

Predictive Validity: SVR-20 Rettenberger, Hucker, Boer, and Eher (2009, pp. 1–22) reviewed the reliability and validity of the *SVR-20* in a variety of North American and European studies.

The results were variable. An early study (Dempster, 1998) found the *SVR-20* to be superior to concurrently used actuarial measures. In a later work, Craig, Browne, Beech, & Stringer (2006), using a small UK sample, a retrospective research design, and file data, found that the *SVR-20* failed to predict sexually violent recidivism. On the other hand, Barbaree, Langton, Blanchard, & Boer (2008), using a large Canadian sample, a retrospective design, and file-based data, found that the instrument showed moderate predictive accuracy. A similar finding in Germany was reported by Stadtland et al. (2005). Rettenberger, Matthes, Boer, and Eher (2009), using a large Austrian sample, a longitudinal prospective research design, *but* using numerical values for item scores, found moderate predictive validity. A later investigation (Rettenberger & Eher, 2009), using a somewhat larger sample, again found moderate predictive validity. Hill, Habermann, Klusmann, Berner, and Briken, (2008), again using a retrospective design and file data, found that *SVR-20* ratings were not associated with recidivism. Meta-analyses (Hanson & Morton-Bourgon, 2005) have generally upheld the predictive accuracy of the *SVR-20*.

Hart and Boer (2010) have made suggestions for improving the accuracy of the *SVR-20* (and these recommendations would apply to all SPJ instruments).

- Numerical coding of the *SVR-20* appears to be as effective as ARAIs. However, summary risk ratings and case prioritization have better predictive accuracy.

- Numerical coding violates the intent of SPJ assessment.
- Clinical interviews together with clinical and criminal data are essential.
- Use of retrospective design limits its usefulness because it is not possible to code changes over time in the risk factors.
- Use prospective longitudinal research designs.
- Use trained raters who are familiar with sex offender issues.
- Coding only lifetime presence ratings limits the predictive power of the *SVR-20*.

In their conclusion Rettenberger et al. (2009) call for a "convergent" approach to risk assessment that incorporates both SPJs *and* ARAIs. This unlikely combination would be anathema to both orthodox and latitudinarian forensic evaluators.

Hart and Boer (2010) also reviewed research on predictive validity of the *SVR-20*. In an early Canadian study, Dempster (1998) numerically coded the *SVR-20* from the files of a group of nonrecidivists, nonsexual violent recidivists, and sexually violent recidivists. Receiver Operating Characteristic (ROC) analysis showed that the *SVR-20* discriminated between sexually violent recidivists and nonrecidivists. In the Netherlands, de Vogel, de Ruiter, van Beek, and Mead (2004), using a retrospective design and a moderate sized sample, found that the *SVR-20* showed good predictive validity. In Spain, Ramirez, Illescas, García, Ferero, and Pueyo (2008), using a retrospective design, coded ratings numerically and summed to total scores. ROC analyses showed that the *SVR-20* had a statistically significant relationship to recidivism (AUC = 0.83, p < 0.001).

Risk for Sexual Violence Protocol (Hart et al., 2003) The *RSVP* could be considered an evolved form of the *SVR-20* (as well as the original Historical-Clinical-Risk-20 (*HCR-20*; Webster, Douglas, Eaves, & Hart, 1997). There is an important distinction. The main task of the *RSVP* is *risk formulation*, not risk prediction. The *RSVP*:

- Identifies potential risk factors (presence).
- Makes a determination of their importance to future offending (relevance).

- Provides explicit guidelines for risk formulation:
  - Risk scenarios
  - Risk management strategies
  - Summary judgments

The primary use of the information contained in the instrument is *preventive*: What steps are needed to minimize *any* risks posed?

The *RSVP* contains 22 items organized in five domains: sexual violence history, psychological adjustment, mental disorder, social adjustment, and manageability as given in the following table (Hart et al. 2003, pp. 43–85):

Domain	Item
Sexual violence history	Chronicity of sexual violence
	Diversity of sexual violence
	Escalation of sexual violence
	Physical coercion in sexual violence
	Psychological coercion in sex violence
Psychological adjustment	Extreme minimization or denial
	Attitudes that support or condone sexual violence
	Problems with self-awareness
	Problems with stress and coping
	Problems resulting from child abuse
Mental disorder	Sexual deviance
	Psychopathic personality disorder
	Major mental illness
	Problems with substance abuse
	Violent or suicidal ideation
Social adjustment	Problems with intimate relationships
	Problems with nonintimate relationships
	Problems with employment
	Nonsexual criminality
Manageability	Problems with planning
	Problems with treatment
	Problems with supervision

Examination of the preceding list shows that many of the *RSVP* items have appeared in risk evaluation instruments dating back to Burgess (1928).

Administration of the RSVP

There are six steps in preparation of the instrument.

Step 1: Case Information It is recommended that the evaluator use multiple methods and multiple sources of information. Static and dynamic risks must both be considered. Information on risk factors should be periodically updated.

The 22 risk factors are coded according to whether they are *present* and/or *relevant*. *Presence* refers to past and recent history of sexual violence. *Relevance* refers to the future likelihood of sexual violence.

Step 2: Presence of Risk Factors These, like the *SVR-20*, are coded on a three-point scale:

- Y = The risk factor is definitely present.
- ? = The risk factor is partially or probably present, or evidence regarding its presence is mixed or inconclusive.
- N = The risk factor is definitely absent, or there is no evidence indicating its presence.

Risk factors may also be coded "O" (omitted) if there is no information, or if the information available is considered unreliable. Omitted factors require an explanation.

Step 3: Relevance of Risk Factors These are also coded on a three-point scale:

- Y = The risk factor is present to some degree and has clear or substantial relevance.
- ? = The risk factor is present to some degree but has unclear or limited relevance.
- N = The risk factor is absent or it is present but not relevant.

Step 4: Risk Scenarios This element is unique to the *RSVP*.

Scenarios are intended to suggest "possible futures," behaviors that the offender might engage in. In constructing scenarios, evaluators are asked to consider the possible nature of a future offense, its possible severity, its possible imminence, how often it might occur, and its likelihood of occurring. Evaluators are encouraged to ideally prepare three scenarios. This is as close as the *RSVP* comes to forecasting the future. It is also a possibly onerous task for the evaluator.

Step 5: Risk Management Strategies Several critical questions must be considered here. How much monitoring will be required? Will periodic visits to a case manager be sufficient or is a more intrusive procedure like house arrest or electronic monitoring required? Is this person a candidate for sex offender treatment? What issues need to be considered? How well will he/she respond to community supervision? What plans will be needed to ensure victim safety?

Step 6: Summary Judgments There are three considerations in making summary judgments regarding case management:

- How urgent is the priority of the case?
  - Low (Routine)
  - Moderate (Elevated)
  - High (Urgent)
- Is there risk of serious harm?
  - Low (Routine)
  - Moderate (Elevated)
  - High (Urgent)
- Is there a need for immediate action?

In making summary judgments, other risks such as nonsexual violence and nonsexual criminality must be considered. The case should be reviewed every 6–12 months routinely but more frequently for moderate to high risk.

Unlike most instruments considered thus far, the *RSVP*, although containing familiar features, is a complex instrument requiring considerable diligence on the part of the forensic evaluator.

Concurrent Validity: RSVP

Kropp (2001) compared past and recent presence ratings from the *RSVP*, recorded as numeric scores and summed to total scores. These total score ratings were correlated with total scores on *MnSOST-R* (r = 0.53), *Static-99* (r = 0.53), and *SORAG* (r = 0.63). A similar study was reported by Klaver, Watt, Kropp, and Hart (2002). Past and recent presence ratings from the *RSVP* were recorded numerically and summed to yield total scores. Total scores for presence ratings were correlated with *Static-99* (r = 0.31), *MnSOST-R* (r = 0.51), and *SORAG* (r = 0.45). Watt, Hart, Wilson, Guy, and Douglas (2006) found that total scores on *Static-99* correlated r = 0.73 with past presence ratings, r = 0.69 with recent presence ratings, r = 0.77 with relevance ratings, and r = 0.77 with case prioritization ratings from the *RSVP*.

Predictive Validity: RSVP

Hart and Boer (2010) have reported that there is very little research in this area. The earliest report (Kropp, 2001) appeared when the *RSVP* was still under development. The focus here was on the case prioritization element of the instrument. The *RSVP* was coded from files, with past and recent ratings converted to numerical scores. Kropp found that *RSVP* case prioritization ratings were significantly related to recidivism (f = 0.40, p<0.05).

Specifically, 8 of 15 offenders rated as high priority were sexually violent recidivists, compared to 5 of 20 rated as moderate priority and 2 of 19 rated as low priority. Hart and Jackson (2008) reported similar results regarding case prioritization. They coded the *RSVP* items from clinical records and divided them according to priority. Most offenders were rated as low to moderate. Recidivism rates were 9% for low priority, 17% for moderate, and 50% for high priority.

The preceding should not be construed to mean that there has been essentially no research on the *RSVP*. In terms of validity, there have been a number of studies on content-related, criterion-related, and concurrent validity. Since we are here comparing the SPJ approach to ARAIs, the most direct comparison should be predictive validity.

Hart and Boer (2010), like Rettenberger et al. (2009), acknowledge the shortcomings of SPJ research: inadequate file information, inexperienced raters, coding only lifetime presence, and numerically converting risk scores.

Conclusions on SPJs

Although the contents of the *SVR-20* and *RSVP* are highly similar, the former is the more flexible and easy to use instrument. It is not difficult to complete and does not require the inclusion of clinical judgment (however professionally structured) in the form of scenarios of future offending or justification of case prioritization. Logan (personal communication, March 13, 2015), one of the coauthors of the *RSVP*, has commented on her use of SPJs in the UK legal system: "The main criticism that I get in terms of feedback from reviewers of my work is that SPJ is too impressionistic and can't help the courts decide yes or no about whether to detain someone whereas the actuarial (pretend to) do that."

Without reference to specific SPJ instruments, Harris and Rice (2015) offer criticism by distinguishing between hypothesis and evidence regarding assessment and communication of risk of recidivism. These are telling criticisms and are routinely ignored by forensic clinicians charged with making judgments about detention. The authors state:

* *Hypothesis 1*: *Final risk ratings are more accurate for the prediction of recidivism than total scores on SPJ tools.* This assertion refers to the SPJ practice of using summary risk ratings of low, moderate, or high. Citing a number of studies, Harris and Rice (2015, pp. 131–132) state that the accuracy of assessments of violence risk is unimproved or slightly worsened by the use of these ratings rather than "untempered raw scores". They argue that (1) "reducing a total score that can range from 0 to 40 to a rating with three values almost certainly means information loss"; (2) "the reliability of the trichotomous judgment has been poor … whereas agreement is better on items and totals"; and (3) "such categories as low, moderate, and high risk have little consensual meaning."

- *Hypothesis 2*: *Assessing both risk and protective factors enhances the accuracy of violence risk assessments.* The issue here is that the inclusion of protective factors adds nothing to the assessment because it cannot be demonstrated that they prevent offending. On the other hand, dynamic risk factors, termed as *criminogenic needs* by Andrews and Bonta (2010), are believed to be empirically linked to reductions in recidivism. Harris and Rice (2015) state that, if protective factors are to be added to an assessment, evidence needs to be provided that they "afford incremental accuracy (above risk factors)" (p. 132.)

- *Hypothesis 3*: *Assessment of dynamic factors, and change in those factors, is critical for assessment of violence risk.* This is an argument against the mixing of static and dynamic factors in the assessment of risk. This is a super-orthodox position that argues that it is clear that "certain characteristics robustly and reliably discriminate those offenders who repeatedly engage in violence (and the most serious violence) from those who are much less likely to do so" (p. 133). And further: "Because items can be selected based on incremental validity, these systems use relatively few items, all reflecting such characteristics. Adhering to specified scoring methods yields large average effects in predicting violent community recidivism...A notable aspect of this is that optimal accuracy can be achieved using items that are exclusively historic—all reflecting prior conduct" (pp. 133–134).

If we put these statements in the context of the RNR model, reliance on actuarial assessment satisfies the "R" portion of the model and assists decisions about custody. If dynamic risk factors are to be considered, they belong to the "N" portion, the treatment of criminogenic needs. Here it would remain to be demonstrated that targeting criminogenic needs is in fact linked to future recidivism.

Hilton, Carter, Harris, and Sharpe (2008) empirically investigated several of the hypotheses just considered. From the orthodox position they state that actuarial risk assessments provide valid numerical information about violence risk but forensic clinicians prefer to communicate risk information in nonnumerical terms (e.g., the use in SPJ practice of *low, moderate,* or *high*). If information could be validly communicated in this fashion, rather than numeric range such as 0–100%, this would simplify enhance communication and promote interrater agreement. The authors recruited 60 forensic clinicians from a variety of disciplines in a large psychiatric hospital. The design was complex and may be described briefly as follows (Hilton et al., 2008, p. 176):

> The study was experimental in that agreement on the numerical risk associated with nonnumerical terms was partly assessed by comparing clinician's responses under two manipulated conditions (a relatively high vs. relatively low risk offender group) and the effect of using nonnumerical terms to describe risk by comparing responses under two manipulated conditions (case summaries with vs. without a nonnumerical term) with participants randomly assigned to conditions).

This study concerned hypothetical forensic decision making and did not include all of the clinical paraphernalia that would be present in an actual forensic situation. The results were interesting but not striking from the orthodox point of view. Although it may seem like a good idea and helpful, two findings from this study stand out. First, the clinicians disagreed on the interpretation of nonnumerical terms, which is not surprising. Second, adding nonnumerical terms to numerical probability statements added nothing to the forensic decisions. "These findings suggest that nonnumerical descriptive terms do not aid effective communication of violence risk and that contextual information might artificially affect estimated risk" (Hilton et al., 2008, p. 171).

In other words, say the orthodox, wherever possible avoid clinical judgment (structured or unstructured). Stick with empirically validated actuarial tools and your risk estimates will always be more right than wrong. And that is where the argument rests at this writing.

References

Andrews, D. A., & Bonta, J. (2010a). *The psychology of criminal conduct* (5th ed.). New Providence, NJ: LexisNexis.

Andrews, D. A., Bonta, J., & Wormith, S. J. (2008). *The Level of Service/Risk, Need, Responsivity (LS/RNR): User's manual.* Toronto: Multi-Health Systems.

Barbaree, H. E., Langton, C. M., Blanchard, R., & Boer, D. P. (2008). Predicting recidivism in sex offenders using the SVR-20: The contribution of age at release. *International Journal of Forensic Mental Health, 7*, 47–64.

Boer, D. P., Hart, S. D., Kropp, P. R., & Webster, C. D. (1997). *Manual for the sexual-violence-risk-20: Professional guidelines for assessing risk of sexual violence.* Burnaby, BC: Simon Fraser University, Mental Health Law and Policy Institute.

Briken, P., & Müller, J. L. (2014). Assessment of criminal responsibility in paraphilic disorder: Can the severity of the disorder be assessed with item of standardized prognostic instruments? *Nervenarzt, 85,* 3040–3311.

Burgess, E. W. (1928). Factors determining success or failure on parole. In A. A. Bruce, A. J. Harno, E. W. Burgess, & J. Landesco (Eds.), *The workings of the indeterminate sentence law and parole in Illinois* (pp. 205–249). Springfield, IL: Illinois State Board of Parole.

Center for Sex Offender Management (CSOM). (2004). *Comprehensive assessment protocol (CAP) of sex offender management strategies.* Silver Spring, MD: Center for Sex Offender Management.

Cooke, D. J. (2011). Violence risk assessment: Things I have learned so far. In T. Bliesener, A. Beelmann, & M. Stemmler (Eds.), *Antisocial behavior and crime: Contributions of developmental and evaluation research to prevention and intervention* (pp. 1–17). Göttingen: Hogrefe.

Craig, L. A., Browne, K. D., Beech, A., & Stringer, I. (2006). Differences in personality and risk characteristics in sex, violent, and general offenders. *Criminal Behaviour and Mental Health, 16,* 183–194.

Craig, L. A., & Rettenberger, M. (2016). A brief history of sex offender risk assessment. In D. R. Laws & W. O'Donohue (Eds.), *Treatment of sex offenders: Strengths and weaknesses in assessment and interventon* (pp. 19–44). New York: Springer, intervention.

de Vogel, V., de Ruiter, C., van Beek, D., & Mead, G. (2004). Predictive validity of the SVR-20 and Static-99 in a Dutch sample of treated sex offenders. *Law and Human Behavior, 28,* 235–251.

Dempster, R. J. (1998). *Prediction of sexually violent recidivism: A comparison of risk assessment instruments.* Unpublished master's thesis, Department of Psychology, Simon Fraser University, Burnaby, BC.

Dietiker, J., Dittmann, V., & Graf, M. (2007). Risk assessment of sex offenders in a German-speaking sample: Applicability of PCL-SV, HCR-20+3, and SVR-20. *Nervenarzt, 78,* 53–61.

Eher, R., Matthes, A., Schilling, R., Haubner-Maclean, T., & Rettenberger, M. (2012). Dynamic risk assessment in sexual offenders using STABLE-2000 and the STABLE-2007: An investigation of the predictive and incremental validity. *Sexual Abuse: A Journal of Research and Treatment, 24,* 5–28.

Eher, R., Rettenberger, M., Gaunersdorfer, K., Haubner-MacLean, T., Matthes, A., Schilling, F., et al. (2013). On the accuracy of the standardized risk assessment procedures Static-99 and Stable-2007 for sex offenders released from detention. *Forensische Psychiatrie, Psychologie, Kriminologie, 7,* 264–272.

Franklin, K., & Abbott, B. (2015, April 19). *Static-99: Yet more bumps on a rocky developmental path* (blog post). Retrieved from http://forensicpsychologist. blogspot.com/

Grubin, D. (1998). *Sex offending against children: Understanding the risk* (Police research series paper 99). London: Home Office, Unpublished report.

Hanson, R. K. (1997). *The development of a brief actuarial risk scale for sexual offence recidivism* (User Rep. 1997-04). Ottawa, ON: Department of the Solicitor General of Canada. www.ps-sp.gc,ca/res/cor/rep

Hanson, R. K., & Bussière, M. T. (1998). Predicting relapse: A meta-analysis of sexual offender recidivism studies. *Journal of Consulting and Clinical Psychology, 66,* 348–362.

Hanson, R. K., & Harris, A. J. R. (1998). *Dynamic predictors of sexual recidivism* (User Rep. 1998-01). Ottawa, ON: Department of the Solicitor General of Canada. www.ps-sp.gc.ca/res/cor/rep

Hanson, R. K., & Harris, A. J. R. (2000a). *The Sex Offender Need Assessment Rating (SONAR): A method for measuring change in risk levels* (User Rep. 2000-01). Ottawa, ON: Department of the Solicitor General of Canada. www.ps-sp.gc.ca/res/cor/rep

Hanson, R. K., & Harris, A. J. R. (2000b). Where should we intervene? Dynamic predictors of sexual offence recidivism. *Criminal Justice and Behavior, 27,* 6–35.

Hanson, R. K., & Harris, A. J. R. (2001). A structured approach to evaluating change among sexual offenders. *Sexual Abuse: A Journal of Research and Treatment, 13,* 105–122.

Hanson, R. K., & Harris, A. J. R. (2004). *STABLE-2000/ACUTE-2000: Scoring manuals for the dynamic supervision project* (Unpublished scoring manuals). Ottawa, ON: Corrections Research, Public Safety Canada.

Hanson, R. K., Harris, A. J. R., Scott, T.-L., & Helmus, L. (2007). *Assessing the risk of sexual offenders on community supervision: The dynamic supervision project* (User Rep.). Ottawa, ON: Corrections Research, Public Safety Canada. www.ps-sp.gc.ca/res/cor/rep

Hanson, R. K., Helmus, L., & Harris, A. J. R. (2015). Assessing the risk and needs of supervised sexual offenders: A prospective study using STABLE-2007, Static-99R and Static-2002R. *Criminal Justice and Behavior, 42*(12), 1205–1224.

Hanson, R. K., Helmus, L., & Thornton, D. (2010). Predicting recidivism among sexual offenders: A multi-site study of STATIC-2002. *Law and Human Behavior, 34,* 198–211.

Hanson, R. K., & Morton-Bourgon, K. E. (2005). The characteristics of persistent sexual offenders: A meta-analysis of recidivism studies. *Journal of Consulting and Clinical Psychology, 73*, 1154–1163.

Hanson, R. K., & Thornton, D. (1999). *Static 99: Improving actuarial risk assessments for sex offenders* (User Rep. 1999-02). Ottawa, ON: Department of the Solicitor General of Canada. www.ps-sp.gc.ca/res/cor/rep

Hanson, R. K., & Thornton, D. (2000). Improving risk assessments for sex offenders: A comparison of three actuarial scales. *Law and Human Behavior, 24*, 119–136.

Harcourt, B. D. (2007). *Against prediction: Profiling, policing, and punishing in an actuarial age*. Chicago: University of Chicago Press.

Hare, R. D. (2003). *Manual for the Hare Psychopathy Checklist: Revised* (2nd ed.). Toronto: Multi-Health Systems.

Harris, A. J. R., & Hanson, R. K. (2010). Clinical, actuarial and dynamic risk assessment of sexual offenders: Why do things keep changing? *Journal of Sexual Aggression, 16*, 296–310.

Harris, G. T., & Rice, M. E. (2015). Progress in violence risk assessment and communication: Hypothesis versus evidence. *Behavioral Sciences and the Law, 33*, 128–145.

Hart, S. D. (2009). Evidence-based assessment of risk for sexual violence. *Chapman Journal of Criminal Justice, 1*, 143–165.

Hart, S. D., & Boer, D. P. (2010). Structured professional judgment guidelines for sexual violence risk assessment: The Sexual Violence Risk-20 (SVR-20) and Risk for Sexual Violence Protocol (RSVP). In R. K. Otto & K. S. Douglas (Eds.), *Handbook of violence risk assessment* (pp. 269–294). New York: Routledge.

Hart, S. D., & Cooke, D. J. (2013). Another look at the (im-)precision of Individual risk estimates made using actuarial risk assessment instruments. *Behavioral Sciences and the Law, 31*, 81–102.

Hart, S. D., & Jackson, K. (2008, July). *The predictive validity of the Risk for Sexual Violence Protocol (RSVP)*. Paper presented at the annual meeting of the International Association of Forensic Mental Health Services, Vienna, Austria.

Hart, S. D., Kropp, P. R., Laws, D. R., Klaver, J., Logan, C., & Watt, K. A. (2003). *The Risk for Sexual Violence Protocol (RSVP): Structured professional guidelines for assessing risk of sexual violence*. Burnaby, BC: Simon Fraser University, Department of Psychology, Mental Health Law and Policy Institute.

Hart, S. D., & Logan, C. (2011). Formulation of violence risk using evidence-based assessments: The structured professional judgment approach. In

P. Sturmey & M. McMurran (Eds.), *Forensic case formulation* (pp. 83–106). Chichester: Wiley-Blackwell.

Helmus, L. (2007). *A multi-site comparison of the validity and utility of the Static-99 and Static-2002 for risk assessment with sexual offenders.* Unpublished Honour's thesis, Carleton University, Ottawa, ON, Canada.

Helmus, L. (2009). *Re-norming STATIC-99 recidivism estimates: Exploring base rate variability across sex offender samples.* Unpublished master's thesis, Carleton University, Ottawa, ON.

Helmus, L., Hanson, R. K., Babchishin, K. M., & Thornton, D. (2015). Sex offender risk assessment with the Risk Matrix 2000: Validation and guidelines for combining with the STABLE-2007. *Journal of Sexual Aggression, 21,* 136–157.

Hill, A., Habermann, N., Klusmann, D., Berner, W., & Briken, P. (2008). Criminal recidivism in sexual homicide perpetrators. *International Journal of Offender Therapy and Comparative Criminology, 52,* 5–20.

Hilton, N. Z., Carter, A. M., Harris, G. T., & Sharpe, A. J. B. (2008). Does using nonnumerical terms to describe risk aid violence risk communication? Clinician agreement and decision making. *Journal of Interpersonal Violence, 23,* 171–188.

Jackson, K., & Healy, J. (2008, July). *Concurrent validity of the RSVP vis-à-vis the SVR-20, Static-99, Static-2002, and SORAG.* Paper presented at the meeting of the International Association of Forensic Mental Health Services, Vienna, Austria.

Klaver, J., Watt, K., Kropp, P. R., & Hart, S. D. (2002, August). *Actuarial assessment of risk for sexual violence.* Paper presented at the meeting of the American Psychological Association, Chicago, IL.

Kropp, P. R. (2001, April). *The Risk for Sexual Violence Protocol (RSVP).* Paper presented at the conference of the International Association of Forensic Mental Health Services, Vancouver, BC.

Langton, C. M. (2003). *Contrasting approaches to risk assessment with adult male sexual offenders: An evaluation of recidivism prediction schemes and the utility of supplementary clinical information for enhancing predictive accuracy.* Unpublished doctoral dissertation, Institute of Medical Science, University of Toronto, Toronto, ON.

Nunes, K. L., & Babchishin, K. (2012). Construct validity of Stable-2000 and Stable-2007. *Sexual Abuse: A Journal of Research and Treatment, 24,* 29–45.

Rettenberger, M., & Eher, R. (2007). Predicting reoffence in sexual offender subtypes: A prospective validation of the German version of the Sexual

Offender Risk Appraisal Guide (SORAG). *Sexual Offender Treatment, 2,* 1–12.

Rettenberger, M., & Eher, R. (2009, November). *A prospective longitudinal study of the reliability and validity of the Sexual Violence Risk-20 (SVR-20).* Poster presented at the conference of the German Association for Psychiatry, Psychotherapy, and Neurology, Berlin.

Rettenberger, M., Hucker, S. J., Boer, D. P., & Eher, R. (2009). The reliability and validity of the Sexual Violence Risk-20 (SVR-20): An international review. *Sexual Offender Treatment, 4,* 2 (unpaginated).

Smeth, A. (2013). *Evaluating risk assessments among sex offenders: A comparative analysis of static and dynamic risk factors.* Unpublished master's thesis, Carleton University, Ottawa, ON.

Sreenivasan, S., Weinberger, L. E., Frances, A., & Cusworth-Walker, S. (2010). Alice in actuarial-land: Through the looking glass of changing Static-99 norms. *American Academy of Psychiatry and the Law, 38,* 400–406.

Stadtland, C., Hollweg, M., Kleindienst, N., Dietl, J., Reich, U., & Nedopil, N. (2005). Risk assessment and prediction of violent and sexual recidivism in sex offenders: Long-term predictive validity of four risk assessment instruments. *Journal of Forensic Psychiatry and Psychology, 16,* 92–108.

Watt, K. A., Hart, S. D., Wilson, C., Guy, L., & Douglas, K. S. (2006, March). *An evaluation of the Risk for Sexual Violence Protocol (RSVP) in high risk offenders: Interrater reliability and concurrent validity.* Paper presented at the meeting of the American Psychology-Law Society, St. Petersburg, FL.

Webster, C. D., Douglas, K. S., Eaves, D., & Hart, S. D. (1997). *HCR-20: Assessing risk for violence, version 2.* Burnaby, BC: Simon Fraser University.

8

Sex Offender Registration and Community Notification

Historical Background

Chapter 6 described the work of Quételet to establish the regularities of crime in the early nineteenth century. Studying the incidence of criminal acts before the courts from 1826 to 1829, he found that young males, poor, uneducated, and unemployed had a greater tendency to commit crimes and be convicted of them. The propensity to commit crimes, he found, was strongest between the ages of 21 and 25.

Logan (2009, pp. 2–16) has provided a brief history of the early years in the development of criminal classification. As we have seen, Quételet's data classified criminals by *groups*.

- As the century progressed, it was noted that some individuals had the propensity to repeatedly commit crimes. The French had a word for it: *récidiviste*. This signaled a shift from a concentration on *classes* of criminals to a focus on *individuals*.
- A serious focus on individual criminals had actually occurred somewhat earlier in the USA. In the late eighteenth century, the Walnut Street Jail in Philadelphia constructed a penitentiary-like structure on its grounds

© The Editor(s) (if applicable) and The Author(s) 2016
D.R. Laws, *Social Control of Sex Offenders*,
DOI 10.1057/978-1-137-39126-1_8

that was unique in that it contained individual cells. Individual offenders were processed in the institution. The information collected included the inmate's name, age, crime of conviction, sentence imposed, and date. However, clerks did not process the information consistently or reliably. Descriptions tended to be vague. The information gathered was peculiar to the institution and not easily retrieved.

- In the not too distant past, offenders could be identified because they had been branded or mutilated. By the early 1800s disfigurement was not considered socially acceptable.

- Photographs of criminals provided an improvement over poorly maintained written records. This approach was introduced in the 1840s by the British and French. In 1850 the New York City police displayed the first rogues' gallery of 450 known criminals—an improvement over text but, similarly, not easily retrieved.

- By the 1850s, we see the emergence of what today would be called a criminal registry. The French introduced *casiers judiciares* (police records). This approach "required that a copy of each conviction and sentence … be sent to the court in the district of the offender's place of birth, or if such a place was not known … to a repository in Paris. With such information consolidated, a 'criminal register' could hold repeat offenders to proper account" (p. 5).

- In 1867 Germany introduced the *Meldwesen* (registration system). All citizens, not just criminals, had to register with the police and report all travel and changes of residence. For police purposes this was supplemented by the *Steckbrief* ("wanted" poster), a daily or weekly notice providing names and descriptions of criminal subjects sought in Germany and elsewhere. This resembles international criminal information exchanges in use today.

- In Britain in the mid-1800s registration and monitoring of offenders was common. If an offender was released before the expiration of his sentence, he was paroled and required to report to the police on a monthly basis. This "ticket of leave" was intended to show that the offender could now be trusted with some freedoms. The practice was later adopted in the USA, Canada, and Ireland.

- During the same period, the British introduced the *Alphabetical Register of Habitual Criminals* and the *Register of Distinctive Marks* (scars, marks, and tattoos).

- Up to this time criminals were only identified by name, historical documentation, and possibly a photograph. The first truly scientific method for identification and classification was the introduction of anthropometry (bodily measurement) by Alphonse Bertillon, a French police officer and biometrics expert. *Bertillonism* was a very intricate approach that

> "depended on three data points: (1) body part dimensions, such as the head, finger, and ear; (2) descriptions of facial features; and (3) notations of 'peculiar marks,' such as scars, birthmarks, and tattoos. Measurements were taken with calipers and other tools by specially trained clerks and complemented by full-face and profile photographs, as were more subjective entries such as complexion, demeanor, voice, and hair color.... Bertillon's appeal, however, also stemmed from its classification system. Measurements taken by clerks were inscribed on index cards and assembled in large specially built cabinets with multiple rows and columns, each concerning a distinct body part.... With each new subject in custody, operators would endeavor to match information taken from the suspect with the anthropometric information filed" (p. 10).

- The array of measurements were reduced to a formula which, it was alleged, would apply to only one person and would not change throughout the offender's adult life. Although Bertillonism was in use from the 1880s to about 1910, it was unevenly adopted. Not surprisingly, the procedure was carried out by humans who recorded the results. The accuracy of measurement was therefore uneven. Illustrations of the measurement system may be seen at www.nlm.nih. gov/visibleproofs (Galleries/Technologies/The Bertillon system).
- Bertillonism survived until about 1910 when it was replaced by fingerprinting, a much simpler and more reliable identification system. Although its origin was in seventh-century China, the procedure did not achieve notice within the criminal justice system until it was endorsed by Sir Francis Galton at the turn of the twentieth century. The approach was well received in the USA and soon emerged as the preferred system of criminal identification, becoming the method of choice by the 1930s. By 1932, J. Edgar Hoover's Bureau of Investigation had over 3 million fingerprints on file with 5000 police agencies reporting.

The Legal Picture: 1930–1980

A senior police officer, August Vollmer, was a strong supporter of the registration of ex-offenders in California. "In 1925, Vollmer urged registration of 'all known criminals coming to California so that police can check their movements.'" His proposal was quite broad, targeting beggars, bigamists, wanted persons, family deserters, escaped prisoners, probation and parole violators, sex offenders, pimps, professional gamblers, and confidence men (Logan 2009, p. 21).

The early history of sex offender registration has also been traced by Logan (2009, pp. 22–49). In September 1931, the Los Angeles District Attorney presented the first criminal registration law. It focused on a diverse list of offenses and was not sex offender specific. The first statewide law in California in 1947 did specifically target sex offenders:

> Compared to the mainly sex offender-related registries of today [ed: 2009] ... sex offender registry laws of the early era were of modest scope. California's law ... specified that persons convicted since 1944 of the following offenses were required to register:
>
> * rape (felony)
> * enticement of a female (felony or misdemeanor)
> * abduction of a minor female to practice prostitution (felony)
> * seduction of a female (felony)
> * incest (felony)
> * crime against nature (felony)
> * lewd and lascivious act on a child under age 14 (felony)
> * oral copulation (felony)
> * indecent exposure (misdemeanor)
> * annoying or molesting a child or loitering near a school (misdemeanor)
> * lewd or lascivious conduct contributing to the delinquency of a child (misdemeanor)

The law further specified that registration information was not to be 'open to inspection by the public or by any persons other than a regularly employed peace or other law enforcement officer' (pp. 31–32).

The scope of the preceding does not appear to be particularly "modest." Despite the sweeping nature of the registration law, there was doubt whether registries produced the desired effect. For example, the *Prison Journal* of the Pennsylvania Prison Society stated that "(I)t is extremely doubtful that the law accomplishes anything. The men who want to be law-abiding and forget their past criminal record will register, while those engaging in criminal activities of course will not" (p. 40).

The decline of registration in this period has also been chronicled by Logan (2009, pp. 46–49):

- States showed little interest in registration during the latter half of the twentieth century.
- No new state registration laws were enacted between 1968 and 1984.
- In California in 1949, 2 years after statewide registration was required, only 550 persons were registered.
- In 1983, the Los Angeles city attorney called the state registry "dysfunctional" because it was overloaded with nonserious sex offenders.
- In 1986, the *Los Angeles Times* described problems with the registry, notably the failure of offenders to register and inaccurate information.
- The attorney general's office did not know the extent of wrong address information in the registry, noting that "we have a people-tracking system of people that don't want to be tracked."
- The *Los Angeles Times* also reported that any effort to construct and maintain a comprehensive and accurate registry was impossible due to resource and personnel limits.
- The Los Angeles County Sheriff's office ceased mailing notices to newly released offenders who did not voluntarily appear for registration because they were receiving a less than 1% response rate.
- By the end of the 1980s sex offender registration appeared to be worthless as a method of social control.

The Reemergence of Registration

Current sex offender legislation describes registration as follows (Tabachnick & Klein 2011, p. 44):

> A system that requires people convicted of sex offenses who are returning to communities post-incarceration to register their whereabouts, and in

many cases check in regularly with law enforcement....Such a procedure can aid in the swift location of individuals if they come under suspicion for a new offense.

That is the simple definition. The reality is considerably more complex.

In Chap. 5, we described the era from 1980 to the present as "The Containment Era." Leon (2011, pp. 107–111 *passim*) provides the idea of the period:

> In the containment era, the public would rather hear about fantastic accusations of satanic ritual abuse of children than address the more common incidents of sexual violence...."Containment" is the designation for a prominent model for managing sex offenders in the community; it also refers to the rhetoric of pollution often used to describe the problem of sex offenders. The containment era features many continuities with the past, including the focus on monstrous offenders rather than the far more typical abuse by familiars.... [S]ince 1980, rehabilitation is rarely promoted, while strategies to prevent and punish have grown exponentially....While satanic abuse hysteria dominated the 1980s and early 1990s, the "sexual predator" eventually became the focus of the containment era. The paradigmatic "sexual predator" is a serial murderer of a child, much like the sexual psychopaths and fiends of the 1930s and 1940s.... In the 1950s and 1960s there was interest in understanding what was normal as well as what was horrible about child molesters.... By 2004 the goal was to gain insight into a monster so that it could be contained.

The containment era, 1980 to the present, is notable primarily for the introduction of repressive legislation aimed at social control of presumably dangerous sex offenders, now called "sexual predators" to underline a sense of fear and loathing. This legislation included civil commitment which was considered in Chap. 5 and will not be repeated here. Sex offender registration and community notification have become central vehicles for social control of sex offenders in the community. Sample and Evans (2009, p. 211) provide a good introduction to this situation:

> Although sex offenders and sexual offenses have received an extraordinary amount of legislative attention over the past two decades, few policy reforms have been as far-reaching as sex offender registration and community

notification. What began as individual state laws, requiring sex offenders to register their addresses with local law enforcement agencies, quickly grew into federal mandates for all states to not only gather information on sex offenders and their whereabouts, but also to release this information to the public.

These procedures seemed new to many but, in fact, similar policies had been around for a long time. As long ago as 1937, Florida passed a registration law requiring offenders of all types to register, the goal being to target felonies of "moral turpitude." It has been mentioned above that California passed a registration statute specifically aimed at sex offenders in 1947. Arizona followed in 1951. In the years 1957–1967 Florida, Alabama, Ohio, and Nevada all passed registration laws focused on sex offenders. In 1986 Illinois passed the *Habitual Child Sex Offender Registration Act*, which became a template for what would follow from the 1990s to the present. The Illinois act required persons convicted of a second offense against a child under 18 to register with law enforcement for 10 years. In the 1990s Illinois expanded the earlier act to now include all offenders convicted of sex crimes against children and adults (Sample & Evans 2009 pp. 212–213).

The legislation that developed in the 1990s and early 2000s was a direct response to horrific crimes against six children: the 1981 sexual assault and murder of Adam Walsh; the 1989 abduction and disappearance of 11-year-old Jacob Wetterling; the 1989 sexual assault and mutilation of a 7-year-old Seattle boy; the 1994 murders of Polly Klaas (age 12) and Megan Kanka (age 7); and the sexual assault and murder of Jessica Lunsford (age 9) in 2005. The following are brief descriptions of these statutes (Laws 2009; Laws & Ward 2011, pp. 130–132; Sample & Evans 2009, pp. 214–221; en.wikipedia.org/wiki/ Sex_offender_registry).

Jacob Wetterling Crimes Against Children and Sexually Violent Offender Registration Act (1994) (Megan's Law)

The law required states to form registries of offenders convicted of sexually violent offenses or offenses against children. The addresses of sex offenders must be verified for 10 years. Those classified as sexually violent offenders must verify addresses quarterly for life. Failure of a state to comply would result in a 10% reduction of federal block grant funding for criminal justice. Congress amended the *Wetterling Act* in 1996 with *Megan's Law* requiring law enforcement to release information about sex offenders to the general public.

Jessica Lunsford Act (2005)

This was a Florida statute that was introduced at the federal level in 2005 but was never enacted into law. The law classified lewd and lascivious molestation of a person under 12 years and a felony carrying a mandatory minimum sentence of 25 years in prison and lifetime electronic monitoring. Lifetime probation would follow imprisonment. *Jessica's Law* introduced residency restrictions.

Adam Walsh Child Protection and Safety Act (2006)

This law is more familiarly known as the *Sex Offender Registration and Notification Act (SORNA)*, Title 1 of the Adam Walsh Act. This is the most sweeping of the acts in this genre and appears to subsume all previously enacted statutes. *SORNA* divides registrants into three "tiers" according to the nature of their offenses:

Tier 3 (most dangerous)

- Update whereabouts every 3 months
- Lifetime registration

Tier 2 (moderately dangerous)

- Update whereabouts every 6 months
- 25 years registration

Tier 1 (least dangerous)

- Update whereabouts each year
- 15 years registration

SORNA created a *national* sex offender registry. States are instructed to apply identical criteria for posting offender information on the Internet (offender's name, address, date of birth, place of employment, photograph, etc.).

Petersilia (2003, pp. 108–109) has shown how intrusive these Internet postings can be. Petersilia noted that "some of the criminal record information in the FBI and state registries has been shown to be inaccurate, and yet it is shared with landlords, financial institutions, and employers as if it was valid." As an example she shows that by entering an inmate's name, date of birth, or a Department of Corrections number in that department's website (Illinois in this case), the screen will show:

- A current picture of the inmate (probationer or parolee)
- The inmate's current status
- Residence location (if paroled)
- Date of birth
- Height and weight
- Race
- Color or hair and eyes
- Any scars or tattoos
- Security classification
- County of commitment (and release)
- Discharge date
- Crime for which convicted
- Number of counts
- Sentences imposed

Petersilia also notes that these sites may also contain information on modus operandi, cars driven, home address, gang affiliation, and substance abuse history.

The *SORNA* notification terms, directed specifically at sex offenders, are broader in scope and include the following (Sample & Evans 2009, p. 214):

- Any aliases used by the offender
- Social Security Number

- Employer and address
- School (if a student)
- License plate number and description of any vehicle owned or operated

Each jurisdiction must also supply the following information for every offender in the registry:

- A physical description of the offender
- The convicted offense
- Criminal history of the offender, including dates of arrests and convictions and correctional or release status
- Fingerprints and palm prints
- A DNA sample
- A photocopy or a valid driver's license or identification card

An additional provision of the Walsh Act requires each jurisdiction in the USA to provide registry information to the public via the *Dru Sjodin National Sex Offender Public Website*. Some nonessential items (e.g., Social Security Number) are not included here (Sample & Evans 2009, p. 220).

Community Notification

Community notification has been defined as:

> A process by which the public broadly and/or a specific community is notified either passively [e.g., information is made available via the Internet] or actively [e.g., information is made available through notices in the newspaper or delivered to homes in a community] about the proximity and presence [e.g., residence, job, or school locations] of a sex offender. (Tabachnick and Klein 2011, p. 44)

Presumably such actions will:

> [E]ncourage community members to keep themselves safe from sexual abuse by knowing that a person previously convicted of a sex offense is in the vicinity of their homes.

Community notification, in fact, can produce devastating effects on the lives of the targeted offenders.

The *Wetterling Act (Megan's Law)* (1994) introduced community notification about sex offenders and *SORNA* (2006) expanded this requirement by the creation of a national sex offender registry. The latter, on the face of it, appears to be a rather draconian response to a perceived threat posed by sex offenders. Velázquez (2008) has asked: What is behind these waves of sex offender laws? We have already considered much of this. There is, says Velázquez, a moral panic underway that exaggerates public response to the perceived threat. This disregards the clear evidence that violent crime rates (including those for sex offenses) have been in decline for 30 years (Chettiar 2015). Velázquez also noted that the presence of 24-hour cable news stations fuels increased awareness of sex crimes.

In the face of considerable evidence, to the contrary, the public embraces persistent myths about sex offenders which seem to validate the imposition of harsh community restrictions. Consider the following survey data from Fortney, Levenson, Brannon, and Baker (2007) (cited in Laws 2009):

Survey Question	Published Data	Public Average
What percentage of sexual assaults were committed by strangers?	27%	49%
What percentage of sex offenders are known to the authorities?	36%	46%
What percentage of adult sex offenders were abused as children?	28%	67%
What percentage of convicted sex offenders will reoffend?	14%	74%
What percentage of rapists reoffend?	20%	74%
What percentage of child molesters reoffend?	13%	76%

A telephone survey along similar lines (Mears, Mancini, Gertz, & Bratton, 2008) produced the same sort of results. Ninety-four percent of respondents stated that tough punishment should be the "top national priority for state and federal policymakers."

Problems in Registration and Notification

Constitutional Challenges

As was the case in sexual psychopath and current civil commitment statutes, there have been constitutional challenges to the registration and notification laws. Two cases, adjudicated before the imposition of *SORNA*, are often cited as examples:

Smith v. Doe, 538 U.S. 84 (2003) This case challenged the *Alaska Sex Offender Registration Act*. John Does I and II had been convicted of aggravated assault prior to the act's passage. Their suit claimed that the act was punitive and violated the ex post facto clause of the US Constitution. A district court ruled that the law was not punitive but an appeals court sided with the Does, ruling that the act was punitive and did violate the ex post facto clause. Subsequently the case was heard by the US Supreme Court. The opinion of the Court was that the intent of the Alaska act was "to create a civil, nonpunitive program to protect the public and that the dissemination of the registration information was not significant enough to declare it debilitating" (retrieved from: http://en.wikipedia.org/w/index.php?title=Smith_v._Doe&oldid=645381461).

Connecticut Department of Public Safety v. Doe, 538 U.S. 1 (2003) This case challenged the *due process* clause of the US Constitution. Connecticut's version of *Megan's Law* required the Department to gather information from the sex offender registry and make it available on an Internet website, making it available to the public in specified state offices. Doe argued that the public disclosure provision denied him due process, a denial of fair treatment. A district court issued an injunction with respect to the public disclosure provisions. An appeals court affirmed that decision and stated that such a disclosure violated the due process clause. The US Supreme Court reviewed the case and determined that "due process does not require the opportunity to prove a fact that is not material to the State's statutory scheme. Injury to reputation itself, even if defamatory, does not constitute deprivation of liberty" (retrieved from: http://en.wikipedia.org/w/index.php?title=Connecticut_Department_of_Public_Safety_v._Doe&oldid=658865297). In other words, the statute is intended to protect the public. If the information disseminated proves harmful to a registrant, that is simply collateral damage.

The Academic Perspective

Proponents of *SORNA* claim that the sweeping statute closes gaps and loopholes in existing sex offender laws. The dissenting voices are many. For example, Sample and Evans (2009, pp. 221–224) outline some of the problematic issues:

- *SORNA* requires that offenders be classified into tiers based on the conviction imposed. Thus, persons convicted of a very serious offense (e.g., sexual acts with a child under the age of 12) would be assigned to Tier III, while a person convicted of a minor or misdemeanor offense (e.g., public indecency) would go to Tier I. This approach ignores history. Opponents say that the Tier assignment should be based, rather, on assessment of risk that the offender poses. For example, Zgoba et al. (2012), examining data from four states, found that recidivism was more accurately predicted by *Static-99R* and *Static-2002* scores than by the prescribed *SORNA* classification system).
- Sex offender laws are more likely to succeed if they target the offenders who pose the most risk. The highest risk offenders should be registered and have their information made available to the public. Meager resources would then be used to focus on those most likely to present public danger. (This would be the recommendation proposed in Andrews and Bonta's (2010a) Risk–Need–Responsivity [RNR] model of intervention.)
- Law enforcement agencies as well as probation and parole officers are required to implement the sex offender laws in addition to their other duties. Many of these individuals are typically overworked and this adds an extra burden.
- The cost of implementing a registration and notification system affects both individual taxpayers and state budgets as states are required to operate these programs. There is a provision in the Walsh Act that

states must implement the act's provisions or suffer a 10% reduction in a federal law enforcement assistance program. Critics have argued that it may be more expensive to implement the Walsh Act than lose the 10% of supplemental funds.

* An apparently insoluble problem is the fact that there are tens of thousands of known sex offenders who are unregistered because they have either refused to do so or have failed to update their registry information. As stated previously these laws may be a people tracking system for people who do not want to be tracked.

I have noted in Chapter 5 that much of public, law enforcement, and governmental judgment about sex offenders is based on myths and faulty conclusions. These conflict with the empirical realities. The prominent myths include (1) sex offenders always reoffend, (2) sex offenders often murder their victims, and (3) sex offenders are often strangers to their victims. Although none of these assertions are true, public support for registration and notification is widespread. Sample and Evans (2009, pp. 231–232) describe a study where Phillips (1998) found that a majority of 400 residents sampled in the Washington state community reported feeling safer because they were aware of a registry of sex offender addresses and information. They also described a study by Anderson and Sample (2008) which surveyed 1800 Nebraska residents. A majority of the sample was aware of the registry but only one third had examined the available information. Most of these individuals received information from newspapers rather than from the registry website.

Levenson and D'Amora (2007) reviewed the history of current sex offender policies and implementation and concluded that "These policies do not appear to be evidence based in their development and implementation because they are founded largely on myths rather than on facts. Little empirical investigation has been conducted to evaluate sex offender policies but extant research does not suggest that these policies achieve their goals of preventing sex crimes, protecting children, or increasing public safety" (p. 168).

Tewksbury and Jennings (2010) reviewed a number of investigations on registration and notification in the first decade of this century and could find no compelling evidence that they had any effect on recidivism.

They then conducted a study which focused on the effectiveness of the Walsh Act (which they term "SORN"). They examined the recidivism rates of two cohorts of Iowa ex-convicts, one released prior to SORN and one released post-SORN. Both were followed up for 5 years. They concluded:

> The results of this study suggest that SORN has not reduced the rate of sex offender recidivism, nor has it led to a decrease in the number of offenses committed by recidivating sex offenders. Among a 10-year cohort of Iowa sex offenders, not only is the sexual recidivism rate virtually identical prior to and following the implementation of SORN, but so too is the distribution of sex offenders into trajectory groups essentially identical....Additionally, the distribution of sex offenders across groups – nonrecidivating, low-rate recidivating, and initially high then decreasing rate of offending – show no differences for before and after the implementation of SORN in Iowa....Overall, the rate of sex offender recidivism is low (12%), corresponding to the results of previous studies....Acknowledging this consistency, it appears that the lack of differences in recidivism and patterns of recidivism prior to and following SORN implementation calls into question the value of SORN policies and procedures. The findings suggest that not only are very few sex offenders likely to sexually recidivate, but the policy also appears to have virtually no impact on sex recidivism. (p. 579)

Nobles, Levenson, and Youstin (2012) also examined recidivism rates before and after the SORN law was passed. No differences were found. A further analysis showed no significant change in sex crime arrest patterns.

Impact of Registration and Notification on the Offender

The community notification provision has the most negative influence on the offender. Being on the registry and being identified through newspaper stories, community flyers, or access to an Internet website can conceivably influence almost every aspect of an offender's life. Laws and Ward (2011, p. 132) have noted that "The 'sex offender' stigma is far more pernicious and far reaching than the 'burglar' or 'car thief' stigma."

Two examples will make this situation clear. Tofte (2007, p.6) notes that "Most registries simply indicate the statutory name of the crime for which a person was convicted, for example, 'indecent liberties with a child.' Such language does not provide useful information about what the offending conduct actually consisted of, and the public may understandably assume the worst."

Tofte (2007, p. 6) provides a verbatim example [ed: email communication to Human Rights Watch, June 4, 2005]:

> When people see my picture on the state sex offender registry they assume I am a pedophile. I have been called a baby rapist by my neighbors; feces have been left on my driveway; a stone with a note wrapped around it telling me to "watch my back" was thrown through my window....What the registry doesn't tell people is that I was convicted at age 17 of sex with my 14-year-old girlfriend, that I have been offense-free for over a decade, that I have completed my therapy, and that the judge and my probation officer didn't even think I was at risk of reoffending. My life is in ruins, not because I had sex as a teenager, and not because I was convicted, but because of how my neighbors have reacted to the information on the internet.

The preceding example is often termed a "Romeo and Juliet" offense. Many professionals believe that such consensual sexual conduct between adolescents does not constitute a crime and should not be prosecuted.

Leon (2011, p. 179) describes a case that legally would be termed "public indecency," an incident that probably should not have happened, but one which hardly merited the consequences that ensued. In 1998:

> Ryan had urinated in the woods because the portable toilets at his jobsite were occupied. A passing police officer spotted him and issued a citation. Ryan was never handcuffed, arrested, or taken to jail. Instead, the State of Florida treated him much like a citizen who is cited for speeding – he was written a ticket, given a date to appear in court, and released. He ultimately pled *nolo contendere* to this single charge and paid $180 in court costs.
> During the years after this citation, Ryan married, had twin boys, lived and worked in New York, and then moved to Arkansas to be near his wife's family. On September 10, 2007, Ryan was arrested by officials from the

Madison County Sheriff's Office for knowingly failing to register as a "sex offender."

In order to earn release on the $15,000 bond, Ryan was forced to register as a convicted sex offender. So that he could comply with the requirements of the state's Community Notification Act, Ryan vacated the home where he resided with his wife of twenty-five years ... because it was purportedly within 2,000 feet of a private day-care facility. The State of Florida had never required Ryan to register as a sex offender, and Arkansas law does not currently treat his conduct as a criminal sex offense that would trigger notification and registration requirements. Nonetheless, as a result of this wrongful conviction [ed: and his voluntary compliance with the Notification Act] ... (he) was ostracized from his community, hounded by the media, and became homeless and unemployed.

To be sure, the two preceding examples represent relatively minor offenses. Persons who have committed more serious crimes would undoubtedly be treated at least as badly, if not worse. However, the examples show that the arm of registration and notification is very long indeed and can sweep up harmless offenders in its ever-tightening net.

Will this ever end? One might expect that, over time, modifications of the more extreme faults could occur. It does not seem likely that registration and notification will disappear given the determination of the general public to ignore the realities of sex crime, the relentless insistence of 24-hour cable news to exploit the sensational while ignoring the commonalities of sex crime, and the pressure on lawmakers to do something, anything, to stop sex offending.

Travis (2005, p. 250) provides a good summary of this situation:

Society does not readily set a place at the communal table for those who have violated the law. We deny ex-felons access to jobs, housing, health care, welfare benefits, voting rights, and other privileges and rights of ownership through a vast network of invisible punishments. On a more fundamental level, we create a symbolic distance between mainstream society and ex-felons by attaching a powerful, seemingly indelible stigma to those who have violated society's laws. Society shuns ex-felons, while simultaneously expecting them to work, support their children, respect the law, and observe their release conditions.

References

Anderson, A. L., & Sample, L. L. (2008). Public awareness and action resulting from sex offender community notification laws. *Criminal Justice Policy Review, 19*, 391–396.

Andrews, D. A., & Bonta, J. (2010a). *The psychology of criminal conduct* (5th ed.). New Providence, NJ: LexisNexis.

Chettiar, I. M. (2015). *The many causes of America's decline in crime.* Retrieved from www.theatlantic.com/features/archive/2015/02/the-many-causes-of-americas-decline-in-crime/385364/

Connecticut Department of Public Safety v. Doe, 538, U.S. 1.

Fortney, T., Levenson, J., Brannon, Y., & Baker, J. N. (2007). Myths and facts about sexual offenders: Implications for treatment and public policy. *Sexual Offender Treatment, 1*, 1–22.

Laws, D. R. (2009, April). *The recovery of the asylum: Observations on the mismanagement of sex offenders.* Keynote presentation at the Tools to Take Home conference, Lucy Faithfull Foundation, Birmingham, UK.

Laws, D. R., & Ward, T. (2011). *Desistance from sex offending.* New York: Guilford.

Leon, C. S. (2011). *Sex fiends, perverts, and pedophiles: Understanding sex crime policy in America.* New York: New York University Press.

Levenson, J. S., & D'Amora, D. A. (2007). Social policies designed to prevent sexual violence: The emperor's new clothes? *Criminal Justice Policy Review, 18*, 168–199.

Logan, W. A. (2009). *Knowledge as power: Criminal registration and community notification laws in America.* Stanford, CA: Stanford Law Books, Stanford University Press.

Mears, D. P., Mancini, C., Gertz, M., & Bratton, J. (2008). Sex crimes, children, and pornography. *Crime & Delinquency, 54*, 532–650.

Nobles, M. R., Levenson, J. S., & Youstin, T. J. (2012). Effectiveness of residence restrictions in preventing sex offender recidivism. *Crime & Delinquency, 58*, 491–513.

Petersilia, J. (2003). *When prisoners come home: Parole and prisoner reentry.* New York: Oxford University Press.

Phillips, D. M. (1998). *Community notification as viewed by Washington's citizens.* Olympia, WA: Washington State Institute for Public Policy.

Sample, L. L., & Evans, M. K. (2009). Sex offender registration and community notification. In R. G. Wright (Ed.), *Sex offender laws: Failed policies, new directions* (pp. 211–242). New York: Springer.

Smith v. Doe, 538 U.S. 84 (2003).

Tabachnick, J., & Klein, A. (2011). *A reasoned approach: Reshaping sex offender policy to prevent child sexual abuse.* Beaverton, OR: Association for the Treatment of Sexual Abusers.

Tewksbury, R., & Jennings, W. G. (2010). Assessing the impact of sex offender registration and community notification on sex-offending trajectories. *Criminal Justice and Behavior, 37,* 570–582.

Tofte, S. (2007). *No easy answers: Sex offender laws in the US.* New York: Human Rights Watch.

Travis, J. (2005). *But they all come back: Facing the challenges of prisoner reentry.* Washington, DC: Urban Institute Press.

Velázquez, T. (2008). *The pursuit of safety: Sex offender policy in the United States.* New York: Vera Institute of Justice.

Zgoba, K. M., Miner, M., Knight, R., Letourneau, E., Levenson, J., & Thornton, D. (2012). *A multi-state recidivism study using Static-99R risk scores and tier guidelines from the Adam Walsh Act* (Document No. 240099). Washington, DC: National Institute of Justice, U.S. Department of Justice.

9

Community Restrictions on Sex Offender Behavior

All ex-prisoners face a considerable array of barriers to reentry and reintegration to society. These apply to general criminal offenders as well as sex offenders. Travis (2005, p. 66) has referred to these barriers as "invisible punishments." The barriers are invisible, he says, because they do not appear in supervision orders governing offender behavior in the community. Travis (2005, p. 73) further states:

> Punishment for the original offense is no longer enough: one's debt to society is never paid....In the modern welfare state, these restrictions on the universe of social and welfare rights amount to a kind of "civil death," in which the offender is deemed unworthy of societal benefits and is excluded from the social compact.

Laws and Ward (2011, p. 124) list some of the less obvious invisible punishments:

- Ineligibility for public assistance, education loans, public housing, or food stamps
- Prohibition of voting, holding public office, or service on a jury

© The Editor(s) (if applicable) and The Author(s) 2016
D.R. Laws, *Social Control of Sex Offenders*,
DOI 10.1057/978-1-137-39126-1_9

• Possible grounds for divorce, termination of parental rights, lifetime registration with the police, or deportation

Other barriers to reintegration are broader in scope and impact (Laws & Ward, 2011, pp. 125–131). Included here are:

Work

Many ex-prisoners are low skilled or unskilled. This is particularly true if they entered prison when young and served a long term. While some prisons have educational and training programs that teach useful skills, many do not. There are prison industries that produce goods useful only in prisons (e.g., shoe factory). Such vocational training as may be imparted (e.g., auto body repair, electronics, welding, office technology) provides skills for state use and only marginal use in the outside world. Travis (2005, pp. 161) comments on this failure: "By failing to prepare prisoners for a return to work, our current prison policies damage the … economy, one prisoner at a time."

Further, Travis notes, many of these prisoners will return to very poor communities that already suffer high unemployment and social dysfunction.

Employment

When prisoners are released, they are presented with supervision orders that they must find and maintain gainful employment. Petersilia (2003, p. 113) has noted a number of barriers to employment that are virtually impossible to put right:

• Very low levels of education and previous work experience
• Substance abuse and mental health problems
• Residing in poor inner-city neighborhoods with weak connections to stable employment opportunities
• Lack of motivation for and attitudes of distrust and alienation from traditional work

That is quite a package but there is more:

• Many offenders, and particularly sex offenders, will be barred from child care, education, or security.
• Some ex-prisoners will not be admitted to trade unions because they cannot be bonded
• It may be difficult to obtain driver's licenses (needed for identity purposes), social insurance cards, or birth certificates
• Employers will not hire or may dismiss employees who deny criminal history
• Ex-prisoners often earn less than employees with no criminal record

Lucken and Ponte (2008, p. 49) conclude that "statutory and regulatory barriers facing ex-offenders in the job market seem antithetical to expectations of good citizenship, familial responsibility, and meaningful [re]integration into community life."

Housing and Homelessness

Employment and housing are essential factors in reentry and reintegration. Ex-prisoners may return to live with their families, who may not want them back. If they are turned away, they may turn to former friends, some of whom may have criminal records or be criminally active.

The US Public Housing Administration (PHA) can "deny applicants whose habits and practices may be expected to have a detrimental effect on the residents or the project environment.... (A) history of criminal activity... would adversely affect the health, safety or welfare of other tenants" (Travis, 2005, p. 229). So, if an offender had formerly lived in public housing he would not be allowed to return. The PHA can terminate leases for any evidence of criminal behavior or use of alcohol or drugs that affects the rights of other tenants. Travis (2005, p. 240) summarizes this situation, noting that ex-prisoners are "a subpopulation that experiences two revolving doors – one that leads in and out of prison, and one that leads in and out of homeless shelters."

Communities

Ex-prisoners often return to poor and broken communities. These are places of extreme economic and social disadvantage. Lack of employment and weak social structure may lead the ex-prisoner to reestablish associations with former pro-criminal friends who may be general criminal offenders if not sex offenders.

Felony Disenfranchisement

Persons convicted of serious crimes (felonies) may be denied the right to vote. This may be permanent or suffrage may be restored after an ex-prisoner has completed a sentence, or completed probation or parole supervision. The Sentencing Project (2014, p. 1) has noted:

- The 12 most extreme states restrict voting rights even after a person has served his or her prison sentence and is no longer on probation or parole.
- Individuals in those states make up approximately 45% of the entire disenfranchised population.
- Only two states, Maine and Vermont, do not restrict the voting rights of anyone with a felony conviction, including those in prison.
- Persons currently in prison or jail represent a minority of the total disenfranchised population.
- Seventy-five percent of disenfranchised voters live in their communities, either under probation or under parole supervision or having completed their sentence.
- An estimated 2.6 million people are disenfranchised in states that restrict voting rights even after completion of sentence.

Residence Restrictions

In 2008, there were 30 states that specified where sex offenders could live (Meloy, Miller, & Curtis, 2008). These residential barriers are the greatest threat to community reentry and reintegration. They are not a part of federal legislation such as *SORNA* but, rather, are a result of the community notification provisions. Since registry information is available on the Internet in many areas in addition to direct notification by criminal justice authorities, citizens in most communities will know who the sex offenders are who live among them and where they live. Therefore, state and local ordinances attempt to restrict where known sex offenders may live. The enactment of these restrictions appears to be a result of the stranger danger myth, that dangerous sex offenders are roaming around the community seeking children to molest. The restrictions prohibit offenders from living near places where children congregate: playgrounds, schools, swimming pools, daycare centers, and school bus stops. Levenson (2009) notes that other protected venues may include arcades, movie theaters, amusement parks, youth sports facilities, and libraries.

Craun and Theriot (2009) examined this misperception by means of a mail survey. They found that "in neighborhoods where registered sex offenders reside, awareness of a local sex offender significantly increases the likelihood that a respondent is worried about a stranger sexually abusing a child" (p. 2057).

Duwe, Donnay, and Tewksbury (2008) looked at the reoffense patterns of 224 sex offenders released from prison between 1990 and 2002. A few contacted victims in close proximity to their residences. No offenders did so near schools, parks, playgrounds, or other locations typically specified in these ordinances.

Chajewski and Mercado (2009) used geographic information systems software to map the residences of sex offenders and the location of schools in a rural, a suburban, and an urban area of New Jersey. The maps showed the schools ringed by buffer zones of 1000–2500 feet. In the rural area, and to a lesser extent in the suburban area, a 1000-foot buffer left enough room for sex offender residences and complies with the law. However, when the buffer zone was increased to 2500 feet in the suburban and urban areas, the zone encompassed nearly all of the space, leaving offenders nowhere to go. The authors noted that since needed offender treatment and monitoring services are most likely to be available in urban and suburban areas, the ordinance produced an unintended result. A similar conclusion was offered by Delson, Kokish, and Abbott (2008), who, speaking for the California Coalition on Sexual Offending

(CCOSO), stated that available research showed no relationship between where a registered offender lived and the pattern of any new sex crimes that the person committed. Rather, the policies appeared to result in significant increases in risk due to the increased number of homeless and transient sex offenders.

Findings highly similar to Chawjewski and Mercado's were reported by Zandbergen and Hart (2006) (summarized by Levenson, 2009, p. 279):

> In Orange County, Florida (the greater Orlando region), researchers found that 95% of over 137,000 residential properties were located within 1,000 feet of schools, parks, day care centers, or school bus stops, and over 99% of housing fell within 2,500 feet of these locations. Restrictions of 1,000 feet resulted in only 4,233 potentially available dwellings; and 2,500-foot buffer zones eliminated all but 37 properties in the entire county. School bus stops were found by far to be the most problematic restrictions (99.6% of properties were within 2,500 feet of a bus stop).

Levenson (2009, p. 271) has described a possible knock-on effect of these restrictions:

> City and county councils appear to fear that if they do not enact laws similar to those of their neighbors, their towns will become a dumping ground for sex offenders. This tends to produce a domino effect as surrounding towns and counties create protected zones in an effort to keep exiled offenders from migrating to their communities.

In a recent review of residence restriction research (Levenson, 2016, pp. 223–242), the author concludes that:

> (T)he research literature provides no support for the assumption that sexual reoffending can be prevented by prohibiting sex offenders from residing near places where children commonly congregate. For the minority of sex offenders who display predatory patterns of seeking out minors in public settings, laws or case management strategies that forbid such offenders to visit such locations might be more effective than laws designating where they can live. Sex offenders do not abuse children because they live near schools, but rather they take advantage of opportunities to cultivate trusting relationships with children and their families to create opportunities for sexual abuse to take place.

Other Restrictions on Social Behavior

While residence restrictions may prove to be the most oppressively burdensome attempt to control offender's social behavior, there are many other, smaller indignities that militate against successful reentry and reintegration. Laws (2009) has referred to these as "a potpourri of creative additions to the sex offender laws." Following are a sample of these:

• 2006, California. Jessica's Law imposes indeterminate sentences on sexually violent predators (SVPs). The main facility housing SVPs is nicknamed "Hotel California," where you can check out any time you like but you can never leave.
• 2006, Georgia. No exemption from residency restrictions for sex offenders living in nursing homes or hospice care facilities.
• 2006, Iowa. Residency restrictions cause sex offenders to change addresses without notification of a new location, register false addresses, or simply disappear.
• 2006, Iowa. Physically and mentally disabled sex offenders are prohibited from living with family members who see to their needs.
• 2007, New Jersey. Sex offenders placed on curfew on Halloween were made to post a sign on their front door: "No Candy at This Residence." (A Washington state attorney reviewed 13 years of sex offenses in a single county. Six offenses of 5560 (0.001%) occurred on Halloween).
• 2008. Change to the *Higher Education Opportunity Act*. Civilly committed sex offenders are no longer eligible for Pell Grants (federal financial aid for education of low-income people).
• 2008, Iowa. Des Moines public schools admit juvenile sex offenders but refuse to provide details on location or nature of the offenses. Parents in the school districts are outraged.
• 2008, Florida. A person designated as a sexual predator may not possess a prescription drug for erectile dysfunction.
• 2008, Iowa. An unmarried parent may not live with a sex offender.
• 2008, Florida. A court may sentence a sex offender to be treated with Depo-Provera (medroxyprogesterone acetate) if convicted of sexual battery or, with voluntary consent, physical castration.

- 2008, Nebraska. Communities tried to develop restrictions that would essentially ban sex offenders from the community. The state stepped in, imposed a 500-foot restriction on the usual locations.
- 2008, Florida. During a hurricane, sex offenders must go to a "designated shelter." Going to other shelters would violate supervision requirements.
- 2008, Florida. CNN reports that sex offenders are living under the Julia Tuttle Causeway in Miami. Probation officer's reponse: "At least we know where they are."

Laws (2009) cited a position paper from the California Coalition on Sexual Offending (2008) regarding residency restrictions.

- The assumptions of residency restrictions are:
  - Strangers pose the major threat of sexual assault.
  - Most new crimes are committed by previously identified sex offenders.
  - Where an offender lives (sleeps at night) has a direct relationship to any new crime he may commit.
- The facts are:
  - In about 20% (or fewer) sex crimes the offender is a stranger.
  - Nearly 90% of new sex crimes are committed by persons with no prior history.
  - 75% or more of registered sex offenders do not commit another sex crime.
  - Available research shows no relationship between where a registered sex offender lives and the pattern of any new sex crime that he commits.
- The Coalition concluded:
  - Residential restriction policies appear to result in a significant increase in the number of homeless and transient sex offenders, thereby increasing risk.
  - Existing laws, policies, and ordinances should be revised or repealed.

Additional challenges to these laws are treated in depth by Huebner et al. (2014); Mustaine (2014); and Socia (2014).

The Containment Model: Is This the Answer for Social Control?

The preceding account of the multitude of restrictions placed upon sex offender behavior in the community reveals the goals of the containment era. They appear to be an effort to place so many restrictions on the social behavior of cooperating offenders that there is little that they can do that will not be under some form of surveillance. The *containment model* refers not only to close criminal justice supervision (probation) but also to sex offender treatment.

English (2009, p. 429) offers a definition of the model:

> The containment approach operates in the context of multiagency — collaboration, explicit policies, and consistent practices that combine case evaluation and risk assessment, sex offender treatment, and intense community surveillance – all designed specifically to maximize public safety.

This approach emphasizes victim protection and public safety as the primary goals of sex offender management. Ideally, multiagency collaboration should include sex offender treatment programs, law enforcement, probation and parole, schools, rape crisis centers, hospitals, prisons, polygraph examiners, victim advocacy organizations, attorneys, emergency room staff, universities, and victim assistance centers (English, 2009, pp. 431–432). This is a very tall order indeed. Those of us who have worked for decades in public service only know too well how difficult it is to cooperatively engage such an array of service organizations in pursuit of a single goal, the containment of a single offender.

The effort is typically focused on what is called the *containment team,* more commonly known as a case management team. The CCOSO (2001, p. 2) describes the function of the team. The team is led by probation or parole officers and is made up of (a) a specially trained supervising officer, (b) a specially trained sex offender treatment provider, and (c) a specially trained polygraph examiner. Additional input may be provided by one or more organizations specified in the preceding paragraph.

Supervision Plans

A full social and criminal history on the offender is required to develop an appropriate supervision plan. Containment-focused case management will be most effective if supervising officers have small caseloads. Twenty-five or less would be the standard. Offenders are pay supervision fees.

Offenders under community supervision are initially presented with a list of probation or parole conditions. This is mainly a list of "thou shall nots," which can be expanded or reduced as supervision develops. Following is a sample list (English, Pullen, & Jones, 1997, pp. 5–6):

- Your employment must be approved by the probation/parole agency.
- You shall participate in treatment with a therapist approved by the probation/parole department.
- You shall participate in periodic polygraph examinations.
- You shall not have contact with children under age 18.
- You shall not frequent places where children congregate.
- You shall not drive a motor vehicle alone without prior permission of your supervising officer.
- You shall maintain a driving log (mileage; time of departure, arrival, return; routes traveled and with whom, etc.).
- You shall not possess any pornographic, sexually oriented, or sexually stimulating visual, auditory, telephonic, or electronic media and computer programs or services that are relevant to your deviant behavior pattern.
- You shall reside at a place approved by the supervising officer, including supervised living quarters.
- You shall abide by a curfew imposed by the supervising officer and comply with electronic monitoring, if so ordered.

- You shall not have contact, directly or through third parties, with your victims.
- You shall abstain from alcoholic beverages and participate in periodic drug testing.
- You shall not have a post office box number without the approval of your supervising officer.
- You shall not use fictitious names.

How is it determined that the offender is in compliance with these rules? The polygraph examination would be one way to do so. Supervising officers can intrude upon offenders' lives in many ways. These include searching residences and vehicles, directly monitoring their activities, making arrests, attending therapy groups, and discussing high-risk issues with their supervisees and continuously assessing their mental status.

Sex Offender-Specific Treatment

The specialized treatment provided should conform to the *Practice Guidelines* recommended by the Association for the Treatment of Sexual Abusers (ATSA, 2014). This would be some form of cognitive–behavioral intervention plus actuarial assessment. Offenders are required to pay for their treatment. The Colorado Sex Offender Management Board (COSOMB, 2014) recommends four group treatment sessions per month or three group sessions and one individual session.

Polygraph Examinations

Pre-conviction polygraph data may be available. The containment model in the community focuses on post-conviction examinations. In order to be most effective, the examiner must be experienced with the patterns of sex offender denial and minimization. Offenders should pay for the polygraph examinations. COSOMB (2014) recommends a polygraph examination every 6 months.

Cost of the Containment Model

The 2014 *Annual Report. Lifetime Supervision of Sex Offenders* stated that most sex offenders in the community in Colorado received intensive supervision. The annual cost per individual in 2014 was $3854; the daily cost was $10.56. The cost of service provision is further illuminated if we examine typical costs in just one judicial district:

Sex-offense-specific group treatment session =	$58.00
Individual or other treatment session =	$75.00
Sex offender evaluation (PPG, viewing time) =	$1000.00
Polygraph examination =	$255.00

PPG = penile plethysmography, the direct measurement of the erection response in males.

Effectiveness of the Containment Model

Colorado was the birthplace of the containment approach, so it will be useful to examine a portion of their data on recidivism following termination of supervision. Recidivism was defined as the occurrence of new court filings within 1 year and within 3 years of termination of supervision. The sample consisted of 689 sex offenders (probation $n = 356$; parole $n = 333$) who were discharged or completed a parole or probation sentence between July 1, 2005, and June 30, 2007. The following are the results:

At 1 year:	
No recidivism	86.9%
New sexual crime	0.7%
New violent, nonsexual crime	5.5%
New nonviolent, nonsexual crime	6.8%
At 3 years:	
No recidivism	72.0%
New sexual crime	2.6%
New violent, nonsexual crime	10.7%
New nonviolent, nonsexual crime	14.7%

Sex offender recidivism rates in Colorado were consistent with national trends. The data also confirm that, if they recidivate, sex offenders are more likely to commit nonsexual than sexual crimes (retrieved from: https://cdpsdocs.state.co.us/somb/RRP/REPORTS2014_Lifetime_ Supervision_Report_Final1.pdf).

Is This a Viable Model?

The data from Colorado would say, yes. There are a number of qualifying issues here. The data suggest that containment is not ruinously expensive if offenders are paying most of the fees. It is important to remember that criminal offenders are not even modestly self-sustaining and many are extremely poor if not indigent. Who pays the fees in these cases?

Geography is a very important issue. Offenders situated in cities and suburbs of large metropolitan areas such as Denver are likely to find a wide variety of services available and the three-part model could be implemented. However, the picture is quite different in rural or even remotely situated exurban areas. Probation and parole services could be maintained there, but exotic services such as sex-offender-specific treatment or polygraph examinations would likely not be available. So, in my judgment, an educated, motivated, compliant, and relatively affluent sex offender living in an urban or suburban area will be most likely to benefit from the containment model. Those conditions severely limit the viability of this approach. "Containment" is an apt word in this case. The worst possible outcome, it seems to me, is that the tightly woven fabric of the containment model, coupled with all the prohibitions and restrictions considered in this chapter, could produce what Travis (2005) has called "civil death."

References

Association for the Treatment of Sexual Abusers (ATSA). (2014). *Practice guidelines for the assessment, treatment, and management of male adult sexual abusers.* Beaverton, OR: Association for the Treatment of Sexual Abusers.

California Coalition on Sexual Offending (CCSO). (2001). *Effective management of sex offenders residing in open communities.* North Highlands, CA: California Coalition on Sexual Offending.

Chajewski, M., & Mercado, C. C. (2009). An evaluation of sex offender residency restrictions functioning in town, country, and city-wide jurisdictions. *Criminal Justice Policy Review, 20*, 44–61.

Colorado Sex Offender Management Board. (2014). *Lifetime supervision of sex offenders. Annual report.* Retrieved from htt;://cdpsdocs.state.co.us/somb/RRP/REPORTS/2014_Lifetime_Supervision_Report_Final1.pdf

Craun, S. W., & Theriot, M. T. (2009). Misperceptions of sex offender perpetration: Considering the impact of sex offender registration. *Journal of Interpersonal Violence, 24*, 2057–2072.

Delson, N., Kokish, R., & Abbott, B. (2008). *Position paper on sex offender residency restrictions.* North Highlands, CA: California Coalition on Sex Offending.

Duwe, G., Donnay, W., & Tewksbury, R. (2008). Does residential proximity matter? A geographic analysis of sex offense recidivism. *Criminal Justice and Behavior, 35*, 484–504.

English, K. (2009). The containment approach to managing sex offenders. In R. G. Wright (Ed.), *Sex offender laws: Failed policies, new directions* (pp. 427–448). New York: Springer.

English, K., Pullen, S., & Jones, L. (1997). *Managing adult sex offenders in the community: A containment approach.* Washington, DC: National Institute of Justice, Office of Justice Programs, U.S. Department of Justice.

Heubner, R. M., Kras, K. R., Rydberg, J., Bynum, T. S., Grommon, E., & Pleggenkuhle, B. (2014). The effect and implications of sex offender residence restrictions: Evidence from a two-state evaluation. *Criminology & Public Policy, 13*, 139–168.

Laws, D. R. (2009, April). *The recovery of the asylum: Observations on the mismanagement of sex offenders.* Keynote presentation at the Tools to Take Home conference, Lucy Faithfull Foundation, Birmingham, UK.

Laws, D. R., & Ward, T. (2011). *Desistance from sex offending.* New York: Guilford.

Levenson, J. S. (2009). Sex offender residence restrictions. In R. G. Wright (Ed.), *Sex offender laws: Failed policies, new directions* (pp. 267–290). New York: Springer.

Lucken, K., & Ponte, L. M. (2008). A just measure of forgiveness: Reforming occupational licensing regulations for ex-offenders using BJOQ analysis. *Law and Policy, 30*, 46–72.

Meloy, M. L., Miller, S. L., & Curtis, K. M. (2008). Making sense out of nonsense: The deconstruction of state-level sex offender residency restrictions. *American Journal of Criminal Justice, 3*, 209–222.

Mustaine, E. E. (2014). Sex offender residency restrictions: Successful integration or exclusion? *Criminology & Public Policy, 13,* 169–177.

Petersilia, J. (2003). *When prisoners come home: Parole and prisoner reentry.* New York: Oxford University Press.

Socia, K. M. (2014). Residence restrictions are ineffective, inefficient, and inadequate: So now what? *Criminology & Public Policy, 13,* 179–188.

The Sentencing Project. (2014). *Annual report.* Washington, DC: The Sentencing Project.

Travis, J. (2005). *But they all come back: Facing the challenges of prisoner reentry.* Washington, DC: Urban Institute Press.

Zandbergen, D., & Hart, T. C. (2006). Reducing housing options for convicted sex offenders: Investigating the impact of residency restriction laws using GIS. *Justice Research and Policy, 8,* 1–24.

10

The International Picture of Social Control

The book thus far has examined various means of social control to manage sex offenders in communities of the USA. The trajectory extends from colonial times but the main focus has been on the past 100 years. It is clear from the materials presented that social control of this population has been variable and never entirely successful. In fact, it has been harsh, unforgiving, often misdirected, and punitive to the extent that outcomes have proven to be the opposite of what was intended. It is reasonable to suppose that not all countries in the world have found it necessary to model their practices on those of the USA. Therefore, I decided to make contact with colleagues around the world and present them with three questions regarding restrictions on sex offenders in the community. These were:

1. Most jurisdictions in the USA require sex offenders to register with the police in their community. This information is then entered into a state and federal sex offender registry.
2. The information in the registry may then be made available to the community through an Internet website or by publication in newspapers or handouts to the public. The ostensible purpose of this is to alert

© The Editor(s) (if applicable) and The Author(s) 2016
D.R. Laws, *Social Control of Sex Offenders*,
DOI 10.1057/978-1-137-39126-1_10

the public that convicted sex offenders are residing in their communities so that they may protect themselves and their children.

3. Most jurisdictions also enforce stringent regulations regarding where sex offenders may live. For example, not less than 1000–2500 feet from a school, playground, swimming pool, school bus stop, etc.

Do any of these, or similar regulations, exist in your country? Please tell me what regulations govern the behavior of sex offenders there.

I did not ask potential respondents to criticize the laws of their country or attempt to contrast them with those of the USA.

I sent these questions to 20 colleagues known by me to be involved in public work with sex offenders. I received 17 replies. In what follows those replies are reduced to brief summaries without editorial comment by me.

Canada (Lawrence Ellerby, Forensic Psychological Services, Winnipeg, Manitoba)

Registration

- Canada has a National Sex Offender Registry for persons convicted of sex offenses and they are ordered to report annually to police.
- The database is accessible to Canadian police agencies through a provincial/territorial registration center.
- The public does not have access to the Registry.

Notification

- In the respondent's province, persons subject to community notification are identified on a provincial website.
- Photographs, history of offending, conditions of release, and participation in treatment are included.

- Users of the website agree:
  - Not to harass or engage in unreasonable conduct against anyone identified on the website.
  - Information will be used solely to protect the user and his or her family.

Residence Restrictions

- The court can impose conditions as part of a probation order specifying where an offender may reside.
- Residence must not be in proximity to a school, playground, or park.
- The order may stipulate as well that the offender may not attend such locations.

England (Mark Blandford, College of Policing, UK)

Registration

- The *Sex Offenders Act 1997* introduced a registry where offenders were required to notify the police of their name, address, and any change of name or address.
  - Criminal sanctions were provided for failing to comply.
- Details are provided on a national database.
- The database is restricted and confidential and is not available to the general public.
- All registered offenders receive a "visit" from the police to ensure compliance and to evaluate current risk concerns.

Notification

- In 2000, there was a public campaign for disclosure of the presence of sex offenders in the community.

- In 2003, the notification requirements were expanded.

  - This action created a requirement for publication of statistics nationally and locally about management of sex offenders
  - These statistics did not provide specific offender details that would identify them.

- In 2007, a new law aimed to provide parents, guardians, and caregivers with information that would enable them to safeguard child safety and welfare.

  - An application must be made to police about a person who has some form of contact with a child where such person is identified as having convictions for sex offenses against children.
  - The presumption is that a disclosure regarding the risk posed will be made available to the applicant.

Residence Restrictions

- The respondent did not provide specific information on residence restrictions.
- The *Sexual Offences Prevention Order* centered on restricting or prohibiting contact with children, discouraging communication with them, and imposing restrictions on locations where children could frequent or be found such as schools or parks.

Northern Ireland (Anne-Marie McAlinden, Queen's University Belfast)

Registration

- Uses the same registration requirement as England.
- Information is held locally within each police district but is searchable via the same registry as used in England.
- In Northern Ireland, all decisions about risk assessment and management are undertaken on a multiagency basis (police, probation, social services, and prisons).

Notification

- "Public disclosure" is the label applied to community notification.
- Community notification and disclosure is based on risk and need to know.
- Thus far, Northern Ireland has not adopted a Megan's Law-type notification scheme such as seen in England, Wales, and Scotland.
- There is a stringent framework for preemployment vetting which places duties and potential liabilities on both employers and sex offenders.

Residence Restrictions

- There are no residence restrictions within the UK.
- Restrictions on their behavior may be imposed such as not attending parks, playgrounds, or other locations where children might congregate.

Republic of Ireland (Caoilte Ó Ciardha, University of Kent, UK)

Registration

- Although the term *Sex Offender Register* is used in Ireland, there is not a register as such.
- Instead, there are certificates held centrally which indicate who is legally subject to the requirements of the *Sex Offenders Act 2001*.
  - These are individuals who have been convicted of the offenses specified in the act or who have been convicted abroad for an equivalent offense(s).
- Individuals subject to the requirements of the *Act* are required to notify the police of the address, changes of names and addresses, and when traveling abroad for more than 7 days.

Community Notification

- There is no provision for information about people subject to the *Act* to be released to the public.

- It is not possible to make requests of information about sex offenders living in certain areas.
- Individuals may request information about themselves.

Residence Restrictions

- A criminal law bill in preparation is intended to improve elements of existing legislation. It does not include restrictions on housing.
- Post-release supervision is conducted by the Probation Service.
  - Particular conditions may be imposed, including mandatory treatment and prohibitions from attending certain locations such as schools.

Germany (Martin Rettenberger, University of Mainz)

Registration

- Registration with the police is not a national law but is part of the police organizations of the federal states.
- The registration is intended to improve risk management and to reduce recidivism risk.
- Registration is usually limited to cases regarded as high risk.

Community Notification

- Registry information is not available to the public.

Residence Restrictions

- There is no general law applicable to all offenders.
- Such regulations would be enforced individually in terms of release, probation, or parole conditions.

- If a court determines that the recidivism risk is high, the offender could be required to live in a certain area.

The Netherlands (Jules Mulder, de Waag, Utrecht)

Registration

- There is no registration law.

Community Notification

- When a sex offender is released from prison, the mayor of the community where he intends to live is informed.
- The risk that the individual poses to the community is evaluated.
- The mayor can inform the community, organize meetings, or persuade the offender to live somewhere else.

Residence Restrictions

- If the offender fails to comply with the mayor's orders, the issue will be taken to court to force the person to live elsewhere.
- Orders of probation may include restraining orders for certain neighborhoods or streets as well as prohibition of contact with designated persons (victims, families).

Switzerland (Andreas Mokros, University Hospital of Psychiatry, Zurich)

Registration

- There is a sex offender registry. However, there is no requirement for sex offenders to register with the police.
- Offenders have access to information about themselves.

Community Notification

- Rap sheets from the registry may be made available to potential employers to determine whether an applicant is an offender who is banned from specific activities.
- There is no publically available registry or website accessible by the public.
- There has been no harassment of offenders by print media ("naming and shaming").

Residence Restrictions

- Restrictions on residence may be imposed by restraining orders.

Norway (Leni Helle Rivedal, Haukeland University Hospital, Bergen)

Registration

- The police maintain a DNA registry of convicted criminals.
- Registry data are not available to the public.

Community Notification

- The data in the registry are used solely for police purposes.
- The public rarely or never know that any given individual is a convicted sex offender.
- For some employment, registered sex offenders are required to present a "criminal record certificate." This could result in exclusion from jobs where children are present.

Residence Restrictions

- When an offender has completed a sentence, there are no restrictions on where he can live or stay in the community.

Sweden (Niklas Långström, Karolinska Institutet, Stockholm)

Registration

* Registration with the police is not required although a registry exists.

Community Notification

* Registry information is not available to the public.
* The *Conviction Register Act* (*1998*) allows a potential employer to demand that applicants provide conviction register records if applying for jobs requiring direct contact with children.

Residence Restrictions

* No information was provided by this respondent.

Finland (Aini Laine, Abo Akademi University, Turku)

Registration

* There is no sex offender registry.

Community Notification

* Community announcements are not made.

Residence Restrictions

* Choice of residence is not restricted.

Czech Republic (Petr Weiss, Charles University, Prague)

Registration

- There is no sex offender registry. Social control of sex offenders is restricted to medical means with an in- or outpatient treatment order by a court on the recommendation of forensic experts.

Community Notification

- Community notification does not exist.

Residence Restrictions

- Choice of residence is not restricted.

Israel (David Cohen, Division of Forensic Psychiatry, Magen Prison, Ramlah)

Registration

- There is a closed sex offender registry administered by the community supervision division of the Israel Prison Service.
- The registry contains information on all sex offenders against whom a community supervision order has been issued.

Community Notification

- The Israeli legislature has taken the position that the public is better served by a closed registry rather than an open one.
- Registry data are available to a restricted group of people—the community supervision officer, the police, risk assessors, and the officer who writes the community treatment plan.

- Divulging information from the registry to unauthorized individuals is a criminal offense.

Residence Restrictions

- There are no restrictions governing where an offender can or cannot live.
- However, restrictions related to an offender's risk situation may be imposed.
  - An offender may be prohibited from approaching or entering a park, playground, or schoolyard but would not be prohibited from living near one.
  - Residence restrictions may be imposed at the request of an offender's victim.

Australia (Andrew Day, Deakin University, Melbourne)

Registration

- There is a sex offender registry. In each state and territory, the police administration is responsible for the maintenance of the register.
- Each state and territory requires the offender to provide similar information, although the period of registration differs, along with some variations in the scope of the offenses.

Community Notification

- By 2012, Western Australia was the only state to have enacted a law to allow community notification.
- There are three forms of disclosure:
  - Information and photographs of dangerous offenders are provided on the Internet.
  - Information is available about the suburbs or surrounding areas where dangerous offenders live.
  - Enquiries from parents or guardians about adults having unsupervised contact with their children are responded to by the police.

Residence Restrictions

- Restrictions on where a sex offender may live would be part of a community corrections order.
- It would be relatively ordinary for an offender to have a condition that he may not reside where children congregate.

New Zealand (Gwenda M. Willis, University of Auckland)

Registration

- A closed register is under development in New Zealand.
- Registry data are available only to designated persons (police).

Community Notification

- Registry data will not be accessible to the public.

Residence Restrictions

- There are no formally enacted residence restrictions.
- There is a problem in that release from detention often requires approved housing.
  - Part of the approval process involves looking at the distance between the residence and the areas where children congregate.

Singapore (Chi Meng Chu, National University of Singapore)

Registration

- There is no sex offender registry.

Community Notification

- There is no publication of information on sex offenders placed on community supervision.

Residence Restrictions

- There are no specific regulations that restrict or govern how and where sex offenders may live.
- Courts may impose specific conditions pertaining to the contact or exposure that offenders may have with disadvantaged persons.

Hong Kong (Judy Hui, Correctional Services Department)

The respondent informed me that although Hong Kong is a "Special Administrative Region" of the People's Republic of China, Hong Kong Law and the criminal code are very different from those on the mainland. Since Hong Kong was a British colony until 1997, the local law retains some residual influence of British law.

What follows are extracts from two documents provided by the respondent: a report from the *Law Reform Commission of Hong Kong* related to sexual offense record checks and an official statement from the *Post-Release Supervision Board* regarding management of sex offenders in the community.

Registration

- There is no registry of sex offenders.
- Police maintain records of persons convicted of sex offenses.
- The records are kept to assist police in prevention, detection, and investigation of crime.
- Police do not provide information to employers regarding whether existing or prospective employees have a criminal record.

Community Notification

- The records kept on sex offenders are not open for public inspection because it would stifle rehabilitation and reintegration.
- A public record could identify victims, affect the offender's family, cause vigilantism, and drive offenders underground.

Residence Restrictions

- The *Post-Release Supervision Board* takes considerable care to be involved in managing the offender's return to the community.
- A supervisee has to comply with the conditions stated in the supervision order:
  - Reside at an address approved by the supervising officer.
  - Undertake only employment as approved.
  - Other conditions (e.g., follow-up treatment) may be imposed as necessary.

Conclusion

In order to obtain a picture of what is going on in the world in terms of social control of sex offenders, I contacted a number of colleagues known to me and asked three questions. These were: (1) Is there a sex offender registry in your country? (2) Is the information in the registry accessible by the public? and (3) Does your country have restrictions regarding where sex offenders may reside? I asked the respondents not to criticize their country's practices and not to compare them with those of the USA. I requested brief responses, perhaps a paragraph or two for each question. I received 17 replies. These varied considerably in length and depth. I decided to reduce their often wordy comments to brief bullet points under the three topical headings.

It is obvious that this is a limited series of snapshots that do not represent the full picture of the situation in any one country. It is also limited by my acquaintance with colleagues in various countries. My contacts are primarily in North America, Western Europe, Scandinavia, and Australasia. There is only one in the Middle East, one in Eastern Europe, and two in Asia. I have no contacts in Central and South America or in Africa.

It is difficult to attempt a summary of this wide-ranging information. It appears to me that practices in the major English-speaking countries, the USA, Canada, the UK, Northern Ireland, Republic of Ireland, Australia, and New Zealand, are, not surprisingly, most similar. The states most similar to these would be Israel and Hong Kong, both of which bear a history of British rule. Germany and the Netherlands have solid but not overly restrictive practices. The Czech Republic appears to stand alone, clinging to old practices with sex offenders, uninfluenced by the social control features of other countries. Although close to the major European countries, Scandinavia appears to have the most relaxed approaches. The greatest surprise to me was the rather relaxed practices in Singapore, a state well known for its harsh treatment of some minor offenses.

While a definitive summary of these responses is not possible here, I think that we can draw two conclusions from them. First, the countries reporting all recognize the need for some variety of social control of sex offenders. Second, none of them employs the more harsh practices of the USA.

11

Psychological Treatment: Risk Reducer or Life Enhancer?

Orders of probation and parole for sex offenders may include a specification that the offender is required to seek, participate in, and complete a course of treatment directed toward his/her sexual deviation. Supervising officers may or may not be aware of treatments available to sex offenders in the community. The general psychological treatment literature is not helpful in this regard. The Society of Clinical Psychology, Division 12 of the American Psychological Association, provides a lengthy list of psychological interventions, including a description, citations of research support, and a bibliography. These are classified by the name of the treatment (e.g., "Cognitive and Behavioral Therapies for Generalized Anxiety Disorder") or by the disorder itself. There is nothing in either of these lists pertaining to sexual disorders in general or sexual deviation in particular (retrieved May 22, 2015, from www.div12.org/Psychological Treatments/treatments.html).

A more definitive source is the report entitled *Current Practices and Emerging Trends in Sexual Abuser Management: The Safer Society 2009 North American Survey* (McGrath, Cumming, Burchard, Zeoli, and Ellerby, 2010). The Safer Society Foundation has been publishing these surveys periodically since 1986. They are relied upon as the major sourcebook for treatment referrals.

© The Editor(s) (if applicable) and The Author(s) 2016
D.R. Laws, *Social Control of Sex Offenders*,
DOI 10.1057/978-1-137-39126-1_11

There is no single treatment intervention that is considered the gold standard. Rather, a large array of possible interventions are mixed and matched to form a coordinated approach. Many theories underlie sex offender treatment. McGrath et al. (2010, pp. 37–39) provide a list of 13 models that are influential in treatment interventions. These are listed alphabetically, not in terms of their supposed importance:

- *Biomedical.* This is the standard medical model of disease. Medications such as antiandrogens and selective serotonin reuptake inhibitors (SSRIs) form a major part of treatment.
- *Cognitive–behavioral.* There are two emphases here. The cognitive element stresses changes in thinking to alter disordered behavior. Behavior therapy is founded on the premise that behavior is learned and can be altered by conditioning methods. The cognitive element is predominant in this approach.
- *Family systems.* The family constellation is seen as a major factor that contributes to and maintains deviant behavior. The goal of the treatment is to change disordered relationship patterns.
- *Good Lives Model (GLM).* This model stresses gaining what are called "primary goods" (respect, love, relationships) in socially acceptable ways rather than through offending. The goal is a good life that is inconsistent with offending. Traditional risk management and avoidance strategies are deemphasized.
- *Harm reduction.* This is more a way of looking at treatment goals rather than a type of treatment. Preventing reoffending is an ideal goal, but any reduction in the magnitude of reoffense is desirable. This is an import from drug addiction treatment.
- *Multisystemic.* Multiple treatment interventions are provided to the client in his/her natural environment. These services would be provided in the home, neighborhood, school, or community.
- *Psychodynamic.* This model is heavily influenced by classical psychoanalytic theory. The goal would be to understand the unconscious forces that shape sexual and other behaviors.
- *Psycho–Social–Educational.* Education is the major method to assist sex offenders to change their behavior. This is usually done in groups with a high level of interaction.

- *Risk–Need–Responsivity (RNR)*. This model focuses services on high- and moderate-risk offenders. The targets for change are those directly linked to reoffending (criminogenic needs).
- *Relapse prevention (RP)*. This is a multimodal, cognitive–behavioral approach. The emphasis is on helping offenders to learn self-management skills to avoid offending in high-risk situations. It is more often used as a framework under which a variety of interventions are organized.
- *Self-regulation*. This model was developed in direct competition with RP. It outlines four pathways to offending and provides interventions appropriate to each.
- *Sexual addiction*. This approach views sex offenders who are seemingly unable to stop offending as similar to drug addicts. The main focus of treatment typically includes the 12-step program and incorporates many of the features from the drug addiction approach.
- *Sexual trauma*. This model argues that being sexually abused as a child may be a major factor in explaining why a person sexually offends as an adult.

Only a handful of these approaches would be considered as standalone treatments. Elements of each can be incorporated to form a credible treatment program as distinguished from a single intervention.

In 2008 McGrath et al. (2010, pp. vii–xii) identified 1379 treatment programs in the USA. This included all 50 states and the District of Columbia. In the USA, in 2009, 53,811 individuals received treatment. Eighty-eight percent of the reporting programs identified group treatment as the most common approach. The median treatment dosage reported was 348 hours over an 18-month period (19 hours/month; 4.8 hours/week).

How many sex offenders are actually engaged in treatment? Laws and Ward (2011, p. 151) described the candidate population:

The Bureau of Justice Statistics (BJS) (2009) reported that, in 2007, there were 826,097 sex offenders on parole and 4,293,163 on probation. In 1994 the BJS reported that 234,000 sex offenders were under the "care, custody or control of correctional agencies in the United States" (Bureau of

Justice Statistics, 1996). Of these, 60% (140,400) were under conditional supervision in the community.

At this writing, nearly 20 years later, we can see from the 2009 BJS report that there are hundreds of thousands of sex offenders in the community. Only a fraction of these could possibly be receiving treatment.

If we view treatment as desirable, we should construct a model that embodies all of the necessary elements. Laws and Ward (2011, pp. 99–100) provided a brief description of current best practice interventions:

> While there are some minor variations in the specifics of treatment programs across the world, any credible program will typically have the following structure, orientation, and elements. Following a comprehensive assessment period where static and dynamic risk factors are assessed and overall level of risk determined, offenders are allocated into a treatment stream. The default etiological assumption appears to be that sexual offenders is a product of faulty social learning and individuals commit sexual offenses because they have a number of skill deficits that make it difficult for them to seek reinforcement in socially acceptable ways. Thus the primary mechanisms underpinning sexual offending are thought to be social and psychological.... Furthermore, treatment is typically based around an analysis of individuals' offending patterns and takes a cognitive-behavioral/relapse prevention perspective. The major goal is to teach sex offenders the skills to change the way they think, feel, and act and to use this knowledge to avoid or escape from future high-risk situations. There are usually discrete treatment modules devoted to the following problem areas: cognitive distortions, deviant sexual interests, social skill deficits, impaired problem solving, empathy deficits, intimacy deficits, emotional regulation difficulties, lifestyle imbalance, and postoffense adjustment or relapse prevention....(T)he length of treatment programs vary but for a medium-risk or higher offender will likely be at least 9 months in duration and frequently quite a bit longer.

A treatment program that follows the model described is likely to produce acceptable results with moderately motivated offenders who actively participate in the program modules. Numerous meta-analyses attest to treatment success, producing modest rates of recidivism (see, e.g., Lösel & Schmucker, 2005; Hanson, Bourgon, Helmus, & Hodgson, 2009).

In their 2008 survey, McGrath et al. (2010. P. viii) found that the three most favored treatment program models were:

1. *Cognitive–behavioral.* Eighty-six percent of programs reported using some variation of this model.
2. *Relapse prevention.* The original model of RP (Marlatt & Gordon, 1985; Laws, 1989) has been largely discredited as a treatment program (Laws, 2003). This selection undoubtedly refers to elements of RP that have survived (e.g., cognitive–behavioral chain).
3. *Good Lives Model.* One-third of US programs reported using GLM.

Two Competing Programs

To illustrate major trends in contemporary sex offender treatment, I have chosen to compare two approaches: the RNR model (Andrews & Bonta, 2010a, 2010b; Bonta & Andrews, 2007) and the GLM (Laws & Ward, 2011; Purvis, Ward & Willis, 2014; Ward & Maruna, 2007). The word "model" requires explanation. The RNR and GLM models are not formal treatment programs with specifically identifiable procedures. Rather, they are frameworks around which a variety of interventions are organized. Although the models view sex offending in strikingly different ways, many of the elements of treatment are common to both.

Risk–Need–Responsivity Model

The development of the RNR model was a reaction to the status of criminology and correctional psychology in the 1970s and 1980s. Criminology was concerned then, as well as now, with the study of crime in the aggregate rather than a primary focus on the individual criminal. Correctional psychology was influenced by the famous "nothing works" meta-analysis by Martinson (1974). The Martinson review considered 231 studies of institutional treatment programs which led to his conclusion that treatment was ineffective. This finding was further reinforced by Lipton, Martinson, and Wilks (1975). Another important publication was the review of sex offender recidivism by Furby, Weinrott, and Blackshaw (1989) which found no evidence to that date that treatment reduced recidivism. Findings such as these encouraged a shift away from rehabilitation programs and toward deterrence.

Despite these discouraging developments, Andrews and Bonta (2010b) noted that through the 1980s new meta-analyses (e.g., Lipsey, 1989) began to show that correctional treatment could have an effect, however modest, on recidivism. A second major development, say Andrews and Bonta (2010b), was the development of what they called a "psychology of criminal conduct." Andrews, Bonta, and Hoge (1990) produced the initial statement of this theory:

> Their psychology is a social learning perspective that assumes that criminal behavior is learned within a social context. Social support for the behavior and cognitions conducive to criminal behavior are central factors, as are criminal history and a constellation of antisocial personality factors [for example, impulsiveness, thrill-seeking, egocentrism]. Other factors of moderate relevance include family/marital functioning, substance abuse, and indicators of social achievement [e.g., education and employment] (Andrews & Bonta, 2010b, p. 44).

Three principles should form the basis of effective correctional programming. All treatment activities should be organized around these rules (Wilson & Yates, 2009, p. 158):

- The *risk* principle. Intervention must be matched to the level of risk posed by the offender. High- to moderate-risk offenders should receive the most intensive interventions. Low-risk offenders should be offered lower intensity programs or nothing at all.
- The *need* principle. Treatment should target those areas that have been empirically determined to be related to recidivism. These are dynamic risk factors and are termed *criminogenic needs*. Although there exists the tendency to offer insight-oriented psychotherapy to offenders, only treatment that specifically targets criminogenic need is likely to affect recidivism.
- The *responsivity* principle. Treatment providers should tailor their interventions to acknowledge individual characteristics and

idiosyncrasies. There are two parts to this principle. *General* responsivity requires the use of cognitive–behavioral social learning methods to influence behavior. *Specific* responsivity (the difficult part) should take into account learning style, personality, motivation, gender, and race of the offender.

Obviously, the goals of risk and need are the most specific and most easily met.

Identification of Specific Needs

Once the level of risk is determined by actuarial assessment (typically *Static-99*, *STABLE-2007*, and *ACUTE-2007* plus the *Level of Service Inventory—Revised* (*LSI-R*) (Andrews & Bonta, 1995), the focus of the RNR turns to the treatment of criminogenic needs. These are presented as the Big Four and the Central Eight.

The Central Eight criminogenic domains are (Andrews & Bonta, 2010b, p. 46):

- Criminal history—extremely relevant but a static risk factor.
- Procriminal attitudes—thoughts, values, and sentiments supportive of criminal behavior.
- Antisocial personality—low self-control, hostility, adventurous pleasure-seeking, disregard for others, and callousness.
- Procriminal associates

The preceding items are considered the Big Four, deserving primary attention.

- Social achievement—education, employment.
- Family/marital—marital instability, poor parenting skills, intrafamilial criminality.
- Substance abuse.
- Leisure/recreation—lack of prosocial pursuits.

The latter four are considered to be important criminogenic needs but perhaps require less attention than the Big Four.

Andrews and Bonta (2010b, p. 46) also list noncriminogenic needs. They do not consider these unimportant but, rather, note that they have not been empirically determined to be related to recidivism. They are:

- Self-esteem.
- Vague feelings of emotional discomfort—anxiety, feeling blue, feelings of alienation.
- Major mental disorder—schizophrenia, depression.
- Lack of ambition.
- History of victimization.
- Fear of official punishment.
- Lack of physical activity.

As we shall see, proponents of the GLM would not consider these to be major needs, but certainly worth attention in that framework.

Treatment of Criminogenic Needs

The psychology of criminal conduct states that criminal behavior is learned within a social context. Therefore, a social learning intervention (cognitive–behavioral therapy) would appear to be the intervention of choice. Bonta and Andrews (2007, pp. 4–5) suggest the following ways to target the major dynamic risk factors. There are seven criminogenic needs shown in the table. The eighth, criminal history, is a static risk factor.

Major risk/ need	Indicators	Interventions
Antisocial personality pattern	Impulsive, adventurous pleasure-seeking, restlessly aggressive, irritable	Build self-management skills, teach anger management
Procriminal attitudes	Rationalizations for crime, negative attitude toward the law	Counterrationalizations with prosocial attitudes; build up a prosocial identity

Major risk/ need	Indicators	Interventions
Social supports for crime	Criminal friends, isolation from prosocial others	Replace procriminal friends and associates with prosocial friends and associates
Substance abuse	Abuse of alcohol/drugs	Reduce substance abuse, enhance alternatives to substance abuse
Family/marital relationships	Inappropriate parental monitoring and disciplining, poor family relationships	Teach parenting skills, enhance warmth and caring
School/work	Poor performance, low level of satisfaction	Enhance work/study skills, nurture interpersonal relationships within the context of work and school
Prosocial recreational activities	Lack of involvement in prosocial recreational and leisure activities	Encourage participation in prosocial recreational activities, teach prosocial hobbies and sports

It is easy to see why I refer to RNR as a "framework." The preceding table is a reasonable summary of what the RNR model purports to do. It is also apparent that it is much easier to identify a problem than it is to alter it. As stated previously, the criminogenic needs identified in the RNR are dynamic risk factors that research has shown to be related to recidivism. The suggested interventions are just that, suggestions. For example, how does one "replace procriminal associates," or "reduce substance abuse," or "nurture interpersonal relationships" in a high-risk career criminal? Types of intervention will vary from one treatment program to another. Treatment program directors and case managers are free to choose whatever intervention they can demonstrate has a positive effect on reducing criminogenic need. Any treatment intervention with important goals such as those described in the preceding table would require very close monitoring. Andrews and Bonta (2010a, p. 318) acknowledge that the RNR approach must go well beyond the identification of risk and criminogenic need. They state that treatment must address the "role of personal strengths in building a prosocial orientation, the assessment of special responsivity factors to maximize the benefits of treatment, and the structured monitoring of the case from the beginning of supervision to the end." The *Level of Service/Case Management Inventory* (*LS/CMI*) would be a major feature for monitoring of treatment. The primary goal is the determination that whatever intervention is chosen adheres closely to the principles of RNR.

Is the RNR Effective?

Considerable support for the RNR has been found in a number of meta-analyses (Andrews & Bonta, 2010b, *passim*). Andrews, Zinger, Hoge, Bonta, Gendreau, and Cullen (1990) reviewed 80 studies and found a significant relationship between adherence to RNR principles and reduced recidivism. Adherence to all three principles proved most effective. Adherence to none showed an increase in recidivism. Punishment alone failed to reduce recidivism. Andrews and Bonta (2010a) compared the effects of treatment versus criminal justice sanctions alone in 374 tests. Not surprisingly, a treatment intervention was found to be superior. Mean effect size in favor of treatment increased to the extent that RNR principles were adhered to. Studies were rated on four levels: 0 = not a human service program or no adherence to RNR; 1 = adherence to one principle; 2 = adherence to two principles; and 3 = full adherence to RNR principles. There were two major findings. First, the greatest magnitude of effect was shown in studies where all three principles were adhered to. Second, in terms of setting where the treatment was delivered, the greatest effect was seen in the community.

Andrews and Bonta (2010b, p. 48) also note that RNR has been shown to be effective with youthful offenders (Dowden & Andrews, 1999a), female offenders (Dowden & Andrews, 1999b), minorities (Andrews, Dowden, & Rettinger, 2001), violent offenders (Dowden & Andrews, 2000), prison misconduct (French & Gendreau, 2006), and gang members (Di Placido, Simon, Witte, Gu, & Wong, 2006).

Almost all of the research of Andrews, Bonta, and their colleagues have focused on general criminal offenders of one type or another. For our purposes, it is essential to know the extent to which RNR applies to sex offenders. Hanson et al. (2009) have provided some confirmatory meta-analytic data. The purpose of the study was to compare the recidivism rates (sexual, violent, general) of a group of treated sex offenders with a comparison group of sex offenders (no treatment, alternate treatment, or less treatment). One hundred twenty-nine studies were initially identified. Using stringent inclusionary criteria, the authors found only a total of 23 studies available for analysis. The RNR principles were carefully observed. The risk principle was met when intensive services were provided to high-risk offenders. The need principle was met if the major treatment targets had been identified as significantly related to sexual or general recidivism. The (general) responsivity principle was met if the program provided cognitive–behavioral treatment or a treatment that made special efforts to involve the offender in treatment. The authors state that the interrater reliability rating of adherence to RNR principles was good (intraclass correlation = .80).

Results showed that the sexual and general recidivism rates for treated sex offenders were lower than those for the comparison groups (10.9% vs 19.22% for sexual recidivism; 31.8% vs 48.3% for any recidivism). Echoing earlier research by Andrews and Bonta (2010a et al., cited above), the authors stated that their results were consistent with adherence to the principles of RNR. When studies adhered to none of the principles, effects were low; for studies adhering to all three, the effects were large. Of the three, they stated, attention to need would produce the largest changes in interventions currently offered to sex offenders. They concluded: "We believe that the research evidence supporting the RNR principles is sufficient so that they should be a primary consideration in the design and implementation of intervention programs for sexual offenders" (p. 886).

The preceding citations represent only a superficial look at the research on various aspects of the RNR principles. This program framework has emerged from a body of research dating back to the 1980s. Readers interested in finer details should consult Andrews, D. A., & Bonta, J. (2010a). *The psychology of criminal conduct* (5th ed.). New Providence, NJ: LexisNexis.

The Good Lives Model

The rehabilitation of offenders should be driven by an enhancement model, not a harm avoidance one. This does not entail ignoring the needs of the community for security and safety; it simply reminds us that all human lives should reflect the best possible outcomes rather (than) the least worst possibilities. Ward and Stewart (2003).

The above statement succinctly summarizes what the GLM is all about. It appears to be an initial statement of a holistic rehabilitation theory and has been so construed by many. It is widely believed that GLM was developed in reaction to RNR and was seen as a possible replacement for it. That is true of the latter stages of its development. The history of research that ultimately led to the development of the GLM is a bit more complex.

The GLM was developed from a lengthy program of research dating, like RNR, from the early 1990s. At that time the original model of RP advanced by Laws (1989) and Pithers (1990, 1991) was falling into disfavor. The single pathway to possible relapse in a motivated, treated offender could not accommodate some obvious alternatives (e.g., unmotivated persons or those with entrenched, pro-offending attitudes). As a result of this conclusion, a program of research was initiated by Ward and his colleagues. Laws (2003, in press) has described the progress of this research. Initially, Ward, Louden, Hudson, and Marshall (1995), using qualitative research methods, identified nine different steps in the offense chain for child molesters and found three pathways to relapse. Subsequent research (Ward & Hudson, 1998) completely revised the cognitive–behavioral model proposed in the original RP model and followed up the 1995 version. Ward and Hudson termed this the *self-regulation model of sexual offending.* Self-regulation, they said, could be used to achieve desired goals as well as avoid risk of relapse. For sex offenders, the emphasis would be on poor self-regulation and they reconceptualized the relapse process in those terms. They retained the nine steps from the 1995 model but now identified four offense pathways: (1) *avoidant-passive,* an underregulation or disinhibition pathway; (2) *avoidant-active,* a misregulation pathway; (3) *approach-automatic,* also an underregulation or disinhibition pathway; and (4) *approach-explicit,* persons with good self-regulation and who have no problem with deviant sexual behavior. Hudson and Ward (2000, pp. 102–122) described the assessment and treatment implications of the improved model. The original RP model was a one-size-fits-all model.

The self-regulation model (SRM), on the other hand, tailored interventions to the type of client being treated. This was a new beginning.

Speaking of the SRM, Ward and Gannon (2006, p. 87) noted:

> A virtue of the SRM is the way it highlights the role of agency and self-regulation in the offence process. The idea that offenders are seeking to achieve specific goals suggests that they are responding to the meaning of events in light of their values and knowledge, they intervene in the world on the basis of their interpretations of personal and social events.

But there were problems (pp. 87–88):

> Perhaps the greatest weakness of the SRM...resides in the privileging of goals relating to behavioral control (i.e., purely offence-related goals concerning deviant sexual activity) and subsequent failure to explicitly document the way human goods and their pursuit are causally related to sexual offending....(S)exual offending is likely to reflect the influence of a multitude of goals and their related human goods....[O]ffenders are psychological agents who are seeking to live meaningful, satisfactory, and worthwhile lives. The fact that they fail to do this suggest(s) there are problems in the ways they are seeking human goods....A further problem with the SRM is that although it does a good job of describing the self-regulatory styles used by sex offenders in the commission of their offences, it gives no indication of the *causal* factors underlying these regulatory styles. In this respect, then, current rehabilitation using identification of SRM pathways is not grounded in either a comprehensive etiological or rehabilitation theory.

It was the recognition of the inadequacies of the SRM and the theoretical propositions of Ward and Stewart (2003) regarding basic needs that led to the development of the GLM. In response to Andrews and Bonta's earlier strict focus on criminogenic needs, Ward and Stewart (2003, p. 137) made their alternative proposition of basic needs. They proposed three basic needs: relatedness, competency, and autonomy. All persons, they said, wish to engage in these valued activities and, if they are unable to, this could result in harm or increased risk of harm in the future. The most valued human goods derived from basic needs were love, friendship, creativity, justice, work, aesthetic pleasure, and sexuality. Here we see the beginnings of what would develop into the GLM.

Proponents of the GLM state that the major shortcoming of the RNR model is its obsessive focus on risk, that attention to criminogenic needs is the primary goal of the treatment. Clients are seen, they say, as "bearers of risk," rather than people seeking primary human goods in inappropriate ways. The GLM is a holistic model of treatment, based on a humanistic rehabilitation theory (Ward & Maruna, 2007). It is described as a "strengths based" approach which emphasizes human agency to gain primary goods common to most people. Offenders are assumed to share the same desires as most nonoffending individuals and seek many of the same goals.

Contrary to popular belief (see Chap. 2), sex offenders are not extraordinary people:

> For the most part, they, like us, come from rather unexceptional backgrounds. Most of them, apart from their sexual deviance, are not criminals. They hunger for the same things that we all do: a good education, a decent job, good friends, home ownership, family ties, children, being loved by someone, and having a stable life. They are, without question, people very much like us (Laws & Ward, 2011, p. 4).

Ward and Marshall (2007, p. 297) continue this theme:

> Offenders, like all other people, attempt to secure beneficial outcomes such as good relationships, a sense of mastery, and recognition from others that they matter....[O]ffending can reflect the search for certain kinds of experience, namely, the attainment of specific goals or goods. Furthermore, offenders' personal strivings express their sense of who they are and what they would like to become....This feature of offending renders it more intelligible and, in a sense, more human. It reminds us that effective treatment should aim to provide alternative means for achieving human goods.

But what about the real phenomenon of risk? GLM does not say that offenders should not be held accountable for their misbehavior. It does say that a comprehensive rehabilitation model must go well beyond the risk management model proposed by Andrews and Bonta (2010a).

Indeed, more recent writings on GLM suggest that addition of GLM principles to RNR programs might form a more comprehensive model that would produce outcomes superior to what we see today (Willis, Ward, & Levenson, 2014).

Primary Goods

Laws and Ward (2011, p. 184) provided this definition:

> In essence, primary goods are states of affairs, states of mind, personal characteristics, activities, or experiences that are sought for their own sake and are likely to increase psychological well-being if achieved. That is, they have intrinsic value and represent the fundamental purposes and ultimate ends of human behavior. In addition to these primary goods, instrumental or secondary goods provide particular ways (i.e., means) fo achieving primary goods, for example, certain types of work or relationships....The notion of instrumental goods is particularly important when it comes to applying the GLM to offending behavior as it is assumed that a primary reason that individuals commit offenses is that they are seeking primary goods in socially and often personally destructive ways. That is, the means chosen to achieve offenders' goals are problematic but not necessarily the goals themselves.

The GLM postulates that there are 11 primary goods (Laws & Ward, 2011, pp. 185–187; Ward & Fortune, 2013, p. 36). Singly and in combination, these goals are presumed to be highly desirable and sought for their own sake.

1. *Life.* Physical needs and factors important for healthy living.
2. *Knowledge.* The tendency of human beings to seek information in order to understand themselves, their natural environment, and other people.
3. *Excellence in play.* The desire to engage in pleasing activities for their own sake.
4. *Excellence in work.* The striving for mastery in work-related activities.
5. *Autonomy.* The desire to formulate one's own goals and to seek ways to realize those goals without undue interference from others.

6. *Inner peace.* Refers to emotional self-regulation and the ability to achieve a state of emotional equilibrium and competence.
7. *Relatedness.* The desire of people to establish warm, affectionate bonds with others.
8. *Community.* The desire of people to belong to social groups that reflect interests, concerns, and values.
9. *Spirituality.* The desire to discover and attain a sense of meaning and purpose in life. This is not necessarily religious.
10. *Happiness.* Refers to the overall experience of being content and satisfied with one's life. Sexual pleasure is included.
11. *Creativity.* Refers to the desire for novelty and innovation in one's life, the experience of doing things differently, or engaging in a specific activity that results in a novel or creative product.

Humanistic goals such as the preceding are notoriously difficult to operationalize. Andrews and Bonta (2010a, p. 512), not surprisingly, were not impressed:

> The fact that personal fulfillment and spirituality do not link with criminal activity does not negate their importance in human and/or social terms. We are not convinced, however, that a focus on noncriminogenic needs will contribute to reduced offending no matter how impassioned the appeal of enhancing personal well-being and personal accomplishment. We wish Tony Ward and his associates all the best as they conduct research on their "good lives model" with due consideration of human motivation.

Difficult or not, the secondary goods must be operationalized. I mentioned above that the GLM does not ignore risk or criminogenic needs. In this respect the model comes closest to the RNR. Risk would be assessed most likely in the manner that Andrews and Bonta (2010a) and Bonta and Andrews (2007) suggest—the use of *Static-99*, *STABLE-2007*, and *ACUTE-2007*. Proper classification by risk would indicate that most intensive services be provided to high- and moderate-risk offenders. Criminogenic needs (dynamic risk factors) would be targeted for cognitive–behavioral treatment with the most attention to Big Four mentioned by Andrews and Bonta (2010a). This portion of the GLM resembles most sex offender treatment programs in operation today.

Attention to primary and secondary goods would constitute the main differences between GLM and RNR-type programs (Laws & Ward, 2011, pp. 185–187; Purvis, Ward, & Willis, 2014, pp. 197–201):

Life	Gaining secure and stable accommodations, engaging in physical exercise and sports, being diet conscious, preparing healthy meals, managing finances correctly, managing health problems
Knowledge	Studying at university or school, participating in training, vocational pursuits, self-study, joining discussion groups, taking lessons to acquire a new skill
Excellence in play	Competitive or social team or individual sports events, having hobbies, socializing with friends, participating in discussion groups
Excellence in work	Gaining meaningful paid employment, engaging in meaningful volunteer work, self-employment, undergoing apprenticeships, taking professional development courses
Autonomy	Asserting oneself and one's needs, self-reflection, achieving financial independence
Inner peace	Achieving a balanced lifestyle, building positive relationships with others, learning emotional control and other self-regulation skills, meditation, counseling, and physical exercise
Relatedness	Engaging in activities centered on relationships—intimate adult romantic relationships, close friendships with others, spending time with family, having and parenting children
Community	Belonging to social service or special interest groups (political party, sports club, craft group, book club, nature group, or religious group), volunteer work, neighborhood or school group
Spirituality	Belonging to a church, studying philosophy, belonging to an environmental association, having a clear vision or plan for one's future and life direction, living according to a particular set of values (ethical behavior, nonviolence)
Creativity	Parenting, gardening, woodwork, painting, attending art exhibitions, playing a musical instrument. May also include how one dresses and presents oneself, decorating a home, selecting furniture

One may reasonably ask—how are you going to do that in a sex offender treatment program? The short answer is: with considerable difficulty (at first).

Obviously, such an approach requires close attention by program personnel who provide information, consistent monitoring, and personal modeling of positive program goals.

Willis et al. (2014, pp. 66–68) have suggested elements that must be respected in introducing a GLM-focused program. The following are slightly modified:

- *Program framing.* Program components (modules, manuals, assignments) emphasize approach goals over avoidant goals, emphasizing coping over avoiding.
- *Individual focus.* Clients are asked to prioritize the list of human goods. Which ones are the most important to them? Integrated care plans for each individual must be developed. Treatment-specific and broader needs (spiritual, recreational, vocational) must be identified.
- *Holistic focus.* The program focus must include noncriminogenic as well as criminogenic needs. The purpose here is to present a wide variety of options.
- *Positive and respectful delivery of service.* Clients are approached as fellow human beings, not moral strangers, and treated with dignity and respect. This is similar to specific responsivity principle of Andrews and Bonta (2010a).
- *Strengths-based approach.* Therapists explicitly identify and reinforce client strengths.
- *Emphasis on the social environment.* Efforts should be made to create an environment that supports working toward treatment goals. This is more easily done in an institution rather than in a community program.
- *Developing client skills.* Skill development is emphasized over fixing and/or managing deficits and problems. This may involve practicing skills that make some clients uncomfortable.
- *Program foundation.* Ideally GLM should be the bedrock of the program rather than a prerelease module at the end of treatment.

None of the preceding could be easily accomplished, particularly in an institutional program that has been providing a risk-focused program for years. However, history has taught us that even seasoned bughousers with entrenched negative attitudes and beliefs about sex offenders can, like their clients, be persuaded to change.

Adaptation to Existing Programs

Willis et al. (2014, p. 61) noted that the evidence base for the GLM is markedly inferior to the support shown for the RNR. Willis et al. (2014) noted that while the GLM has the potential for enhancing the effectiveness of existing programs, this potential requires the correct operationalization of the GLM in practice. The recent Safer Society survey (McGrath et al., 2010) found that one-third of US programs and half of Canadian programs reported that they used GLM as one of the three main theories (GLM, RP, and RNR) guiding their work. The Willis et al. (2014) study had two aims: (1) to examine how the GLM was operationalized into a sample of North American programs, and (2) to evaluate the degree to which GLM had been integrated into those programs. Responding to a list serve, 27 programs expressed interest in participating. Thirteen programs met the authors' inclusionary criteria and all sites were visited. A coding protocol was developed to rate major aspects of each program. The findings can be briefly summarized (pp. 72–74):

- *Program aims.* Twelve of the 13 programs communicated the dual foci of risk reduction and well-being enhancement.
- *Assessment.* Eight of the 13 programs used a standardized assessment of static and dynamic risk factors as well as a psychosocial history. All programs used a static risk assessment and ten used a dynamic risk assessment.
- *Intervention planning.* Following assessment, 7 of the 13 programs adopted a collaborative approach to treatment planning.
- *Intervention content.* Eight of the thirteen programs used strengths-based manuals or guides. Aims of each treatment component were approach oriented and linked to one or more primary goods. Treatment content varied from an RP influence to more standard cognitive–behavioral approaches. Three programs incorporated a GLM component in the final module of treatment.

- *Intervention delivery.* Although some characteristics were more evident than others, treatment personnel presented positive therapist behavior. There was considerable variability with some therapists showing warmth, praise, and empathy while others were directive and confrontational. Some groups appeared to be education based. The degree to which treatment components were tailored to individuals varied substantially.

It seemed to me that the authors were rather generous in their appraisal of what they found in these site visits. In conclusion they stated (p. 79):

> The GLM is a relatively new theory of offender rehabilitation and it is encouraging to see its application in so many North American treatment programs. Although this study has revealed some areas of weakness in the implementation of the GLM, the majority of programs examined appeared to effectively use the model to create positive, motivationally engaging, and risk reducing therapeutic approaches.

What Willis et al. (2014) found is approximately what I would expect. I am quite familiar with RP/cognitive–behavioral programs in use in the 1980s and 1990s. These programs tended to be risk based, with a heavy focus on avoidance, personally confrontational, with strict adherence to treatment manuals, and rigid in implementation. Attempting to introduce something as radical as the GLM into those programs would not have been possible. The therapeutic climate in the treatment of sex offenders has loosened up a bit since then, but incorporating GLM principles remains a major task. This softening is, I think, what Willis et al. (2014) observed.

Empirical Support for the GLM

The GLM stands in stark contrast to sex offender treatment practices that have been evolving since about 1975. While most clinicians would acknowledge that GLM principles are sound in nature and should be major components of treatment, there remains a caution, a concern that such an approach could make happy criminals of people widely believed to be bearers of significant risk. We see an example of this caution in the Willis et al. (2014) study just reviewed. They recruited their subjects from the list serve of the Association for the Treatment of Sexual Abusers. This is the largest organization of its kind in the world and the list serve is widely used. The Safer Society survey (McGrath et al., 2010) identified 1379 programs yet Willis et al. (2014) could only recruit 13 out of 27 volunteering. It is therefore not surprising that the empirical base for the GLM is meager. However, what we see to date is promising.

Willis and Ward (2013) have provided summaries of some recent research on various aspects of the GLM. Ward, Mann, and Gannon (2007) described a group-based application of GLM based on seven modules generally used in treatment and their links to primary goods. For example, the primary good of knowledge is contained within a cognitive restructuring module. A social skills module is seen as associated with the goods of friendship, community, and personal agency. Ward et al. (2007) stress that the good(s) associated with any particular module ought to be directly linked to an individual's good lives (GL) plan. They note that several studies have supported the underlying assumptions of the GLM (Barnett & Wood, 2008; Purvis, 2010; Willis & Grace, 2008; Willis & Ward, 2011).

There have been several studies on what Willis and Ward (2013) call "GLM-consistent interventions." Simons, McCullar, and Tyler (2006) reported on the shift from a program using an RP framework focusing on criminogenic needs and avoidance goals to a GLM-based format. In the GLM approach treatment goals were arrived at collaboratively and framed as approach goals. Compared to the RP framework, clients who received the GLM approach were more likely to stay in treatment longer and complete it, and be rated by therapists as highly motivated. Post-treatment, GLM clients showed better coping skills and were more likely to have a support system.

A modified version of the GLM was offered by Marshall, Marshall, Serran, and O'Brien (2011). They collapsed the 11 primary goods into six categories:

- *Health.* Good diet and exercise.
- *Mastery.* In work and play.

- *Autonomy.* Self-directiveness.
- *Relatedness.* Intimate/sexual relationships, family friends, kinship, and community.
- *Inner peace.* Freedom from turmoil and stress, and a sense of purpose and meaning in life.
- *Knowledge and creativity.* Satisfaction from knowing and creating things, job- or hobby-related knowledge, playing music, and writing.

Marshall et al. have historically used a cognitive–behavioral approach in their treatment program. Evaluation of this program (535 clients) showed a 3.2% recidivism rate at 5.4 years and 5.6% rate at 8.4 years. These results fall well below the rates typically reported in meta-analyses.

Gannon, King, Miles, Lockerbie, and Willis (2011) conducted what they called a "descriptive study" of the application of a GLM program with mentally disordered offenders. The GLM content was incorporated into assessment, treatment planning, and the program modules. The treatment modules included:

- Understanding GL and risk factors.
- Understanding offending.
- Sexual arousal and fantasy.
- Coping skills.
- Offense-supportive thinking.
- Victim awareness and empathy.
- Intimacy and relationships.
- Recognizing risk.
- Leading a good life.

Despite the fact that participating clients were mentally disordered and residing in an inpatient unit, Gannon et al. (2011) reported that all clients understood what primary goods are and why prosocial attainment of goods was important. Some clients had difficulty connecting the links between GLM concepts and their own risk factors. Thus, clients must understand that addressing their criminogenic needs is part of the treatment package.

Harkins, Flak, Beech, and Woodhams (2012) evaluated what they called a "Better Lives" module, a replacement for an RP-based module in a community treatment program. Better Lives used a GLM approach emphasizing prosocial attainment of each of the 11 primary goods. The Better Lives approach ($n = 76$) was compared with the existing RP program ($n = 701$). The Better Lives approach was rated by clients and facilitators as more positive although there were no differences in attrition rates or treatment change.

Conclusion

The evidence for the efficacy of the GLM, such as it is, is promising. In my view, what it promises is a great deal of work to promote a new framework that is so contrary to standard sex offender programs that have been in existence for at least 40 years. A complete bibliography for GLM may be found at: www.goodlivesmodel.com/publications (2015).

Is RNR–GLM Integration Possible?

Willis et al. (2014, p. 59) have stated that "Operationalized appropriately, the GLM offers potential for improving outcomes of programs operating in accordance with the Risk, Need, and Responsivity (RNR) principles." If this is so, then would it be possible to integrate the best elements of each into a single comprehensive model? The major proponents of the RNR (Andrews, Bonta, & Wormith, 2011) think it is not. Their position, carefully detailed in the cited paper, is that the attempt to incorporate GLM concepts and practices would add nothing to RNR that is not already there. This paper is a truly impassioned defense of a solid empirically based position and is highly recommended to the reader.

References

Andrews, D. A., & Bonta, J. (1995). *The level of service inventory—Revised*. Toronto: Multi-Health Systems.

Andrews, D. A., & Bonta, J. (2010a). *The psychology of criminal conduct* (5th ed.). New Providence, NJ: LexisNexis.

Andrews, D. A., & Bonta, J. (2010b). Rehabilitating criminal justice policy and practice. *Psychology, Public Policy, and Law, 16*, 39–55.

Andrews, D. A., Bonta, J., & Hoge, R. D. (1990). Classification for effective rehabilitation: Rediscovering psychology. *Criminal Justice and Behavior, 17*, 19–52.

Andrews, D. A., Bonta, J., & Wormith, S. J. (2011). The risk-need-responsivity model: Does adding the good lives model contribute to effective crime prevention? *Criminal Justice and Behavior, 38*, 735–755.

Andrews, D. A., Dowden, C., & Rettinger, J. L. (2001). Special populations within corrections. In J. A. Winterdyk (Ed.), *Corrections in Canada: Social reactions to crime* (pp. 170–212). Toronto: Prentice-Hall.

Andrews, D. A., Zinger, I., Hoge, R. D., Bonta, J., Gendreau, P., & Cullen, F. T. (1990). Does correctional treatment work? A psychologically informed meta-analysis. *Criminology, 28*, 369–404.

Barnett, G., & Wood, J. L. (2008). Agency, relatedness, inner peace, and problem solving in sexual offending: How sexual offenders prioritize and operationalize their good lives conceptions. *Sexual Abuse: A Journal of Research and Treatment, 20*, 444–465.

Bonta, J., & Andrews, D. A. (2007). *Risk-need-responsivity model for offender assessment and rehabilitation* (User Rep. No. 2007-06). Ottawa, ON: Public Safety Canada.

Bureau of Justice Statistics. (1996). *Correctional populations in the United States 1994*. Washington, DC: Office of Justice Programs, US Department of Justice.

Di Placido, C., Simon, T. L., Witte, T. D., Gu, D., & Wong, S. C. P. (2006). Treatment of gang members can reduce recidivism and institutional misconduct. *Law and Human Behavior, 30*, 93–114.

Dowden, C., & Andrews, D. A. (1999a). What works in youth offender treatment: A meta-analysis. *Forum on Corrections Research, 11*, 21–24.

Dowden, C., & Andrews, D. A. (1999b). What works for female offenders: A meta-analytic review. *Crime & Delinquency, 45*, 438–452.

Dowden, C., & Andrews, D. A. (2000). Effective correctional treatment and violent reoffending. *Canadian Journal of Criminology, 42*, 449–467.

French, S., & Gendreau, P. (2006). Reducing prison misconduct: What works! *Criminal Justice and Behavior, 33*, 185–218.

Furby, L., Weinrott, M. R., & Blackshaw, L. (1989). Sex offender recidivism: A review. *Psychological Bulletin, 105*, 3–30.

Gannon, T. A., King, T., Miles, H., Lockerbie, L., & Willis, G. M. (2011). Good lives sexual offender treatment for mentally disordered offenders. *British Journal of Forensic Practice, 13*, 153–168.

Hanson, R. K., Bourgon, G., Helmus, L., & Hodgson, S. (2009). The principles of effective treatment also apply to sexual offenders: A meta-analysis. *Criminal Justice and Behavior, 36*, 865–891.

Harkins, L., Flak, V. E., Beech, A. R., & Woodhams, J. (2012). Evaluation of a community-based sex offender treatment program using a good lives model approach. *Sexual Abuse: A Journal of Research and Treatment, 24*, 519–543.

Hudson, S. M., & Ward, T. (2000). Relapse prevention: Assessment and treatment implications. In D. R. Laws, S. M. Hudson, & T. Ward (Eds.), *Remaking relapse prevention with sex offenders: A sourcebook* (pp. 102–122). Thousand Oaks, CA: Sage.

Laws, D. R. (1989). *Relapse prevention with sex offenders.* New York: Guilford.

Laws, D. R. (2003). The rise and fall of relapse prevention. *Australian Psychologist, 38*, 22–30.

Laws, D. R. (in press). The rise and fall of relapse prevention: An update. In L. E. Marshall & W. L. Marshall (Eds.), *The Wiley-Blackwell handbook on the assessment, treatment, and theories of sexual offending. Volume: Treatment.* Chichester: Wiley-Blackwell.

Laws, D. R., & Ward, T. (2011). *Desistance from sex offending.* New York: Guilford.

Lipsey, M. W. (1989, November). *The efficacy of intervention for juvenile delinquency: Results from 400 studies.* Paper presented at the meeting of the American Society of Criminology, Reno, NV.

Lipton, D. S., Martinson, R., & Wilks, J. (1975). *The effectiveness of correctional treatment: A survey of treatment evaluation studies.* New York: Praeger.

Lösel, F., & Schmucker, M. (2005). The effectiveness of treatment for sexual offenders: A comprehensive meta-analysis. *Journal of Experimental Criminology, 1*, 117–146.

Marlatt, G. A., & Gordon, J. R. (Eds.). (1985). *Relapse prevention: Maintenance strategies in the treatment of addictive behaviors.* New York: Guilford.

Marshall, W. L., Marshall, L. E., Serran, G. A., & O'Brien, M. D. (2011). *The rehabilitation of sexual offenders: A strengths-based approach.* Washington, DC: American Psychological Association.

Martinson, R. (1974). What works? Questions and answers about prison reform. *The Public Interest, 10*, 22–54.

McGrath, R. J., Cumming, G. F., Burchard, B. L., Zeoli, S., & Ellerby, L. (2010). *Current practices and emerging trends in sexual abuser management: The Safer Society 2009 North American Survey.* Brandon, VT: Safer Society Press.

Pithers, W. D. (1990). Relapse prevention with sexual aggressors: A method for maintaining therapeutic gain and enhancing external supervision. In W. L.

Marshall, D. R. Laws, & H. E. Barbaree (Eds.), *Handbook of sexual assault* (pp. 343–361). New York: Plenum.

Pithers, W. D. (1991). Relapse prevention with sexual aggressors. *Forum on Corrections Research, 3,* 20–23.

Purvis, M. (2010). *Seeking a good life: Human goods and sexual offending.* Saarbrücken: Lambert Academic Publishing GmbH & Co KG.

Purvis, M., Ward, T., & Willis, G. (2014). Applying the good lives model of offender rehabilitation to sex offenders. In M. Carich & S. Mussack (Eds.), *The Safer Society handbook to adult sexual offender assessment and treatment* (pp. 193–220). Brandon, VT: Safer Society Press.

Simons, D., McCullar, B., & Tyler, C. (2006, September). *Evaluation of the good lives model approach to treatment planning.* Workshop presented at the conference of the Association for the Treatment of Sexual Abusers, Chicago.

Ward, T., & Fortune, C.-A. (2013). The Good Lives Model: Aligning risk reduction with promoting offenders' personal goals. *European Journal of Probation, 5,* 29–46.

Ward, T., & Gannon, T. A. (2006). Rehabilitation, etiology, and self-regulation: The comprehensive good lives model of treatment for sexual offenders. *Aggression and Violent Behavior, 11,* 77–94.

Ward, T., & Hudson, S. M. (1998). The construction and development of theory in the sexual offending area: A meta-theoretical framework. *Sexual Abuse: A Journal of Research and Treatment, 10,* 47–63.

Ward, T., Louden, K., Hudson, S. M., & Marshall, W. L. (1995). A descriptive model of the offence chain for child molesters. *Journal of Interpersonal Violence, 10,* 452–472.

Ward, T., Mann, R., & Gannon, T. A. (2007). The Good Lives Model of offender rehabilitation: Clinical implications. *Aggression and Violent Behavior, 12,* 87–107.

Ward, T., & Marshall, W. L. (2007). Narrative identity and offender rehabilitation. *International Journal of Offender Therapy and Comparative Criminology, 51,* 279–297.

Ward, T., & Maruna, S. (2007). *Rehabilitation: Beyond the risk paradigm.* London: Routledge.

Ward, T., & Stewart, D. (2003). Criminogenic needs and human needs: A theoretical model. *Psychology, Crime & Law, 9,* 125–143.

Willis, G. M., & Grace, R. C. (2008). The quality of community reintegration planning for child molesters: Effects on sexual recidivism. *Sexual Abuse: A Journal of Research and Treatment, 20,* 218–240.

Willis, G. M., & Ward, T. (2013). The Good Lives Model: Does it work? Preliminary evidence. In L. A. Craig, L. Dixon, & T. A. Gannon (Eds.), *What works in offender rehabilitation: An evidence-based approach to assessment and treatment*. Chichester: Wiley-Blackwell.

Willis, G. M., Ward, T., & Levenson, J. S. (2014). The Good Lives Model (GLM): An evaluation of GLM operationalization in North American treatment programs. *Sexual Abuse: A Journal of Research and Treatment, 26*, 58–81.

Willlis, G. M., & Ward, T. (2011). Striving for a good life: The Good Lives Model applied to released child molesters. *Journal of Sexual Aggression, 17*, 290–303.

Wilson, R. J., & Yates, P. M. (2009). Effective interventions and the Good Lives Model: Maximizing treatment gains for sexual offenders. *Aggression and Violent Behavior, 14*, 157–161.

12

Conclusions and Future Outlook

After reading this book the major conclusion that readers will perhaps reach is that the war against sex offenders cannot be won. However, neither will it be lost as the demands for ever more control increase. We may reasonably ask what has been accomplished in this 100-year conflict.

It is apparent that the authors of multitudes of legislation and practices intended to control the social behavior of sex offenders have been very creative indeed. However, what has been accomplished has turned out to be far less than what was expected. The efforts have not been total failures but the consequences have been devastating for those affected. In many cases what has been accomplished is that a large number of ex-offenders, their partners, and families live in fear, may be homeless, jobs have been lost, families have been destroyed, and children are left without a parent. This is what wars usually accomplish.

In this concluding chapter, I will revisit the major subject matter areas covered in the book and consider the long-term impact of the legislation, practices, and beliefs that underlie those efforts at social control. Where possible I make recommendations on what may reasonably be expected to change in the future. Those recommendations would continue not only to stress the need to keep society safe but also to provide means to

© The Editor(s) (if applicable) and The Author(s) 2016
D.R. Laws, *Social Control of Sex Offenders*,
DOI 10.1057/978-1-137-39126-1_12

encourage ex-offenders to rehabilitate themselves and live in a legal and socially acceptable manner.

Moral Panic

This phenomenon is ever with us and, although the concern that it incites ebbs and flows, it never really goes away. The concern that sex offenders pose a continuing threat to the social order is always present, erupting from time to time as knowledge of a particularly brutal sex crime becomes known. In my view, print and television media are the engines that drive this panic. In the 1940s and 1950s newspapers and radio could make sensational presentations to excite public interest. Such stories could not remain front-page news or the opening of a radio broadcast for long and the coverage tended to fade away fairly quickly. This is no longer so. Cable news coverage can keep a sensational story alive around the clock. Newsreaders can dwell on tiny details supplemented by visuals. Small groups of experts discuss the issues. Pundits offer learned opinions. This can be stretched out indefinitely, occasionally shelved, and then resurrected as needed. The panic thus created is exacerbated by less reasoned presentations on Internet postings. Newspapers also carry this information but many people today rely on television and the Internet for current news.

Are there ways to counter the irresponsible incitement to a panic over sex offenders? There are several options, all of which require devotion to the subject and hard work.

- It is not going to be possible to constrain some of the major media outlets. Sex crime bleeds and it leads. It is possible to insert sane voices into the debate about social threat. It is possible for a TV network to include a commentator who is willing to say things like, "You know, (news anchor), what you just said about the danger that strangers pose to children is not really accurate. Let me inform our viewers what the facts really are." Such a commentator would not be welcome in all venues.
- Numerous writers publish accurate accounts of the supposed menace of sex offenders in respected periodicals. This is a welcome event. For

this to have an effect, however, one must assume that people actually read magazines with serious content. Most do not.

- A bright spot in the media can be found in nonnetwork Internet news outlets. These unique sources often publish quite accurate information on supposedly sensational crime issues.
- Public engagement is essential to dispelling myths. One way to do this might be to stage public debates in schools, churches, or other public venues. These would be pro and con debates on the sex offender menace. The value here would be to show the public that there is another side of the story than the supersensational one.
- Politicians and legislators are understandably timid to take a position on any issue that seems to excuse or minimize criminal behavior. It is not too much to ask them to consider that some of the draconian laws in force actually imperil society rather than protect it. There is ample evidence supporting repeal of a number of these laws.
- It would seem that law enforcement would be the most difficult group to assist in dispelling moral panic. Where sex offenses are concerned I doubt that this is true. Law enforcement officers are often the first responders to complaints about sex offenses. They see on a daily basis what the public almost never sees, that the bulk of sex offending is small-scale abuse carried out repeatedly by unknown offenders. It is abuse to be sure and it is perpetrated far too often, but it is far from the kidnap, rape, and murder tales trumpeted by the media. Police officials can speak to this truth. Someone should ask them.

Tabachnick and Klein (2011) stress the need for communicating accurate information about perpetration to the public:

Because policy is often created in response to public demands, sharing accurate and evidence-based information with the public will increase the likelihood of public demand for appropriate and effective policy for sex offenders and for preventing child sexual abuse. Involving the media in the dissemination of accurate and non-sensational stories about child sexual abuse and its perpetrators and victims will also help shift the public's response to sexual offending and motivate the community's desire to prevent child sexual abuse. (p. 40)

Efforts such as those suggested above may serve to quell but not entirely eliminate the moral panic about sex offenders. The point is to introduce rational voices into the discourse regarding the supposed threat to the social order.

Early Treatment of Sexual Deviance

Chapter 3 traced the attempts to control sex offenders from the early years of the republic through the nineteenth century. Today it seems incomprehensible that people were displayed publicly in stocks, made to stand holding signs that described their deviant behavior, whipped in public, or branded with symbols that indicated their crime. Today, such practices are no longer considered acceptable.

There are alternatives, however, that are no less reprehensible. For example, in 2000 a young British girl, Sarah Payne, was murdered by a convicted pedophile. The public outrage was such that a London tabloid, the *News of the World*, initiated what was called a "naming and shaming" campaign in which the names of known pedophiles were made public. Some were accurately named and some were not. The campaign resulted in vigilante attacks on some of the named persons. The *News of the World* eventually suspended the effort after the Home Office introduced a program that allowed community members to inquire about the criminal records of people they suspected of sexual abuse. This is similar to some of the community notification laws passed in the USA.

Similar efforts have appeared in the USA. Sex offenders have been made to display signs on their home property that say "Danger! Sex Offender Lives Here." It has been suggested that similar signs appear on the sides of automobiles and that sex offenders be issued vehicle license plates of a color that would distinguish them from the population at large. This is eerily reminiscent of the Nazi practice of making sexual deviants wear a pink triangle in prison camps.

Public humiliation of sexual deviants encourages hatred, discrimination, and acts of vigilantism. While these practices seem to surface at the height of a moral panic, they fade away as the panic subsides. My future outlook is that they should be banned since they serve only to keep the panic alive.

Medicalization

Until the latter part of the nineteenth century, deviant sexual behavior was considered sinful or criminal or both. By the mid-nineteenth century, the new science of psychiatry began to categorize various forms of deviant social behavior rather than accept a highly general term such as "perversion." As a result of this effort, behaviors that had been dealt with at a civil level became the province of medicine (Link, 2009, p. 3). Now, 150 years later, medicalization of deviant behavior is a standard component of what Goffman (1961) called the "tinkering trades." All levels of treatment providers and managers, all levels of treatment provision, are subject to some extent by medicalization.

In my view, medicalization introduces surplus terminology into assessment and treatment provision. In Chap. 4, I gave the example of *transsexualism* being renamed as *gender dysphoria*. Transsexualism is a term acceptable and widely used in the lesbian, gay, bisexual, and transgender (LGBT) community and, hence, should be acceptable to us. The efforts of psychiatry to slice the diagnostic salami ever thinner seem to never end. The recent disputes over definitions of supposed paraphilias to be included in the *Diagnostic and Statistical Manual of Mental Disorders, Fifth Edition (DSM-V)* offer some examples of this. The inclusion of *paraphilic coercive disorder* as a synonym for *rape* is a particularly egregious example. Rape, a physical assault masked as a sexual act, will never be accepted as a mental disorder. *Pedo-hebephilia* was an attempt to nest the disputed term, *hebephilia*, in an already well-accepted category. *Hypersexual disorder* would likely be called by its more common label of "sexual addiction." Since 1980 treatment programs for this problem, modified from the Alcoholic Anonymous 12-step model, have proliferated throughout North America. No officially sanctioned diagnosis was necessary.

Medicalization is a necessary feature for supplying population statistics to official government bodies, for submitting claims for service to insurance companies, for providing diagnoses for medication, and for providing diagnoses to justify certain legal practices such as civil commitment. Other than these or similar uses, it is not useful. It wraps a medical cloak around common terms and practices and simply confuses the issues.

Sexual Psychopath/Predator Laws

"Wicked people exist," said political scientist James Q. Wilson (1985, p. 193). "Nothing avails except to set them apart from innocent people" (p. 235). The indeterminate confinement of the supposed worst of the worst has been tried twice. These efforts appeared in two eras: the first from the early 1930s to the late 1970s and early 1980s; the second from 1990 to the present.

Today, the early era is generally considered to have been a failure. The laws were unevenly, inconsistently and, some cases, unenthusiastically applied, suffered many challenges over the years, and gradually fell into disuse and eventual repeal.

The present era of the so-called sexual predator laws has been marginally more successful although the statutes contain serious problems that remain unresolved. In terms of eligibility for confinement, it has been relatively easy to identify the more serious cases, the life-course persistent, repetitive, and violent sex offenders. However, those same criteria are sufficiently broad, that much less dangerous, although repetitive sex offenders such as voyeurs, exhibitionists, and fetishists can be swept into the net. The eligibility criteria all specify a diagnosis of mental illness which is much more difficult to prove. The supposed mental illness is considered to be the engine that drives the deviant sexual behavior. Thus, as has been the case in the past, remediation of this problem, restoration of a reasonable degree of sanity, is the key to release from civil commitment. Although a few civil commitment programs claim to release offenders who have undergone treatment in these facilities, it is repeatedly reported that most programs never release anyone due to the concern about reoffense.

It seems to me that there are possible solutions to the civil commitment problem:

- It is not difficult to identify the worst of the worst. Abundant documentation in the criminal justice system shows who these people are. The central problem of civil commitment is the mandatory condition of sex offender treatment. Why should one believe that lifelong-persistent sex offenders would benefit from treatment? The USA has no problem with confining serious criminal offenders for life. Instead of pretending that civil commitment programs contain a redemptive factor, a much simpler solution would be a life sentence.

- Canada, for example, has a provision in its Criminal Code called a "Dangerous Offender (DO)" designation. An offender may be designated DO during sentencing if the court determines that the offender presents a danger to the life, safety, physical, or mental well-being of the public. Once designated a DO, the offender is likely to be sentenced to an indeterminate prison sentence with no chance of parole for 7 years. If the offender subsequently shows repeated offenses, the DO designation could result in a life sentence.

- Civil commitment programs are enormously expensive to construct and operate. This may be why only 40% of American states contain them. I agree with Janus and Prentky (2009) that states may eventually simply run out of money to continue or implement these programs. They promise a solution but they fail to deliver.

Assessment of Risk to Reoffend

Chapters 6 and 7 considered the development of instruments that purport to predict future criminal behavior. It is quite clear that, from the 1920s to the present, actuarial assessment in numerous variations has been the predominant approach. This is a solid body of research and it is not surprising that elements of instruments developed in the early twentieth century (Burgess, 1928) persist to this day (Andrews & Bonta, 2010a). Indeed, criminological discoveries from the early nineteenth century, for example, the age–crime curve, continue to influence current actuarial prediction (see Hanson, 2002; Nicholaichuk, Olver, Gu, & Wong, 2014).

Since 1997 there has been a large volume of research on actuarial prediction and considerably less on the use of structured professional judgment. Actuarial prediction of sexual reoffense has been, by far, the most popular approach. There has been considerable opposition to these methods (see, Franklin & Abbott, Appendix 1), but this has not materially affected their enthusiastic adoption. I have tried to fairly present the current status of these methods. I was initially adamantly opposed to actuarial prediction. However, after closely reviewing what has been accomplished, in particular by Hanson and his colleagues, I have developed a certain guarded respect for these methods. What the future holds is more to come. I say this in the hope that many of the outstanding objections may be resolved. The procedures are here to stay.

It seems to me that the best use of an actuarial instrument such as the *Static-99* is to use it as a baseline judgment of risk, a tentative judgment, not a final one. This judgment must be supplemented by other actuarials such as the *STABLE-2007* and *ACUTE-2007*. It would not be inappropriate to further supplement the evaluation with instruments such as the *SVR-20* and the *Psychopathy Checklist—Revised*. Such an approach would provide a fairly firm initial grounding for a defensible forensic evaluation.

Registration, Community Notification, and Residence Restrictions

This package of statutes, ordinances, and prohibitions represent, for the most part, the greatest threat to the rehabilitation of sex offenders in the community.

Registration with the police has the longest history, dating back to the mid-nineteenth century. This practice will not cease despite the fact that many offenders simply ignore the requirement and fail to register. Those who wish to comply with the law readily register and maintain that status as they move from place to place. The purpose of registration has been to provide the police with knowledge of the whereabouts of the most dangerous offenders in their jurisdiction, presumably to aid in the investigation of future crimes. Maintaining a registry is burdensome and the utility of it is questionable.

Community notification has been unevenly applied. Wholesale communication of all offenders' names and whereabouts has proven to be a harmful practice, as shown by the "Naming and Shaming" campaign in the UK. Providing information in this manner has been shown to encourage discrimination and vigilantism. A less noxious practice would be to provide information to parties who have a genuine need to know. Community notification has not proven to be useful in preventing future crime and it has made life for ex-offenders extremely difficult.

Residence restrictions have proven to be the least successful community control measure. Chajewski and Mercado's (2009) evaluation of buffer zones around areas where children would be expected to congregate showed that the largest buffer zones occupied so much space that they left little or no space where sex offenders could live. This result simply drives sex offenders underground and defeats most if not all efforts at community control.

Some Possible Solutions

Tofte (2007, pp. 15–20), speaking for Human Rights Watch, offered a broad set of recommendations on these issues. Although presented in 2007, they do not appear to be substantially dated.

Adam Walsh Act (SORNA)

- Congress should repeal all provisions of the Act that deal with state registration and community notification requirements.
- If Congress fails to act, states should not adopt those provisions

State Sex Offender Registries

- Former offenders who have committed minor, nonviolent offenses, or consensual activity with a minor who is within 5 years of age of the offender should not be required to register.
- No offender under the age of 18 at the time of offense should be required to register. If states require this registration, a determination must be made that the child presents a high risk of sexual reoffense and that public safety cannot be adequately protected by any other means.
- States should remove offenders from the registry if they are exonerated, convictions overturned, set aside, or otherwise vitiated, or if their conduct is no longer considered criminal.

- Registration information should be periodically reviewed to ensure its accuracy.
- Ex-offenders should not be required to register with their schools or places of employment. A criminal background check may be run on employees who will be working with children.
- Registration should be limited to former offenders who pose a high or medium risk of a future offense, either of sexually abusing children or a violent sex crime against adults.
- Ex-offenders considered to be low risk for reoffending should not be required to register.
- The period of inclusion on the registry for ex-offenders assessed as medium to high risk should be determined by individual risk assessment and then be subject to periodic review with a view to extension of termination. Lifetime inclusion should not be permitted. At periodic review registrants should be able to present:

  - evidence of rehabilitation,
  - change in life circumstances,
  - incapacitation (disease or disability), or
  - substantial time living offense-free in the community

  to obtain termination of the requirement to register or to change level of risk.

Community Notification

- Access to sex offender registries should be limited to law enforcement.
- Information about registered sex offenders should only be released on a need to know basis. This includes notification to the person(s) victimized by the offender. Information released should enhance the recipient's personal safety and that of their children.
- Law enforcement officials should eliminate the use of posters, flyers, and other easily replicable materials to alert communities of the presence of a registered sex offender in their neighborhood. Possibly affected community members should be informed individually.
- All community members must be kept safe, including persons convicted of sex offenses. Officials must assess the potential for com-

munity hostility against registrants and take steps to mitigate that threat.

- All registrants should be able to appear periodically before a panel to review the requirement that law enforcement publicly release their personal information.

Online Sex Offender Registries

- States should eliminate public access to online registries of sex offenders as a form of community notification.
- States maintaining online registries should only include information about offenders assigned a high level of risk.
- No member of the public should be able to search the entire database. States should also take steps to ensure that registry information may not be accessed by Internet search engines.
- Accountability for those who search online databases should be ensured by requiring the user to specify the purpose of the search.
- Online databases should provide enough information to enable a layperson to understand the nature of the offense of which the offender was convicted and the registrant's risk of recidivism.
- Information about a registrant revealed online should be limited to what is necessary to promote public safety.
- Online registries must prominently display warnings against misuse of information on the registry. Misuse of registry information should be prosecuted.
- Registrants should have a periodic opportunity to petition to be removed from the online registry.

National Sex Offender Registry

- Congress should eliminate public access to the national sex offender registry.
- If a national registry is to be maintained, it must include only such information from state registries as is consistent with the criteria specified above.

Residency Restrictions

- Neither states nor localities should have residency restriction laws that apply to entire classes of former offenders.
- Authorized residency restrictions should be limited to individually tailored restrictions for certain offenders as a condition of probation, parole, or other mandated supervision.

Psychological Treatment: Two Models

Chapter 12 provides a somewhat brief overview of two psychological interventions, the Risk–Need–Responsivity (RNR) model and the Good Lives Model (GLM). I will stress again that the use of the word "model" does not signify a prescriptive structure for treatment intervention. Rather, as models they provide organizing principles under which a variety of specific interventions may be grouped. Each states that focus must be directed to important structural features (e.g., "criminogenic needs" in RNR and "primary goods" in GLM). These interventions were not chosen for review because they are necessarily the "best" treatments. Rather, they were chosen because they were identified in the 2009 Safer Society Survey (McGrath, Cumming, Burchard, Zeoli, & Ellerby, 2010) as two of three most prominent choices by treatment providers. I leave it to the reader to choose his or her favorite. If we were to rely solely upon empirical support over the past 20 years, the RNR model appears to be the most frequently used.

There are questions regarding psychological treatment of sex offenders which remain unresolved. These include:

Who Gets Treatment?

Laws and Ward (2011, p. 97–98) argued, based on arrest and conviction data from 2004, that only a tiny fraction of prosecuted sex offenders were mandated to treatment. Being mandated to treatment does not mean that an individual will certainly attend, participate, and complete treatment.

Statistics on sex offenders in community supervision are notoriously difficult to locate. For example, the Center for Sex Offender Management (CSOM, 2000), citing a 1997 Bureau of Justice Statistics report, stated that 265,000 adult sex offenders were in the "care, custody, or control of correctional agencies in the United States. Of these, almost 60% are under some form of community supervision" (p. 1). That means that, 18 years ago, 159,000 sex offenders were in community supervision, with very few likely in a treatment program. More recently, the Bureau of Justice Statistics (BJS, 2013) reported that 4,751,400 persons were on probation and parole, with no specification of how many of these were sex offenders. The sex offender community supervision population has grown enormously since 1997.

Consider now that the Safer Society 2009 survey (McGrath et al., 2010) reported, in that year, that 53,811 sex offenders received treatment in 1379 treatment programs in the USA. It is quite clear, and disappointing, to conclude that a miniscule number of sex offenders in the community are receiving treatment.

Does Treatment Work?

In my view it has been established beyond question that sex offender treatment "works," that is, reasonably objective outcome measures show that treatment completers can be shown to have gained benefit from the program. The stringent meta-analyses by Lösel and Schmucker (2005) and Hanson et al. (2009), to cite two major investigations, attest to this fact. That treatment is effective is typically measured in post-treatment recidivism rates. Here lies the problem with treatment efficacy. Recidivism rates are obtained from rap sheets and other public records. The post-treatment period for determining recidivism is usually too brief, about 5 years. Some treatment programs make no effort to determine recidivism, basing their conclusions of effectiveness on treatment completion data. The major problem is that follow-up is not based on intensive supervision; rap sheets are consulted at some time in the post-treatment future and conclusions about treatment effectiveness are made. This is an all too frequently ignored problem. To consult rap sheets 20–30 years in the future and claim that treatment was so effective that, essentially, it completely prevented reoffense is nonsense. If treatment does nothing else, it attempts to demonstrate that there are other ways of living one's life than sex offending. Treatment is not an inoculation producing immunity to evildoing.

Are There Alternatives?

My colleague Tony Ward has suggested that perhaps the main function of treatment is that it serves as a catalyst, providing alternative ways of behaving, options that may be tried out, and options for behaving in a nonoffensive way. Forensic psychology has devoted a lot of attention to changing behavior in the here and now and has paid almost no attention to the natural processes of desistance from crime that criminologists have advocated for decades. Indeed, some have argued that treatment just gets in the way. The phenomenon of natural desistance has been evident since the time of Quételet in the early nineteenth century. Laws and Ward (2011, pp. 15–95) have traced much of this work through the twentieth and into the twenty-first centuries. Readers interested in this work should consult Sampson and Laub (1993) and Laub and Sampson (2003) for information on encouraging and tracking desistance. Forensic psychology has not been entirely remiss in this regard (see Hanson, 2002; Nicholaichuk et al., 2014) but they have tended to regard desistance as a phenomenon rather than an area of study worth examining and pursuing.

Laws and Ward (2011, p. 105) make several observations regarding desistance in sex offenders:

- If we accept that treatment is effective, at best the results are modest.
- We should adopt a rehabilitation model that incorporates desistance research and ideas, that is more constructive, and thereby improves the effectiveness of current treatment practice.
- Considering that treated sex offenders reoffend at a lower rate than untreated ones, we do not know why this is so.
- We do not really know how treatment works or what mechanisms are operating to promote successful reintegration.

- A very evident problem is that sex offenders are not followed up long enough or in their natural (personal, unique) environments.

A Final Word

I do not declare that this is a totally objective work. I have attempted to trace the development of attempts to control sex offenders in the community and have attempted to provide sufficient historical background to demonstrate how these practices came about and why they persist. This account is of course colored by my own experience in research and practice over nearly 50 years. I am no bleeding heart for criminals and particularly not for sex offenders. What has concerned me as a professional and a member of the same community is that we have erected a prejudicial framework so immense that it strongly militates against desistance from crime and living a responsible and law-abiding life in that community. If I have made this clear and offered some suggestions regarding how we can make this situation better in ways that promote rehabilitation of offenders, I am satisfied with my efforts.

References

Andrews, D. A., & Bonta, J. (2010a). *The psychology of criminal conduct* (5th ed.). New Providence, NJ: LexisNexis.

Bureau of Justice Statistics. (2013). *Probation and parole in the United States, 2013*. Washington, DC: Office of Justice Programs, US Department of Justice.

Burgess, E. W. (1928). Factors determining success or failure on parole. In A. A. Bruce, A. J. Harno, E. W. Burgess, & J. Landesco (Eds.), *The workings of the indeterminate sentence law and parole in Illinois* (pp. 205–249). Springfield, IL: Illinois State Board of Parole.

Center for Sex Offender Management (CSOM). (2000). *Community supervision of the sex offender: An overview of current and promising practices*. Silver Spring, MD: Center for Sex Offender Management.

Chajewski, M., & Mercado, C. C. (2009). An evaluation of sex offender residency restrictions functioning in town, country, and city-wide jurisdictions. *Criminal Justice Policy Review, 20*, 44–61.

Goffman, E. (1961). *Asylums: Essays on the social situation of mental patients and other inmates*. Garden City, NY: Anchor Books.

Hanson, R. K. (2002). Recidivism and age: Follow-up data from 4,673 sex offenders. *Journal of Interpersonal Violence, 17*, 1046–1062.

Hanson, R. K., Bourgon, G., Helmus, L., & Hodgson, S. (2009). The principles of effective treatment also apply to sexual offenders: A meta-analysis. *Criminal Justice and Behavior, 36*, 865–891.

Jackson, K., & Healy, J. (2008, July). *Concurrent validity of the RSVP vis-à-vis the SVR-20, Static-99, Static-2002, and SORAG.* Paper presented at the meeting of the International Association of Forensic Mental Health Services, Vienna, Austria.

Laub, J. H., & Sampson, R. J. (2003). *Shared beginnings, divergent lives: Delinquent boys to age 70.* Cambridge, MA: Harvard University Press.

Laws, D. R., & Ward, T. (2011). *Desistance from sex offending.* New York: Guilford.

Link, S. (2009). *The medicalization of deviance.* Retrieved January 3, 2015, from: www.dswleads.com/Ebsco/The%20Medicalization%20of%20deviance.pdf

Lösel, F., & Schmucker, M. (2005). The effectiveness of treatment for sexual offenders: A comprehensive meta-analysis. *Journal of Experimental Criminology, 1*, 117–146.

McGrath, R. J., Cumming, G. F., Burchard, B. L., Zeoli, S., & Ellerby, L. (2010). *Current practices and emerging trends in sexual abuser management: The Safer Society 2009 North American Survey.* Brandon, VT: Safer Society Press.

Nicholaichuk, T. P., Olver, M. E., Gu, D., & Wong, C. P. (2014). Age, actuarial risk, and long-term recidivism in a national sample of sex offenders. *Sexual Abuse: A Journal of Research and Treatment, 26*, 406–428.

Sampson, R. J., & Laub, J. H. (1993). *Crime in the making: Pathways and turning points through life.* Cambridge, MA: Harvard University Press.

Tabachnick, J., & Klein, A. (2011). *A reasoned approach: Reshaping sex offender policy to prevent child sexual abuse.* Beaverton, OR: Association for the Treatment of Sexual Abusers.

Tofte, S. (2007). *No easy answers: Sex offender laws in the US.* New York: Human Rights Watch.

Wilson, J. Q. (1985). *Thinking about crime.* New York: Basic Books.

Appendix 1: Static-99 and 99R Developmental Timeline: A Rocky Developmental Path

Source: Karen Franklin, PhD and Brian Abbott, PhD, reproduced with permission.

The Static-99 is the most widely used instrument for assessing sex offenders' future risk to the public. Indeed, some state governments and other agencies even mandate its use. But bureaucratic faith may be misplaced. Conventional psychological tests go through a standard process of development, beginning with the generation and refinement of items and proceeding through set stages that include pilot testing and replication, leading finally to peer review and formal publication. The trajectory of the Static-99 has been more haphazard: Since its debut 15 years ago, the tool has been in a near-constant state of flux. Myriad changes in items, instructions, norms and real-world patterns of use have cast a shadow over its scientific validity. Here, we chart the unorthodox developmental course of this tremendously popular tool.

© The Editor(s) (if applicable) and The Author(s) 2016
D.R. Laws, *Social Control of Sex Offenders*,
DOI 10.1057/978-1-137-39126-1

Date	Event
1990	The first Sexually Violent Predator (SVP) law passes in the United States, in Washington. A wave of similar laws begins to sweep the nation
1997	The US Supreme Court upholds the Constitutionality of preventive detention of sex offenders
1997	R. Karl Hanson, a psychologist working for the Canadian prison system, releases a four-item tool to assess sex offender risk. The Rapid Risk Assessment for Sex Offence Recidivism (RRASOR) uses data from six settings in Canada and one in California[1]
1998	Psychologists David Thornton and Don Grubin of the UK prison system release a similar instrument, the Structured Anchored Clinical Judgment (SACJ-Min) scale[2]
1999	Hanson and Thornton combine the RRASOR and SACJ-Min to produce the Static-99, which is accompanied by a three-page list of coding rules.[3] The instrument's original validity data derive from four groups of sex offenders, including three from Canada and one from the UK (and none from the United States). The new instrument is atheoretical, with scores interpreted based on the recidivism patterns among these 1208 offenders, most of them released from prison in the 1970s
2000	Hanson and Thornton publish a peer-reviewed article on the new instrument[4]
2003	New coding rules are released for the Static-99, in an 84-page, unpublished booklet that is not peer reviewed.[5] The complex and sometimes counterintuitive rules may lead to problems with scoring consistency, although research generally shows the instrument can be scored reliably
2003	The developers release a new instrument, the Static-2002, intended to "address some of the weaknesses of Static-99."[6] The new instrument is designed to be more logical and easier to score; one item from the Static-99—pertaining to whether the subject had lived with a lover for at least 2 years—was dropped due to issues with its reliability and validity. Despite its advantages, Static-2002 never caught on, and did not achieve the popularity of the Static-99 in forensic settings
2007	Leslie Helmus, A graduate student working with Karl Hanson, reports that contemporary samples of sex offenders have much lower offense rates than did the antiquated, non-US samples upon which the Static-99 was originally developed, both in terms of base rates of offending and rates of recidivism after release from custody[7]

Date	Event
September 2008	Helmus releases a revised actuarial table for Static-99, to which evaluators may compare the total scores of their subjects to corresponding estimates of risk.[8] Another Static-99 developer, Amy Phenix, releases the first of several "Evaluators' Handbooks"[9]
October 2008	At an annual convention of the Association for the Treatment of Sexual Abusers (ATSA), Andrew Harris, a Canadian colleague of Hanson's, releases a new version of the Static-99 with three separate "reference groups" (Complete, CSC and High Risk) to which subjects can be compared. Evaluators are instructed to report a range of risks for recidivism, with the lower bound coming from a set of Canadian prison cases (the so-called CSC, or Correctional Service of Canada group), and the upper bound derived from a so-called "high-risk" group of offenders. The risk of the third, or "Complete," group was hypothesized as falling somewhere between those of the other two groups[10]
November 2008	At a workshop sponsored by a civil commitment center in Minnesota, Thornton and a government evaluator named Dennis Doren propose yet another new method of selecting among the new reference groups. In a procedure called "cohort matching," they suggest comparing an offender with either the CSC or High-Risk reference group based on how well the subject matched a list of external characteristics they had created but never empirically tested or validated[11]
December 2008	Phenix and California psychologist Dale Arnold put forth yet a new idea for improving the accuracy of the Static-99: After reporting the range of risk based on a combination of the CSC and High-Risk reference groups, evaluators are encouraged to consider a set of external factors, such as whether the offender had dropped out of treatment and the offender's score on Robert Hare's controversial Psychopathy Checklist-Revised (PCL-R). This new method does not seem to catch on[12, 13]
2009	An official Static-99 website, www.static99.org, debuts[14]
Winter 2009	The Static-99 developers admit that norms they developed in 2000 are not being replicated: The same score on the Static-99 equates with wide variations in recidivism rates depending on the sample to which it is compared. They theorize that the problem is due to large reductions in Canadian and U.S. recidivism rates since the 1970s–1980s. They call for the development of new norms[15]

(continued)

Date	Event
September 2009	Hanson and colleagues roll out a new version of the Static-99, the Static-99R.[16] The new instrument addresses a major criticism by more precisely considering an offender's age at release, an essential factor in reoffense risk. The old Static-99 norms are deemed obsolete. They are replaced by data from 23 samples collected by Helmus for her unpublished Master's thesis. The samples vary widely in regard to risk. For estimating risk, the developers now recommend use of the cohort matching procedure to select among four new reference group options. They also introduce the concepts of percentile ranks and relative risk ratios, along with a new Evaluators' Workbook for Static-99R and Static-2002R. Instructions for selecting reference groups other than routine corrections are confusing and speculative. Research is lacking to demonstrate that selecting other than routine corrections reference group produces more accurate risk estimates[17]
November 2009	Just 2 months after its introduction, the Evaluators' Workbook for Static-99R and Static-2002R is withdrawn due to errors in its actuarial tables.[18] The replacement workbook provides the same confusing and speculative method for selecting a nonroutine reference group, a method that lacks scientific validation and reliability
2010	An international team of researchers presents large-scale data from the United States, New Zealand and Australia indicating that the Static-99 would be more accurate if it took better account of an offender's age.[19] The Static-99 developers do not immediately embrace these researchers' suggestions
January 2012	Amy Phenix and colleagues introduce a revised Evaluators' Workbook for Static-99R and Static-2002R.[20] The new manual makes a number of revisions both to the underlying data (including percentile rank and relative risk ratio data) and to the recommended procedure for selecting a reference group. Now, in an increasingly complex procedure, offenders are to be compared to one of three reference groups, based on how many external risk factors they had. The groups included Routine Corrections (low risk), Preselected Treatment Need (moderate risk), and Preselected High Risk Need (high risk). Subsequent research shows that using density of external risk factors to select among the three reference group options is not valid and has no proven reliability.[21] A fourth reference group, Nonroutine Corrections, may be selected using a separate cohort-matching procedure. New research indicates that evaluators who are retained most often by the prosecution are more likely than others to select the high-risk reference group,[22] which has base rates much higher than in contemporary sexual recidivism studies and will thus produce exaggerated risk estimates[23]

Date	Event
July 2012	Six months later, the percentile ranks and relative risk ratios are once again modified, with the issuance of the third edition of the Static-99R and Static-2002R Evaluators' Handbook.[24] No additional data is provided to justify that the selection of nonroutine reference groups produces more accurate risk estimates than choosing the routine corrections reference group
October 2012	In an article published in *Criminal Justice & Behavior*, the developers concede that risk estimates for the 23 offender samples undergirding the Static-99 vary widely. Further, absolute risk levels for typical sex offenders are far lower than previously reported, with the typical sex offender having about a 7% chance of committing a new sex offense within 5 years. They theorize that the Static-99 might be inflating risk of reoffense due to the fact that the offenders in its underlying samples tended to be higher risk than average[25]
2012	The repeated refusal of the Static-99 developers to share their underlying data with other researchers, so that its accuracy can be verified, leads to a court order excluding use of the instrument in a Wisconsin case[26]
October 2013	At an annual ATSA convention, Hanson and Phenix report that an entirely new reference group selection system will be released in a peer-reviewed article in Spring 2014.[27] The new system will include only two reference groups: Routine Corrections and Preselected High Risk High Need. An atypical sample of offenders from a state hospital in Bridgewater, Massachusetts dating back to 1958 is to be removed altogether, along with some other samples, while some new data sets are to be added
October 2014	At the annual ATSA convention, the developers once again announce that the anticipated rollout of the new system has been pushed back pending acceptance of the manuscript for publication. Helmus nonetheless presents an overview.[28] She reports that the new system will abandon two out of the current four reference groups, retaining only Routine Corrections and Preselected High Risk Need. Evaluators should now use the Routine Corrections norms as the default unless local norms (with a minimum of 100 recidivists) are available. Evaluators will be permitted to choose the Preselected High Risk Need norms based on "strong, case-specific justification." No specific guidance nor empirical evidence to support such a procedure is proffered. A number of other new options for reporting risk information are also presented, including the idea of combining Static-99 data with that from newly developed, so-called "dynamic risk instruments"

(continued)

Date	Event
January 2015	At an ATSA convention presentation followed by an article in the journal *Sexual Abuse*,[29] the developers announce further changes in their data sets and how Static-99R scores should be interpreted. Only two of the original four "reference groups" are still standing. Of these, the Routine group has grown by 80% (to 4325 subjects), while the High-Risk group has shrunk by 35%, to a paltry 860 individuals. Absent from the article is any actuarial table on the High-Risk group, meaning the controversial practice by some government evaluators of inflating risk estimates by comparing sex offenders' Static-99R scores with the High-Risk group data has still not passed any formal peer review process. The developers also correct a previous statistical method as recommended by Ted Donaldson and colleagues back in 2012,[30] the effect of which is to further lower risk estimates in the high-risk group. Only sex offenders in the Routine group with Static-99R scores of 10 are now statistically more likely than not to reoffend. It is unknown how many sex offenders were civilly committed in part due to reliance on the now-obsolete data

[1]Hanson (1997)
[2]Grubin (1998)
[3]Hanson and Thornton (1999)
[4]Hanson and Thornton (2000)
[5]Harris, Phenix, Hanson, and Thornton (2003)
[6]Hanson, Helmus, and Thornton (2010)
[7]Helmus (2007)
[8]Helmus (2008)
[9]Phenix, Helmus, and Hanson (2008)
[10]Harris, Hanson, and Helmus (2008)
[11]Doren and Thornton (2008)
[12]Phenix and Arnold (2008)
[13]Abbott (2009)
[14]Helmus, Hanson, and Thornton (2009)
[15]*Ibid*
[16]Hanson, Phenix, and Helmus (2009)
[17]DeClue and Zavodny (2014)
[18]Phenix, Helmus, and Hanson (2009)
[19]Wollert, Cramer, Waggoner, Skelton, and Vess (2010)
[20]Phenix, Helmus, and Hanson (2012a)
[21]Abbott (2013)
[22]Chevalier, Boccaccini, Murrie, and Varela (2014)
[23]Abbott (2013) *op. cit*
[24]Phenix, Helmus, and Hanson (2012b)

[25]Helmus, Hanson, Thornton, Babchishin, and Harris (2012)
[26]*State of Wisconsin v. Homer L. Perren Jr.*, La Crosse County 2010-CI000003.
   See Franklin (2012)
[27]Hanson and Phenix (2013)
[28]Helmus (2014)
[29]Hanson, Thornton, Helmus, and Babchishin (2015)
[30]Donaldson, Abbott, and Michie (2012)

References

Abbott, B. (2009). Applicability of the new Static-99 experience tables in sexually violent predator risk assessments. *Sexual Offender Treatment, 1*, 1–24.

Abbott, B. R. (2013). The utility of assessing "external risk factors" when selecting Static-99r reference groups. *Open Access Journal of Forensic Psychology, 5*, 89–118.

Bureau of Justice Statistics. (2000). *Probation and parole in the United States, 2000*. Washington, DC: Office of Justice Programs, US Department of Justice.

Chevalier, C., Boccaccini, M. T., Murrie, D. C., & Varela, J. G. (2014). Static-99R reporting practices in sexually violent predator cases: Does norm selection reflect adversarial allegiance? *Law & Human Behavior, 38*, 337–345.

Davy v. Sullivan, 354F Supp. 1320 (MS Ala. 1973).

DeClue, G., & Zavodny, D. (2014). Forensic use of the Static-99R: Part 4. Risk communication. *Journal of Threat Assessment and Management, 1*(3), 145–161.

Donaldson, T., Abbott, B., & Michie, C. (2012). Problems with the Static-99R prediction estimates and confidence intervals. *Open Access Journal of Forensic Psychology, 4*, 1–23.

Doren, D., & Thornton, D. (2008). New norms for Static-99: A briefing. A workshop sponsored by Sand Ridge Secure Treatment Center on November 10, 2008. Madison, WI.

© The Editor(s) (if applicable) and The Author(s) 2016
D.R. Laws, *Social Control of Sex Offenders*,
DOI 10.1057/978-1-137-39126-1

Franklin, K. (2012, December 14). Judge bars Static-99R risk tool from SVP trial: Developers staunchly refused requests to turn over data. *In the News blog.*

Grubin, D. (1998). *Sex offending against children: Understanding the risk* (Police research series paper 99). London: Home Office, Unpublished report.

Hanson, R. K. (1997). *The development of a brief actuarial risk scale for sexual offence recidivism* (User Rep. 1997-04). Ottawa, ON: Department of the Solicitor General of Canada. www.ps-sp.gc,ca/res/cor/rep

Hanson, R. K., Helmus, L., & Thornton, D. (2010). Predicting recidivism among sexual offenders: A multi-site study of STATIC-2002. *Law and Human Behavior, 34*, 198–211.

Hanson, R. K., & Morton-Bourgon, K. E. (2009). The accuracy of recidivism risk assessments for sexual offenders: A meta-analysis of 118 prediction studies. *Psychological Assessment, 21*, 1–21.

Hanson, R. K., & Phenix, A. (2013, October). *Report writing for the Static-99R and Static-2002R.* Preconference seminar presented at the 32nd annual research and treatment conference of the association for the treatment of sexual abusers, Chicago, IL, October 30, 2013. See also: Static-99 'norms du jour' get yet another makeover. *In the News blog*, November 17, 2013

Hanson R. K., Phenix, A., & Helmus, L. (2009, September 28). *Static-99(R) and static-2002(R): How to interpret and report in light of recent research.* Paper presented at the 28th Annual Research and Treatment Conference of the Association for the Treatment of Sexual Abusers, Dallas, TX.

Hanson, R. K., & Thornton, D. (1999). *Static 99: Improving actuarial risk assessments for sex offenders* (User Rep. 1999-02). Ottawa, ON: Department of the Solicitor General of Canada. www.ps-sp.gc.ca/res/cor/rep

Hanson, R. K., & Thornton, D. (2000). Improving risk assessments for sex offenders: A comparison of three actuarial scales. *Law and Human Behavior, 24*, 119–136.

Hanson, RK, Thornton, D, Helmus, L-M, & Babchishin, KM. (2015). What sexual recidivism rates should be associated with Static-99R and Static-2002R scores? *Sexual Abuse: A Journal of Research and Treatment.* Advance online publication.

Harris A. J. R., Hanson, K., & Helmus, L. (2008). *Are new norms needed for Static-99?* Workshop presented at the ATSA 27th annual research and treatment conference on October 23, 2008, Atlanta, GA. www.static99.org

Harris, A. J. R., Phenix, A., Hanson, R. K., & Thornton, D. (2003). *Static-99 coding rules: Revised 2003.* Ottawa, ON: Solicitor General Canada.

Helmus, L. (2007). *A multi-site comparison of the validity and utility of the Static-99 and Static-2002 for risk assessment with sexual offenders.* Unpublished Honour's thesis, Carleton University, Ottawa, ON, Canada.

Helmus, L. (2008, September). *Static-99 Recidivism percentages by risk level.* Last Updated September 25, 2008. Unpublished paper.

Helmus, L. M. (2014, October). *Absolute recidivism estimates for Static-99R and Static-2002R: Current research and recommendations.* Paper presented at the 33rd annual research and treatment conference of the association for the treatment of sexual abusers, San Diego, CA, October 30, 2014.

Helmus, L., Hanson, R. K., & Thornton, D. (2009). Reporting Static-99 in light of new research on recidivism norms. *The Forum, 21*(1), 38–45, Winter 2009.

Helmus, L., Hanson, R. K. Thornton, D., Babchishin, K. M., & Harris, A. J. R. (2012). Absolute recidivism rates predicted by Static-99R and Static-2002R sex offender risk assessment tools vary across samples: A meta-analysis, *Criminal Justice & Behavior.* See also: Static-99R risk estimates wildly unstable, developers admit. *In the News blog,* October 18, 2012.

Levenson, J. S. (in press). Community control of sex offenders. In D. R. Laws & W. T. O'Donohue (Eds.), *Treatment of sex offenders: Strengths and weaknesses in assessment and intervention.* New York: Springer.

Levenson, J. S., Ackerman, A. R., & Harris, A. J. (2014). Catch me if you can: An analysis of fugitive sex offenders. *Sexual Abuse: A Journal of Research and Treatment, 26,* 129–148.

Logan, C. (2014). The HCR-20 version 3: A case study in risk formulation. *International Journal of Forensic Mental Health, 13,* 1–9.

McGuire, R. J., Carlisle, J. M., & Young, B. G. (1965). Sexual deviations as conditioned behaviour: A hypothesis. *Behaviour Research and Therapy, 3,* 185–190.

National Crime Victimization Survey (NCVS). (2013). Washington, DC: Bureau of Justice Statistics, Office of Justice Programs, U.S. Department of Justice.

Pérez Ramírez, M., Redondo Illescas, S., Martinínez Garcia, M., García Forero, C., & Andrés Pueyo, A. (2008). Predicción de riesgo de reincidencia en agresores sexuales. *Psicothema, 20,* 205–210.

Phenix, A., & Arnold, D. (2008, December). *Proposed considerations for conducting sex offender risk assessment draft 12-14-08.* Unpublished paper.

Phenix, A., Helmus, L., & Hanson, R. K. (2008, September 28). *Evaluators' workbook.* Unpublished.

Phenix, A., Helmus, L., & Hanson, R. K. (2009, November 3). *Evaluators' workbook.* Unpublished.

Phenix, A., Helmus, L., & Hanson, R. K. (2012a, January 9). *Evaluators' Workbook.* Unpublished.

Phenix, A., Helmus, L., & Hanson, R. K. (2012b, July 26). *Evaluators' workbook.* Unpublished.

Ramsey, C. B. (2013). Sex and social order: The selective enforcement of colonial American adultery laws in the English context. *Yale Journal of Law & the Humanities, 10,* 191–228.

Rettenberger, M., Matthes, A., Boer, D. P., & Eher, R. (2010). Prospective actuarial risk assessment: A comparison of five risk assessment instruments in different sexual offender subtypes. *International Journal of Offender Therapy and Comparative Criminology, 54,* 169–186.

Watson, J. B. (1913). Psychology as the behaviorist views it. *Psychological Review, 20,* 158–177.

Wollert, R., Cramer, E., Waggoner, J., Skelton, A., & Vess, J. (2010). Recent research (N = 9,305) underscores the importance of using age-stratified actuarial tables in sex offender risk assessments. *Sexual Abuse: A Journal of Research and Treatment, 22*(4), 471–490. See also: "Age tables improve sex offender risk estimates," *In the News blog,* December 1, 2010.

Index

© The Editor(s) (if applicable) and The Author(s) 2016
D.R. Laws, *Social Control of Sex Offenders,*
DOI 10.1057/978-1-137-39126-1